Federal Social Policy
The Historical Dimension

FEDERAL SOCIAL POLICY

The Historical Dimension

Edited by
DONALD T. CRITCHLOW
AND ELLIS W. HAWLEY

With a Foreword by
ROBERT KELLEY

The Pennsylvania State University Press
University Park and London

HN57
.F43
1988

Library of Congress Cataloging-in-Publication Data

Federal social policy: the historical dimension
  edited by Donald T. Critchlow and Ellis W. Hawley.
        p.   cm.
  Includes index.
  ISBN 0-271-00617-X
  1. United States—Social policy. I. Critchlow, Donald T., 1948–
II. Hawley, Ellis Wayne, 1929–
HN57.F43 1988
361.6'1'0973—dc19   87–19395
                                                        CIP

Contents

PART TWO
THE HISTORICAL AND INSTITUTIONAL
CONTEXTS OF POLICY-MAKING

Acknowledgments

THE editors want to thank David Leege, director of the Hesburgh Program in Public Service, who played an essential role in organizing a conference to study federal social policy, held at the University of Notre Dame in the fall of 1985, which brought together many of the scholars who have contributed to this volume. Although many of the essays in this volume were contributed after the conference, the meeting provided the occasion for the authors to plan this collection. Support for the conference and for editing the volume was graciously provided by the Center for the Study of Contemporary Society, under the direction of Roger Skurski, at the University of Notre Dame.

Other people should be acknowledged for their assistance as well: Theda Skocpol, Harvard University, Roger Daniels, University of Cincinnati, and the readers for the Pennsylvania State University Press offered their insights and critical comments on early drafts of the collection; Ann Bates provided editorial supervision; and Nila Gerhold and Nancy Kegler typed more drafts of this manuscript than either they or the editors would care to remember. Finally, a great debt is owed to Patricia Powers Critchlow, who lived with this collection from the beginning and who indexed it at the end.

ROBERT KELLEY

FOREWORD
The History of Public Policy:
Does It Have a Distinctive Character and Method?

H ISTORIANS have been studying the history of public policy for many generations, indeed for many centuries. We can begin with Thucydides, more than 2,000 years ago, in his study of warmaking by the Athenian state. From Gibbon writing about the fall of the Roman Empire in his eighteenth-century study to our colleagues writing their many histories of policy issues today, politics and public policy have traditionally fascinated the historical mind. Our colleagues write foreign policy history, economic policy history, family policy history (that is, studies of the birth control and abortion movements), cultural policy history (as in histories of prohibition or of immigration), educational policy and race policy history, military policy history, resource-management policy history, urban policy history, constitutional policy history, gender policy history, and on and on.

Only recently, however, have a few historians begun thinking of themselves specifically as *policy* historians. (The first meeting of a group of historians to talk self-consciously about policy history took place only in the fall of 1979, when Morton Keller and Thomas McCraw convened such a meeting at Harvard University.) The tardiness of this sense of being a policy historian is a curious matter. What has happened, we have to note, is a shift in our perceptions. Somehow, in recent years, a particular realm in our environment, hitherto simply part of the of-course universe, has separated itself out to become visible to us as a distinct human activity worth being thought of as an appropriate, in fact, a most important subject for historical study: the making of public policy. Just as historians have earlier created the history of technology as a focus of disciplined examination, and the history of the family or of immigration, so now we witness the emergence of the history of public policy. Our colleagues in political science, long fascinated by exactly this dimension of public life, are in their studies of public policy well ahead of us. And why not? Political scientists have much to tell historians about the making of public policy. They have insights and models and ways of ordering and categorizing and talking about the phenomenon which we need.

Note how much historians are in their debt. If there is any central organizing paradigm for political scientists, it is an abstraction called the state: its structure, how it works, how it is moved to do this or that, and, above all, its policies. This is essentially what Ellis Hawley and Morton Keller, as historians of public policy, have told historians about the nature of the kind of state that has emerged in the United States, its origins, what it does, where it is going.

Among political scientists, consequently, public policy has a recognizable identity and method. We know what it is they are doing when we see courses listed in the university catalogue in their department under that rubric. Students go there to learn how the budget is made in the Office of Management and Budget and how laws are passed and implemented. They learn primarily how the process works right now, since political scientists, with a few important exceptions, are present-oriented. We can say, then, that historians come to this picnic bringing their own special commodity: time. Historians are usually not very good on process, but they are superb on the time dimension, on how things have evolved over generations. That is what fascinates them, telling that particular story. It is only when we bring in the dimension of time, historians say, that we gain a real understanding of human affairs.

By contrast with political scientists, who have their quasi-Platonic concern with abstractions like the state, and their appetite for theory, historians are Aristotelians, inveterate empiricists interested almost entirely in particulars, in concrete and specific events in time. They like to study particular people doing particular things in particular locations.

What historians bring to this enterprise, then, is the habit of digging deeply into particular policy streams, such as foreign policy or economic policy, and showing how they evolved over decades and generations, or into specific policy controversies, great and powerful events in time like the Reformation and the American Civil War. In this tradition, Andrew Achenbaum's work on the aged is classically historical, the study not of the state but of a particular policy over time. His essay in this volume is centered on a particular *problem*; it does not arise out of reflecting on a theoretical issue in the discipline and seeing how a study of the aging could illuminate it.

Historians are by nature clinicians. Their role, as many of them see it, is to concentrate in a generally untheoretical fashion on putting together a narrative of the course of events and analyzing them more or less in their own terms, relying upon that act in itself to create understanding. This has given what historians have written a richness in narrative content, in empirical concreteness, from which we all benefit. However, this means that the field of public policy history and its literature remains formless; that it has little that is clear and distinct or intellectually manageable to offer our colleagues in history who are, without knowing it, doing policy history. The work of policy historians runs along many separate railroads that rarely converge.

However, if the field of policy history persists in its formless condition among scholars in the field, without a distinctive characteristic or method, a paradigm, a clear focus of shared attention, then it will have but modest community-building power among historians. Can we go beyond the pure empiricism of histories of particular policies, running this way and that, described in their own ad hoc terms? We must turn to that ancient activity which lies essentially at the core of human society, as it has from our earliest beginnings—the *policy process*, its nature and history. The various policy streams appear to be separate from each other, but they all share this at their core: there is a process of making and implementing public policy which pumps away like the heart in every human body, recognizably unique in each separate location but recognizably the same, displaying universal characteristics and shared inner dynamics.

Policy history should exist, it seems to me, in two dimensions: as studies of separate policy questions or themes and as studies of *the process itself*. All share that process; it runs horizontally across the lines of inquiry, and it presents us over and over again with the same human contextual dynamics. And yet at the same time the policy process itself has a history, for in every society it evolves and changes over time. The policy-making dynamics that we may observe in the American Revolution are profoundly universal in nature, and yet the process of making public-policy history in this country now is infinitely more complex. We need, in fact, histories specifically of the process in given times and circumstances, histories we do not presently have.

As it happens, a focus on the policy process opens for historians a rich and well-populated interdisciplinary conversation. The field of *policy analysis*—that is, the explicit study of how the policy process works, so as to be able to give advice to policy decision makers—has over the past generation come widely into being. It has produced for us a copious literature to learn from and a numerous array of methods and insights and paradigms.

Drawing upon the social sciences for methods and insights is a traditional habit among historians. Policy historians therefore become part of a long, honorable, and often fruitful tradition if they reach over to the policy analysts to make use of their experiences and perspectives. Doing so will also align with the historian's instinctive habit of being empirical and particular-problem oriented; that is, it will align with the historian's natural habit of being a clinician, whose role is to sit down with a particular group of people in a particular time and context and come to an understanding of the specific problems they face and try, in their policy-making, to solve.

There is a profound intellectual difficulty here, however. The methods generally used in policy analysis grate on the historical consciousness, setting up fundamental disagreements. The most widely used model is that of cost-benefit, evolved out of the work of economists, and most historians simply cannot agree with them in their psychological model of human nature: that the ultimate factor in politics is single, and that it always revolves around motives related to cost or material benefit. So, too, most historians are put off by the models political scientists often rely upon. The underlying assumption is that people act rationally—as in the input-output model of the policy process—or only incrementally, and do not break out in new directions guided by compelling moral values and ideologies. The rational cost-benefit model lay at the heart of our nation's policies in Vietnam—as Robert McNamara would say, "If we can only make it *cost* the North Vietnamese enough, they'll quit!"—and we know where that led us. Those overmastering motives which could not be quantified, the ideas and values of the North Vietnamese, and their determination to win no matter what it cost were not only those factors that were consciously left out, they were the ones that in the long run counted.

In fact, however, policy analysis is a many-sided field, and contemporaneously with its many failures in the 1960s and 1970s, through its reliance on shallow models, a variant for the consideration of policy historians has been steadily developing—as political scientists are well aware, having used it successfully. I speak of the "policy sciences" approach developed out of the intellectual tradition founded by Harold Lasswell at Yale and further evolved not only at Yale but at the Rand Corporation. In an absorbing work written by Garry Brewer and Peter deLeon, *The Foundations of Policy Analysis* (1983), we can learn of the policy-sciences approach in what I think is a wise, subtle, and gracefully written book.

How wrong it is, they write, pointing to the many failures of this approach, to build policy-analysis models on a single-factor, rationalist, quantified basis. To begin with, they are openly skeptical of theory as a guiding framework, just as they question approaches which arise fundamentally from a need to answer theoretical questions within the discipline. Policy analysis, they write, must begin first with the client's *problem*, not with theory; it must proceed in immediate and lively consideration of the human factor, that is, of ideas, moral values, emotions, mind-sets, and the impact of particular individuals; and it must pay close attention to the element of *time*, which, as it passes, keeps changing the problem and its terms of reference.

Brewer and deLeon place great emphasis on the actors themselves and their ways of thinking. How did the parties involved define the issue? What did they know about the issue (i.e., how was the information system working for them)? What were their interests, conceived of not simply in material terms but also professionally, organizationally, and culturally? In its many dimensions, what was the context within which the actors worked? That context is structural, and it is also social, historical, intellectual, and moral. What was the impact on the actors of affective, as against rational and instrumental, habits of mind, of fears and anxieties, of stereotypes, of nationalism and team spirit, of hatreds? And then, most important, what happened during the stage of implementation? It is particularly in making historical studies of what happened to adopted policies when they were put into operation—and often, in that process, effectively changed—that historians can make an especially important contribution.

The policy-sciences model, in short, is one which is most congenial to the way historians think about human nature and human affairs. There is a sentence in Brewer and deLeon's book that should particularly appeal to the historical mind: "There is nothing quite so irrational—and misguided—as [analytical] approaches that claim to be rational and then operate as if the world ought to be the same— neat, simple, and orderly" (p. 23). Their method, too, has the great benefit of being the fruit of many years of close analysis by many scholars of recent public-policy issues of great complexity and enduring power, so that the historian who is beginning to study policy during the period of Reconstruction in United States history, say, has through the policy-sciences method the accumulated insights and painful failures of many years of professional labor devoted specifically to this task: analyzing policy problems. Policy history would benefit from making use of a now well-matured analytical method, although this should not preclude the use and development of other methods. Whatever the method, the field should be marked by a *systematic* study of the policy process over time. This should be its distinguishing characteristic of policy history, as the essays in this volume show.

To sum up: We are at a moment when a new focus of historical attention is coming into view and is being named, and we have the happy fortune of participating in the shaping of what this new approach will be like, what will characterize it, and what will give it a living and important identity. We also have, at the same time, a most fulfilling subject for further study. The making of public policy is as deeply human as anything else about humanity that scholars examine. Nothing else is more central to our nature and existence as human communities than the crucial work of making and carrying out public decisions on issues of great importance. The process therefore is enormously complicated. It is subtle, surprising, the prey of chance, filled with nuances and the unexpected. It is moved as much by emotions and passions as by logic and reason, as much by ideas and cultural dynamics as by material, economic factors. Politics and public policy-making in this country form, in reality, a kind of national theater in which most Americans participate in one way or another; therefore, it draws on the full theatrical armamentarium of symbol, gesture, rhetoric, and expressive action, just as it lays heavy claims, in its highest moments, on our minds and hearts.

Since policy-making is as complex in nature as anything else that is fundamentally human, it has the potentiality of being both creative and destructive; it can, as we know, be both at the same time. The making of public policy is certainly one of the few human arenas in which lasting accomplishments of wide significance may, for better or for worse, not only be conceived of but brought to reality. To be successful at the task is a rare art which is at all times, and in every society, in high demand. However, those who are gifted at it are almost always in short supply, if indeed they are available at all in any given generation. To be the historians of this ancient human enterprise is to have a task that never loses its savor, though it may severely test our inner sense of human possibilities. We are specially favored in our profession to have it given to us to study and to teach.

DONALD T. CRITCHLOW

INTRODUCTION
Social-Policy History:
Past and Present

THE relationship between social-science
research and social policy presents a cru-
cial problem for scholars concerned with the meaning of knowledge
and its application in a democratic society. Yet the relationship
between the two is not readily discernible either to social scientists
or to policymakers.[1]

This relationship cannot be easily dismissed, however, especially
by those social scientists concerned with social policy as history.
After all, history should offer the social sciences, if nothing else, the
distance which imparts objectivity. And while history may not provide clear policy directives, it should correct misperceptions concerning past policies while establishing a relatively neutral ground
for reflection on current policy.

Whether history has these capacities remains to be seen, because
the history of social policy remains only in the preliminary stages of
investigation. Only within the last decade has policy history emerged
as a recognized subfield in the discourse of the social sciences. Yet,
historians since the late nineteenth century, the period when the
social sciences emerged as professions within the university, have
expressed a deep interest in social policy.[2] Indeed, one of the first
volumes in the influential Johns Hopkins Historical and Political
Science Monographs was Herbert Baxter Adams's *Notes on the Litera-*

ture of Charities, while subsequent volumes explored public health, charities, and corrections in various states.[3]

The Johns Hopkins Monographs gave special attention to the role of the state in economic and social development in American history. Herbert Adams and his associates had been greatly influenced by German scholarship which showed that the expansion of a strong government was necessary for reform and that the emergence of a centralized state was completely in accord with the evolutionary tendencies of society. Thus behind their claims to scholarly objectivity lay strong tendencies toward ideological advocacy.[4]

Later generations of scholars who followed Adams's pioneering work in policy history were no less free of tendencies toward ideological advocacy, but any interest in the state per se often was subsumed in more explicit attention to other topics in policy history, including the development of social welfare, the nature of reform, the meaning of liberalism, and the role and culture of expertise within social institutions. These topics often seemed to circle without directly examining the nature of the American liberal state. Invariably, however, these very topics raised questions directly related to the character of the liberal state in American history. As a consequence, historians in the 1970s gave increasing attention to the place and meaning of the liberal state in the American polity.

This is not to deny that other social scientists working in other disciplines with little familiarity with the historiography of policy history were also drawn toward explorations of the state in their own research. Nor is this to suggest that a teleological design should be imposed on the historiography of social policy itself as somehow leading inevitably to the study of the state. This is to suggest, however, that as historians explored other topics within policy history, as it was broadly conceived, the nature of the liberal state reappeared as a primary concern of historians in the field. In turn, policy history increasingly has gained clarity and coherence as a distinctive field of study since the 1970s. Without presuming to offer a full discussion of the historiography of the field, a brief overview of the literature illustrates how historians in their discussion of a plethora of related topics arrived at the fundamental question: What is the meaning of the liberal state in the American polity?

Following the pioneering efforts of Herbert Adams and his students at Johns Hopkins University, the history of social policy was largely taken over by those associated with professional social work. As a consequence, many of the scholarly studies of the 1920s reflected a preoccupation with endowing social work with its own history and in strengthening the emerging sense of professionalism among welfare practitioners.[5] Authors such as Sophonisba Breckenridge and Edith Abbott were leaders in the field of social work as well as activists in the reform movement. Their activism led them to focus much of their work on the transformation of private charity into public social insurance. In the decades of the 1930s and 1940s the University of Chicago School of Social Service Administration extended this work through a series of state welfare histories. These histories offered narrow institutional and administrative studies, which often focused on the legislative history of one reform or another, or on the administration of welfare agencies and programs within a single state. Thus reform-minded scholars, equally interested in the professionalization of social work, projected their concerns with contemporary welfare issues in their historical studies of poor laws and public welfare on the state level.[6] The result was, as Michael Katz observes in his survey of policy history in this period, that public-welfare history remained more or less in the domain of social workers until the post–World War II period.

In the 1950s and 1960s, social-policy history entered a new phase when a group of professional historians led by Robert Bremner, Clarke Chambers, Allen Davis, Walter Trattner, James Leiby, Blanche Coll, and others initiated major studies in the field.[7] Their interest in the history of social welfare in America manifested a general interest in social history, particularly in the rise of the city and industrialization in modern America. At the same time, new professional standards were introduced to social-policy history and fitted it into a broader interpretive framework. While sharing a humanistic faith, and a critical sensibility, in the progressive ideal that American society was getting better, they portrayed the nineteenth century as a period of laissez-faire capitalism which left the poor, women, children, the aged, and the disabled to the vicissitudes of the marketplace and in the care of charity organizations that made callous distinctions between the "deserving" and "undeserving" poor. They then depicted the Progressive Era and the New Deal as watersheds in social policy as liberalism now addressed, although not always successfully, the fundamental problems of social dislocation in a capitalist society. A sharp contrast was made between what one historian called the "negative" laissez-faire state in the nineteenth century and the "positive" welfare state in the twentieth century.[8] In addition, the resulting studies offered new insights into social history and urban history.

While seeking to introduce scholarly objectivity to the history of social policy, these historians remained critical of much of what had been accomplished by way of social reform. The exclusion of blacks and other ethnic groups from various welfare programs, the continued inequalities in opportunity and wealth, and the elitist nature of many of the reformers were all critically noted. In *American Philanthropy* (1960), Robert Bremner concluded that "charity was subject to abuse, by the giver as well as the taker."[9] These historians maintained a liberal faith in progress, in humanitarian reform, and in benevolent state intervention. In the 1960s, they would be attacked by a group of historians who dismissed reformers as self-serving, neurotic, and elitist, and who saw liberal reform as conservative, disingenuous, and defensively designed to maintain social control.

A group of radical historians led by William A. Williams, Gabriel Kolko, and James Weinstein projected a new view of the modern liberal state as an instrument of class control over the economic and social life of the nation for the benefit of private profit and corporate interests. While liberal historians assumed that federal intervention in areas of economic regulation and social welfare was the result of popular pressure for reform, radical historians believed that the public interest had been subverted by private corporate interests that sought increased state intervention in order to rationalize the market and to maintain their monopolistic positions. While liberal historians saw Progressive and New Deal reform as having extended democratic participation in a pluralistic society, radical historians described reform in modern America as a "successful effort to guide and control the economic and social policies of federal, state, and municipal governments by various groups in their own long range interest as they perceive it."[10] In the process of attacking the Progressive and New Deal reforms and the regulatory state, radical historians also provided new perspectives on the history of social welfare as it emerged in the late nineteenth and early twentieth centuries. Specifically, New Left historians raised questions concerning the role of elites and class interests in social policy, and this posed further questions concerning the nature of the American welfare state.

One of the earliest criticisms of welfare work as a class tool to preserve social order came in 1963 in a series of articles by Marvin E. Gettleman in *The American Journal of Economics and Sociology*.[11] Gettleman showed that charity workers in the nineteenth century had sought more than the humanitarian care of the poor. Indeed, influenced by Social Darwinism and distrustful of the poor, they had seen themselves as agents "for the protection of the rich." Therefore, they had opposed "charity" per se and instead had hoped to maintain social control over the masses through a systematic program designed to inculcate the middle-class values of hard work, independence, and participation in the marketplace.

Subsequently, this theme of social control became a focus for myriad other studies that explored the history of social institutions, deviancy, and reform in the nineteenth and twentieth centuries. Social control as a theme in American liberalism received its clearest articulation in Christopher Lasch's *The New Radicalism in America* (1965). In a series of brilliant essays on the emergence of reform-minded intellectuals in the Progressive Era, which he described as the "new radicals," Lasch showed how women and men such as Jane Addams, John Dewey, and Edward A. Ross sought to find a place and meaning for themselves in a world profoundly different from that of their parents. As a result of the immediate and specific anxieties felt by this emergent generation of young intellectuals, they developed a class identity as the new managers of society. In their desperate search for meaning and order, they came to "insist again and again on the importance of discipline, mastery, and control, the control of environment by the means of will." And desiring to liberate the unused energies of industrial America, they also enthusiastically called for social planning as a way to enhance social welfare. This, said Lasch, reflected "the planners' confidence in themselves as a disinterested elite" and "their abiding anxiety lest the voice of reason be overwhelmed by the uproar of social conflict."[12] In tracing the emergence of this new class, Lasch showed that behind the call for reform lay the concerns of a self-interested class motivated to ensure their own position and status in the world while maintaining social control over the masses. The humanitarian reformer had been replaced by the neurotic, self-promoting, fully bourgeois intellectual, less concerned with altruism than with social position and social order. Lasch's critique of progressive reformers was devastating and immediately influential.

Anthony Platt, a sociologist writing shortly after Lasch, took social control and professional self-aggrandizement as major themes in his study of juvenile reform in the Progressive Era.[13] Platt argued that middle-class reformers and a new class of professionals had arbitrarily designated certain children as delinquents in order to maintain social control in a rapidly changing industrial order. He found little altruism in the movement to reform juvenile offenders. Instead, he traced the roots of the juvenile-reform movement in the Progressive Era to a need by the middle class to control the dangerous classes and to the strivings of those involved in prison institutions to raise their status as professionals. Like Lasch, Platt maintained that the motivation and the results of Progressive social policy were to maintain social order in the capitalist system. Reform was elitist in nature and anti-democratic in impulse.

Platt's work addressed only a small part of the American social-reform movement—juvenile reform in the Progressive period. Moreover, his characterization of reformers as self-promoting professionals and his easy dismissal of any altruistic impulse appeared to many historians as mechanistic.[14] Writing only two years after Platt's study appeared, David Rothman presented a more sophisticated understanding of social reform in his impressive study of public institutions in antebellum America. In his examination of the development of the penitentiary, the almshouse, the mental asylum, the house of refuge, and the medical dispensary, Rothman portrayed the creators of these institutions as humanitarians concerned with maintaining social order. Drawing upon the work of French sociologist Michel Foucault, Rothman showed how deviants were institutionalized by bourgeois society in order to inculcate inmates with middle-class moral and social values.[15] In a changing economic and social environment, evidenced in the rise of urban centers, reformers sought to isolate, cure, and prevent social problems such as crime, insanity, and pauperism. The institutions were intended to provide a "model" environment of the good society, but they tended over time to degenerate into harsh and brutal instruments for punishing the deviant. As a consequence, the ideology of reform appeared to be self-serving in its search to teach deviants the value of hard work, discipline, and temperance. Rothman's reformers were no less elitist than Platt's child savers, but Rothman understood the importance of republican values and Christian humanitarianism in antebellum America and laid considerable stress on ideas.[16]

The task of integrating a social-control perspective and social welfare into an explicit economic interpretation of capitalism fell to two sociologists, Frances Piven and Richard A. Cloward, in their influential study *Regulating the Poor.* Piven and Cloward explicitly dismissed the "humanistic" character of social welfare and instead found that the key to relief-giving in capitalist society could be found in a political-economic cycle. During times of economic downturn, Piven and Cloward argued, ruling elites would institute relief and work programs designed to "mute civil disorder." When the economy recovered, welfare programs were disbanded or drastically reduced in order to "reinforce work norms" among those working as well as those unable or unwilling to work.[17] The Piven-Cloward thesis gave rise to immediate debate within scholarly circles.[18]

While the social-control thesis elicited a counterattack from an array of historians, liberal social programs and social policy also came under attack from another and generally unexpected quarter—social scientists concerned with studying the relationship between electoral politics and the policy process. Led by such scholars as James Sundquist, Martha Derthick, and Edward Tufte, social scientists began to frame the history of modern social policy in terms of a political means to appease voters and to win support at the polls, especially from the middle classes. Edward Tufte, a political scientist, showed through regression analysis that the timing of elections generally influenced the rate of employment, the growth of disposable income, and the flow of transfer payments through Social Security and unemployment benefits. In turn, Martha Derthick in her important study of Social Security since 1935 showed that Congress and the Executive Office, whether under the control of Democrats or Republicans, consciously expanded benefits payments and coverage for political reasons, seemingly impervious to the costs of the system. Tufte and Derthick, along with others, raised serious questions as to whether the public interest was indeed being served in the liberal democratic state.

These criticisms of the welfare state, coming from both the radicals and establishment social scientists, challenged previous understandings of the meaning of "liberalism" in the American polity. Both radical historians and "objective-minded" social scientists shared a common perspective that welfare was motivated less by charitable and humanistic impulses than by a desire to maintain social and political control for established interests. While critics of the radical perspective might dismiss much of the social-control argument as reductionist and at times too cynical in imputing conscious manipulation by elites of ideas and programs, most scholars agreed that radicals had raised fundamental questions concerning "class divisions, power differentials, ideology, and the relationship between ideas and social-economic reality."[19]

In the decade that followed, a number of works appeared which explored social policy as it related to the aged, the family, women and children, and education, as well as traditional groups for study—the poor and the mentally ill and mentally retarded.[20]

This increased interest in social-policy history opened new lines of inquiry for historians who wanted to create a more detailed and complex picture of the history of social policy as it evolved in modern

America. Two areas of exploration proved to be especially rewarding: the role of elite groups in social-policy formulation and implementation, and the nature of the liberal welfare state. Both areas of study grew largely in response to the issues raised by radical historians in their characterization of reformers as disingenuous and the liberal state as inequitable. In evaluating the earlier work of radicals, historians entered into an interdisciplinary discourse which addressed fundamental questions concerning the meaning of expertise, bureaucracy, and the state in a liberal democracy. In the process, expertise, bureaucracy, and the state came to be viewed as autonomous entities with their own unique identities and character, influenced, but not directly responsive to, the larger social and economic forces operating in society.

"Social order" and "bourgeois moral values" were vague concepts in themselves, since all societies seek to maintain social order and in a capitalist society most values will appear "bourgeois." Nevertheless, the meaning of social order and bourgeois morality was given new meaning by Paul Boyer in *Urban Masses and Moral Order* (1978). In a masterful study of moral reform in the city from 1820 to 1920, Boyer showed how urban reformers responded to the urban masses whom they feared. In seeking to maintain the values of the republican village, these reformers sought moral control, but Boyer did not see this campaign to purify the city as overt cynicism or as an explicit movement to repress the working classes. In showing the diversity in urban-reform movements, even as they shared common anxieties about the urban masses and the threat from below, Boyer imparted a more sophisticated understanding of social control.[21]

While offering new insights into the meaning of reform, Boyer remained within a tradition which saw that beneath the catchwords of humanitarian reform lay profound concerns with moral order and efficiency and economy in industrial society. In this way, Boyer saw reform as a reflection of the social fears and economic needs of modern society. Little attention was given to the influence of professional values as providing an independent impetus to social policy.

Scholarship over a wide array of subjects suggested the importance of professional and bureaucratic autonomy in shaping social policy. Gerald Grob, for example, found that the key to understanding the crisis in the treatment of mental illness in modern America lay in the ideology of professionalism and a coinciding status anxiety experienced by mental-health professionals in the decades from 1875 to 1940.[22] In painting his complex picture of the treatment of the mentally ill in these decades, Grob maintained that custodial care was undermined in large part by a crisis in the psychiatric profession. Doctors involved in the treatment of the mentally ill came under criticism from others in the medical profession as well as the educated public for being out of touch with current medical research, particularly related to the etiology of mental illness and neurological advances. Mental-health professionals therefore gradually redirected their attention away from the care of institutional patients toward scientific research and toward the organizing of societies which enhanced their professional status. At the same time, institutional problems concerning overcrowding, improper care of patients, and inadequate appropriations for asylums created a crisis in the custodial care of the mentally ill. Nonetheless, mental-health experts saw little advantage in remaining involved in issues related to custodial care when new opportunities for professional advancement could be found in research and private practice.

Other studies suggested that a similar process of bureaucratization and professionalization had overwhelmed the efforts of compassionate and dedicated reformers working with dependent children at the turn of the century. Similarly, one study suggested that gender differences in the administration of charity organizations determined relief expenditures and welfare programs in the nineteenth century.[23] These studies indicated that professional and administrative values were more than mere abstractions used to rationalize social policies designed to control the masses, either through confinement, dependence, or moral persuasion.

Historians also discovered that professional values and bureaucratic politics had great importance for understanding the evolution of federal social policy in the twentieth century. Many times they have found experts and professionals playing unusual and unexpected roles in the policy process. For instance, following the stock-market crash of 1929 and continuing well into the depression, social workers opposed federal intervention into local relief efforts in fear that a permanent class of dependents might be created. And later, in 1934, social workers opposed the highly successful work-relief program of the Civil Works Administration as being too expensive, mostly because the administration was controlled by engineers unsympathetic to the professional aspirations of the social workers.[24] Experts, moreover, often played contradictory roles in the politics of Social Security during the formative years of the program. In 1938 Social Security administrators allowed the program to be expanded not for humanitarian reasons or as a way of enlarging their power base but in order to reduce the general trust fund which was under attack by conservative

Republicans, who feared that the fund, with its large capital resources, would be used to socialize the economy.[25] Equally interesting is the Brookings Institution's opposition to Truman's Fair Deal
program, which called for the further expansion of Social Security,
national health insurance, and a full employment program. Brookings
economists consistently opposed these Fair Deal measures because
they felt that federal civil servants, the experts in government, were
too vulnerable to partisan political control.

If experts during the New Deal–Fair Deal era took positions that
are not easily explained by social control or simple legitimization
models, surely the actions of experts in the Johnson-Nixon years are
even more perplexing. In planning the War on Poverty program,
experts such as Walter Heller readily abandoned discussion of income transfers, redistribution, and inequality issues, in large part
because they perceived the political liabilities of such issues. In so
doing, they showed that they were more than mere technocrats.[26]
The Nixon administration's involvement in welfare reform, through
a guaranteed national income program, presents an even more convo-
luted story, a script more from a comedy of errors than from rational
men intent on preserving their class interests. How can we explain a
tale which has federal bureaucrats left over from the previous Democratic administration turning to a guaranteed national income proposal, originally made by conservative economist Milton Friedman,
a proposal which, while cutting off aid to certain welfare recipients,
would have greatly expanded the overall rolls and radically increased
federal social spending?[27]

Clearly a larger view of the liberal state was necessary to make
any sense of the politics of social policy, which involves experts,
bureaucrats, politicians, and political constituents playing a variety
of roles with seemingly little continuity from one act to the next.
Realizing this, social scientists in the last decade have paid growing
attention to the formation of the modern state.

Robert Kelley, one of the pioneers in the development of policy
history, makes exactly this point in the Foreword when he observes
that policy history as a distinct field remains primarily concerned
with "an abstraction called the state: how it works, how it is moved
to do this or that, and, above all, its policies." Historians, he continues, have drawn heavily from political scientists in describing the
nature of the state as it has emerged in the United States. Yet he
adds that historians offer a perspective frequently not found in the
other social sciences: historians provide a dimension of time which

illuminates the evolution of the state and the development of particular policies as they have evolved over decades and generations.

Historians are by nature interested in policy (foreign policy, economic policy, family policy, business policy), but because they usually study only one country or one time period, or one theme, their work runs along innumerable separate paths which rarely connect. As a consequence, policy history persists in its presently formless condition without a distinctive method, paradigm, or clear focus of shared attention. Therefore, Kelley recommends that policy history, if it is to succeed as a separate field which goes beyond pure empiricism, must turn to the policy process itself. In doing this, policy history will approach its subject in two dimensions—as a study of separate policy themes and as a study of the process itself. By approaching policy history within these two dimensions—particular policies over time and the policy process within time—policy history becomes a set of problems which can be analyzed in systematic ways. Moreover, historians will confront basic issues concerning the nature of the state in the American polity.

The essays in this volume show the value of approaching policy formation as a set of problems which informs the historian about the development of particular policies in the political arena, the policy process itself, and the nature of the democratic state as it has emerged over time.

In his essay, "Interests, Political Parties, and Policy Formation in American Democracy," Jack Walker, a political scientist, examines the current complaint that American democracy has become gridlocked by competing interest groups which operate through well-financed and highly organized lobbies. Critics of contemporary democracy warn that given the number of these interest groups and organizations vying to be heard in Washington the system is now incapable of conducting a coherent foreign or domestic policy.

By placing the American party system and the emergence of interest groups within a historical perspective, Walker maintains that the American policymaking system is actually stronger today than it was in the nineteenth century. Although critics of contemporary American politics express misgivings about the prevalence of interest groups in the national policymaking process, Walker argues that interest groups, as they have evolved, are a preferable mechanism for the political mobilization of citizens in a democracy.[28] Walker bases his conclusion on his understanding of the changing nature of the American party system, which has entailed the breakdown of well-organized political parties capable of mobilizing masses of voters on election day. As the traditional party system came under attack by reformers and new professional groups who denounced partisanship while praising the virtues of scientific values, the sources of patronage were eliminated and social services expanded and professionalized at the state and local level. In the twentieth century, the traditional party system confronted other organizational setbacks, so that by the 1960s parties could no longer control the national policy agenda. On the state and local levels, party organizations proved unable to adjust to the problems related to the growth of suburban areas and the decline of the inner city. Without a responsive party system, urban and suburban voters supported reapportionment in order to gain representation in previously rural-dominated state legislatures. In the process, reapportionment further fractured local political organizations and carefully constructed state coalitions.

While the older party system found itself in the throes of change, new interest groups emerged to fill the power vacuum left by the the decline of party organizations. These interest groups provided new channels for the expression of public concerns in the political and policy arena. Moreover, the successful organization of these interest groups often occurred in large part because of the assistance offered by sympathetic governmental agencies seeking to develop constituencies for their own programs.

Interest groups therefore evolved to fit the needs of the political environment, both for constituents and for governmental bureaucracies. As these new interest groups developed, elaborate networks of policy professionals grew around public issues, including agriculture, housing, welfare, health care, and employment. These policy networks brought together public officials, activists, and policy specialists from Congress, governmental bureaucracies, the Executive Office, university research centers, private consulting firms, and think tanks into the policy process. As a consequence, this allowed a dramatic increase in the range of interests being represented and the number of issues being debated in Washington. These policy communities, by allowing citizens to voice their concerns, showed that American democracy was adaptive and responsive to public interests. Democracy had risen to a higher level of political participation, thereby creating a highly engaged, conflictual political environment.

The role played by the elderly and women in the policy process further suggests that a new political environment has been created that allows for greater citizen participation. At the same time, the organization of the elderly and women has been encouraged by government agencies concerned with issues related to these groups.

Andrew Achenbaum reconstructs federal policy of the aged since 1920 as an example of how federal policies in one area have affected a range of policies in other areas. With the growth of federal policies in many new areas, a network of policy specialists and constituent interests has arisen which affects the course of policy evaluation, reform, and innovation. Social Security through Medicare/Medicaid has directly influenced health care and has given incentive to the creation of groups concerned with health-care policy in the United States. Yet for all of its accomplishments, Social Security, the cornerstone of the American welfare system, suggested that our federal system was only a patchwork of welfare and employment initiatives, administered through a decentralized system of federal and state agencies and dominated by an array of conflicting bureaucracies and constituent interests. In tracing the incremental growth of the Social Security programs, Achenbaum suggests the importance of the American tradition of self-reliance, voluntarism, and anti-statism in shaping American social policy, characterized by its lack of an explicit policy agenda.

Achenbaum also finds that essential to understanding the evolution of Social Security in America is the emergence of a sprawling policy network of service providers, area agencies on aging, and senior-citizen organizations, which provide an effective advocacy forum. The development of this network of specialists and organizations concerned with the aged has reshaped the environment in which policy issues are debated. As a result, social scientists need to see federal agencies and the recipients of these federal programs as leading actors playing decisive roles in the policy process. The interaction of these interests gives policy formulation an ephemeral and incremental character. Thus the incremental and patchwork character of public policy in the United States, he conjectures, is best explained in developmental terms which recognize the differential rates of societal change and group activism over time, and the autonomous nature of many of the institutions and agencies involved in the policy process.

The importance of recipients as actors and the autonomous role federal bureaucracy can play in the policy process is examined by Brian Balogh in his review of Social Security policy during the formative years between 1935 and 1939. Balogh stresses the importance of the Social Security Board (SSB) as an independent political actor in shaping policy in these years. He portrays the SSB as primarily concerned with ensuring political support for its program in the first crucial years of the agency. Social Security Board members Arthur J.

Altmeyer, Wilbur Cohen, and Vincent Miles were well experienced in the art of politics before joining the agency. Their previous experience enabled them to cut a fine line in maintaining pensions as a right of all citizens and pensions based solely on need.

In these early years, Balogh maintains, the board paid close attention to public relations in order to enhance the program's reputation as an efficient, well-managed organization. The board also sought to build relations with Congress and the states through various ways, including technical assistance in drafting legislation and administrative guidelines, selecting personnel for state agencies, and forming alliances with groups such as the National Civil Service Reform League and the American Public Welfare Association. Further, to ensure continuing support for the Social Security program, the SSB came out strongly for a compulsory program which offered benefits to all citizens, not based on income, instead of just a program for the needy. The SSB deemed it essential to build a broad constituency in support of Social Security, if the program was to survive political attacks in Congress.

Following the election of 1936, the SSB launched a full publicity campaign, using newsreels, movies, pamphlets, and newspapers, to maintain and strengthen its public support. At the same time, the board assigned the able Wilbur Cohen to act as a liaison with Congress. As a result of this activity, the board proved to be more than a passive federal bureaucracy, but instead established itself as a political actor able to form political alliances with legislative bodies, other governmental agencies, and private interests in order to shape the policy agenda in future years.

The effective roles played by lobbying organizations, policy networks, and governmental agencies suggest a democracy at work. Through the interaction of activist bureaucracies, involved policy networks, and constituent interests, it appears that program goals are repr_ented and defended in the policy process. Judith Sealander in her study of federal policy toward women shows that the representation of women's interests in government and the organization of women's groups active in the political arena failed to ensure that issues involving women's employment, child-care centers, and birth control would be necessarily addressed in the policy arena. Sealander maintains that changes in federal policy toward women in such areas as legal equality, equal pay, and abortion availability occurred when a conducive "social climate" was created by the entrance of millions of women into the labor force, especially in white-collar occupations.

The changing status of women workers and its effect on the "social climate" explains the difference in federal policy toward women during World War II and the postwar years. While the Women's Advisory Comittee to the War Manpower Commission during World War II failed to influence in any decisive way federal policy toward women workers, significant changes occurred in the postwar years, particularly with the establishment by John F. Kennedy of the Commission on the Status on Women in 1961. The commission's report two years later revealed a new understanding and commitment toward women. The report also set the stage for Robert Kennedy, as U.S. Attorney General, to rule that federal hiring policies which favored men were illegal. In the next few years, further legislation and executive orders addressed equal pay, civil rights, education, and affirmative action for women. In the late 1970s, women workers gained further attention when philanthropies such as the Rockefeller Foundation funded research projects and organizing efforts concerning federal policies toward women and employment practices in the private sector. By the late 1970s the American people and their government had moved "painfully and uncertainly" toward new ideas concerning the status of women in the work force and in society.

The interaction of federal agencies, policy networks, and interests groups, as seen in issues related to the aged and women, tells us much about the policy process and suggests much about the nature of the democratic state in the United States. To understand fully the public-policy process historically and as it stands today, social scientists have begun to reexamine the nature of the state.[29] Historians, Edward Berkowitz maintains in his essay, have been more reticent in studying the nature of the state because they have often focused their work on the Presidency. Nonetheless, he argues that such work has led historians to overlook the institutional development of the federal government, especially its reliance on local administration and close connection to fiscal policy. If historians are to explore fully the nature of the state and its role in social policy, Berkowitz feels, they will need to understand the incremental nature of its growth and the ability of its institutions and bureaucracies to survive even at times of policy innovation.

Surely any understanding of the liberal state in America must begin with a distinction between the state in the nineteenth century and the state in the twentieth century. In describing the state in the first half of the nineteenth century, Walter Dean Burnham declared, "The chief distinguishing characteristic of the American political system before 1861 is that *there was no state*";[30] and as Morton

Keller observes, social policy came from several sources primarily centered around a party system which was well organized, participatory, and machine-dominated. The major federal social-welfare programs of this time—the pension system for Union veterans—came from politicians, not reform intellectuals, planners, or bureaucrats. If the modern administrative state was beginning to take shape, as evidenced in the rise of state boards of charities and public health, bureaus of labor statistics, railroad commissions, and movements for civil-service reform and army reorganization, its activities, as Keller notes, were "far from the realm of the issues that most concerned Americans: housing and living conditions, education, social welfare, and race relations." Further, while signs of national welfare policy were seen in calls for workmen's compensation, social insurance, and child labor, little progress was in fact made in instituting these programs on the federal level. Instead, the major accomplishments of early twentieth-century policy emerged from issues of the previous century—prohibition and immigration restriction. As a consequence, the Eighteenth Amendment and the Volstead Act—and the quota system for immigration—stand as the most important achievements of national American social policy in these years.

The twentieth century marks the full emergence of a welfare administrative state characterized by policy elites, bureaucratic infighting, and incremental politics. Federal social policy expanded to include health care and assistance to the aged, the unemployed, the disabled, families and children, the mentally ill, and numerous other dependent groups. With the emergence of the modern welfare system and its expansion into spheres once the domain of voluntaristic and local interests, scholars concerned with the history of social policy have had to confront a broad array of questions involving the social and political dynamics of the liberal state. Questions arose concerning the growth of the state and its instrumentalities for policy formulation and implementation.

A number of explanations has been offered, acccompanied by much debate. In their search for answers, scholars have turned to broader interpretations of the state, including liberal pluralist models as well as New Left or neo-Marxist models.[31] These interpretations have provided new insights into the social-policy process and the meaning of power within a democracy, but pluralist and neo-Marxist models revealed inherent inadequacies when applied to the history of social policy.

A recent line of inquiry into the nature of the liberal welfare state is suggested by a group of social scientists who interpret the modern state in terms of "regime imperatives."[32] As Ellis Hawley explains in his essay, this emphasis on "regime imperatives" combines the strengths of pluralist and neo-Marxist views by focusing attention on the political environment and the market forces which affect a liberal regime in maintaining power. The regime approach places the liberal democratic state within a context which enables social scientists to see the ebb and flow of social policy, both in the short run and over an extended period of time, as being a result of the interaction between political forces in the public arena and economic forces within the marketplace.

The modern liberal state, as viewed from this perspective, is characterized by this tension between public-welfare concerns and private economic interests which are mediated by public officials concerned with preserving their own political and institutional bases of support. In formulating and managing social programs, public officials have to be concerned with two constituencies—a political one that imparts authority to the regime, and an economic one that provides legitimacy to the regime by ensuring the economic well-being of the nation. If they are to maintain their political and bureaucratic base of support while enhancing their own power, they must look to the social welfare of their political constituents, but do so in ·a way designed not to alienate or hurt their economic constituency, which operates within the property-based marketplace.

The regime approach has much to offer. Within this view the state is given an autonomy which allows scholars to examine the interrelationship of political, administrative, and economic forces. By approaching the liberal state in terms of regime imperatives, historians can potentially discern the unique historical evolution of individual liberal democracies as well as understanding the varying degrees of state intervention and the diversity of welfare systems which so distinguishes, for example, the regimes of Great Britain, France, and the United States.

Although the regime approach is only in its early stages of development, its application for understanding social policy from John F. Kennedy through Ronald Reagan is apparent. The interplay between the imperative to maintain the general welfare and the imperative to maintain the economic well-being of the nation sets a context for the formulation and implementation of a social-policy program in each of the administrations. John F. Kennedy, intent on distinguishing his administration from the previous Republican administration, and witnessing the first signs of political mobilization of blacks, students, and white liberals activated by the civil-rights movement, developed an extensive and innovative social program for health, education, and welfare. Yet Kennedy's estranged relations with the business community, especially after the controversy over steel prices in 1962, and with a conservative Congress, doomed the program from the outset.[33]

Subsequently, in the Johnson administration, the growth of a militant civil-rights movement and the eruption of urban rioting, combined with his good relations with business, allowed Lyndon Johnson to fulfill the Kennedy promise. During the years of the Great Society, general welfare and economic well-being appeared to be momentarily balanced. But this did not last. Stagflation and early signs of economic instability pressured Nixon to call for welfare reform, but even as he did so the political rewards from income transfers led him to expand expenditures for social welfare. By 1975 social services financed by the federal government were on their way to having universalistic coverage not only for the poor but for the middle classes as well. By 1975 government social expenditures totaled approximately $388.7 billion, which covered an estimated 72.7% of all social-welfare expenditures in the nation. Per capita social-welfare expenditures had climbed from 38% of the poverty index for an urban family of four in 1960 to 107% by 1978. As Neil Gilbert observed in *Capitalism and the Welfare State* (1983), "If these public expenditures were directly distributed to the entire population in the form of cash grants, nobody would have fallen below the established poverty line of $6,000 in 1978."[34]

After 1978, a fiscal crisis caused by deficit spending, runaway inflation, and a commitment to increased defense spending finally forced Jimmy Carter to retrench social-welfare programs in order to ensure, as he saw it, the economic well-being of the nation. The emergence of a highly politicized business community in the late 1970s and the gradual erosion of leftist politics, which coincided with the inability of blacks and other disadvantaged groups to counter the forces of reaction, were major factors allowing Ronald Reagan to undertake drastic cuts in social spending.[35] Economic well-being now took precedence, at least in the short run. A robust, unfettered economy, the Reagan administration believed, was enough to ensure the general welfare.

Whether the regime model fulfills its promise to explain the history of social policy in modern America remains to be seen. Still in the 1980s historians had entered into an interdisciplinary discourse which was exploring new issues and approaches to policy history. They had moved beyond the interests of the first generation of welfare historians. The new policy historian had enlarged the research agenda to include more than the evolution of poor relief in history and was using new methodological approaches adapted from the social-sciences methods. Moreover, an entirely new set of questions concerning the state and the polity was being considered.

Historians in looking at the history of public policy became engaged in a rewarding dialogue with other social scientists, including political scientists, sociologists, and economists. Interdisciplinary exchange has long been the rhetorical tool of the social sciences. Now historians, by bringing their perspective to bear on fundamental issues involving the nature of social policy in the American polity, offer to help fulfill the promise of interdisciplinary discourse.

NOTES

1. Henry Aaron points to exactly this ambiguity when he observed that social-science research "reflects prevailing moods at least as much as it influences them; and that research, insofar as it exercises independent influences on opinions about social questions, tends over time to be profoundly conservative in its impact." Henry Aaron, *Politics and the Professors: The Great Society in Perspective* (Washington, D.C., 1978), 17. To suggest that social scientists are biased, influenced by the prevailing moods of the day, is to challenge their capacity for scholarly objectivity; in turn, it remains certain that most politicians and policymakers cannot tolerate analytical ambiguity. In this way, Aaron suggests, social science as it relates to policy satisfies neither the scholar nor the policymaker.

2. This can be explained in part by the reformist origins of the professionalized social sciences in the United States, as traced by Thomas Haskell, *The Emergence of Professional Social Science: The American Social Science Association and the Nineteenth-Century Crisis of Authority* (Urbana, 1977).

3. Often this early interest in social policy came under the guise of studying efficiency and economy in government administration, so it should not come as a surprise that Woodrow Wilson, then a graduate student in history at Johns Hopkins, called for the establishment of a national social-science research center to be located in the nation's capital, Washington, D.C. Yet many questioned the utility of history for policy studies, and some wondered whether scholarship could remain objective if history became a servant to the state. This concern was most clearly articulated later by Robert S. Lynd in *Knowledge for What? The Place of Social Science in American Culture* (Princeton, 1939).

4. This phrase is taken from Mary Furner, *Advocacy and Objectivity: A Crisis in the Professionalization of American Social Science, 1865–1905* (Lexington, 1975).

5. This point is developed by Raymond A. Mohl, "Mainstream Social

Welfare History and Its Problems," *Reviews in American History* (December 1979), 469–476.

6. Michael Katz, *Poverty and Policy in American History* (New York, 1983), 183–241, especially 219.

7. Robert H. Bremner, *Up From the Depths: The Discovery of Poverty in the United States* (New York, 1956); Clarke A. Chambers, *Seedtime of Reform: American Social Science and Social Action, 1918–33* (Minneapolis, 1963); Chambers, *Paul U. Kellogg and the Survey: Voices for Social Welfare and Social Justice* (Minneapolis, 1971); Allen Davis, *Spearheads for Reform: The Social Settlements and the Progressive Movement* (New York, 1967); Sidney Fine, *Laissez Faire and The General Welfare State: A Study of Conflict in American Thought, 1865–1901* (Chicago, 1956); Walter Trattner, *Crusade for the Children: A History of the National Child Labor Committee and Child Labor Reform in America* (Chicago, 1970); Blanche Coll, *Perspectives in Public Welfare* (Washington, D.C., 1969); June Axinn and Herman Levin, *Social Welfare: A History of the American Response to Need* (New York, 1970).

8. Sidney Fine, *Laissez Faire and the General Welfare State: A Study of Conflict in American Thought, 1865–1901* (Chicago, 1956).

9. Robert H. Bremner, *American Philanthropy* (Chicago, 1960), 186.

10. James Weinstein, *The Corporate Ideal and the Liberal State* (Boston, 1968), 157. Also, see Gabriel Kolko, *Railroads and Regulation* (Princeton, 1965); Kolko, *The Triumph of Conservatism* (New York, 1963); Martin J. Sklar, "Woodrow Wilson and the Political Economy of Modern U.S. Liberalism," *Studies on the Left* (1960), 17–47; and William A. Williams, *The Contours of American History* (Chicago, 1966).

11. Marvin E. Gettleman, "Charity and Social Classes in the United States, 1874–1900," *The American Journal of Economics and Sociology* 22 (April 1963), 313–331; (July 1963), 417–427.

12. Lasch, *The New Radicalism in America, 1889–1963: The Intellectual as a Social Type* (New York, 1965), 171, 168.

13. Anthony Platt, *The Child Savers: The Invention of Delinquency* (Chicago, 1969).

14. William A. Muraskin, "The Social Control Theory in American History: A Critique," *Journal of Social History* 9 (June 1976), 559–570.

15. David Rothman, *Discovery of the Asylum* (Chicago, 1969).

16. Rothman's study appeared to certain of his critics as only a "highly idealistic intellectual history of the period." Muraskin argued that Rothman failed to develop a "social control perspective and for this reason his book was more stimulating than convincing." Muraskin in "Social Control Theory in American History: A Critique," *Journal of Social History* 9 (June 1976), 561.

17. Frances F. Piven and Richard A. Cloward, *Regulating the Poor: The Functions of Social Welfare* (New York, 1971).

18. For instance, see Lois Banner, "Religious Benevolence as Social Control: A Critique of an Interpretation," *Journal of American History* 60 (June 1973), 23–41. Also, Richard Fox, "Beyond 'Social Control': Institutions and Disorder in Bourgeois Society," *History of Education Quarterly* 16 (Summer 1976), 559–569; and Walter I. Trattner, ed., *Social Welfare or Social Control?* (Knoxville, 1983), a collection of essays which challenges Piven and Cloward's specific, and sometimes narrow, issues.

19. Muraskin, "The Social Control Theory in American History," 568.
20. Representative studies include W. Andrew Achenbaum, *Shades of Gray: Old Age, American Values, and Federal Policies Since 1920* (Boston, 1983); LeRoy Ashby, *Saving the Waifs: Reformers and Dependent Children, 1890–1917* (Philadelphia, 1984); William Graebner, *A History of Retirement: The Meaning and Function of an American Institution, 1885–1978* (New Haven, 1980); Hugh Davis Graham, *The Uncertain Triumph: Federal Education Policy in the Johnson Years* (Chapel Hill, 1984); Gerald N. Grob, *Mental Illness in American Society* (New York, 1973); Grob, *Mental Illness and American Society, 1875–1940* (Princeton, 1983); Judith Sealander, *As Minority Becomes Majority: Federal Reaction to the Phenomenon of Women in the Work Force, 1920–1963* (Westport, CT, 1983); Gilbert Steiner, *The Children's Cause* (Washington, D.C., 1976); and Peter L. Tyor and Leland Bell, *Caring for the Retarded in America: A History* (New York, 1983). For general surveys of social-welfare policy, see Walter I. Trattner, *From Poor Law to Welfare State: A History of Social Welfare in America* (New York, 1974); James Leiby, *A History of Social Welfare and Social Work in the United States* (New York, 1978); James T. Patterson, *America's Struggle Against Poverty, 1900–1980* (Cambridge, MA, 1981). Still, major areas remained unexplored, including the nature of poverty in the nineteenth century, the economics of aggregate welfare expenditures in the nineteenth century, and a synthetic account of the emergence of the welfare state in modern America. As a consequence, James Patterson, in his later survey of the welfare state in the twentieth century, confessed that any comparison of the poor in the nineteenth century with the poor in the twentieth century was impossible in the "absence of longitudinal studies of poor people" in the period following the Civil War (James T. Patterson, *America's Struggle Against Poverty*, 13). It should be noted that Michael Katz addressed this problem in part in his demographic study of the Erie County poorhouse, 1829–1886, in Katz, *Poverty and Policy in American History* (New York, 1983), 55–87, while Alexander Keyssar shows that unemployment was endemic to industrial society in the early twentieth century, and because unemployment affected the lives of most workers, this suggests that poverty was a transitory state (Alexander Keyssar, *Out of Work: The First Century of Unemployment in Massachusetts* [New York, 1986]). Further studies of nineteenth-century poverty can be found in Eric H. Monkkonen, *The Dangerous Class: Crime and Poverty in Columbus, Ohio, 1880–1885* (Cambridge, MA, 1975); Priscilla Clement, *Welfare and the Poor in the Nineteenth City: Philadelphia, 1800 to 1850* (Carlisle, PA, 1985); and Stephen Edward Wiberly, Jr., "Four Cities: Public Poor Relief in America, 1700–1775" (Ph.D. dissertation, Yale University, 1975). See also John U. Hammon, "Poor Relief Policy in Antebellum New York State: The Rise and Decline of the Poorhouse," *Explorations in Economic History* 22:3 (July 1985); Frank R. Levstik, ed., "Life Among the Lowly: An Early View of the Ohio Poorhouse," *Ohio History* 88 (Winter 1979); Ethel McClure, "An Unlamented Era: County Poor Farms in Minnesota," *Minnesota History* 38:8 (December 1963).

It is interesting to note that as the field expanded the definition of social policy became an inclusive term which came to mean, as Gerald Grob noted, all "actions taken by government to deal with social and economic distress and other problems of an urban-industrial society." Gerald N. Grob,

"Reflections on the History of Social Policy in America," *Reviews in American History* 7 (September 1979), 293–306.

21. Paul Boyer, *Urban Masses and Moral Order in America, 1820–1920* (Cambridge, MA, 1978). For an excellent review of Boyer, along with Paul E. Johnson's study of evangelical reform in a factory town, *A Shopkeeper's Millennium: Society and Revivals in Rochester, New York, 1815–1837* (New York, 1978), see Bertram Wyatt-Brown, "The Mission and the Masses: The Moral Imperatives of the City Bourgeoisie," *Reviews in American History* 7 (December 1978), 527–534. Further nuance was given to social reform by David Rothman in his examination of institutional reform in the Progressive Era. Rothman showed that philanthropic reformers concerned with the abhorrent conditions in mental institutions and prisons at the turn of the century proposed a variety of humanitarian reforms, which when implemented by administrators and public officials were subverted in the interest of efficiency and economy.

22. Gerald N. Grob, *Mental Illness and American Society, 1875–1940* (Princeton, 1983).

23. LeRoy Ashby, *Saving the Waifs: Reformers and Dependent Children, 1890–1917* (Philadelphia, 1984). John T. Cumbler, "The Politics of Charity: Gender and Class in Late 19th-Century Charity Policy," *Journal of Social History* 14 (Fall 1980), 99–113.

24. Social workers' initial opposition to federal intervention is discussed by William W. Bremer, *Depression Winters: New York Social Workers and the New Deal* (Philadelphia, 1984). It should be noted that by 1931, as local and voluntaristic efforts were overwhelmed by the unemployed seeking relief, social workers became major proponents of federal intervention. Social workers' opposition to the CWA is discussed by Bonnie Fox Schwartz, *The Civil Works Administration, 1933–1934: The Business of Emergency Employment in the New Deal* (Princeton, 1984).

25. This fascinating story of the expansion of Social Security in these years is traced in Edward Berkowitz's much overlooked "The First Social Security Crisis," *Prologue* 15 (Fall 1983), 133–151.

26. Carl M. Bauer, "Kennedy, Johnson, and the War on Poverty," *Journal of American History* 69 (June 1982), 98–119.

27. Vincent J. Burke and Vee Burke, *Nixon's Good Deed: Welfare Reform* (New York, 1974); M. Kenneth Bowler, *The Nixon Guaranteed Income Proposal: Substance and Process in Policy Change* (Cambridge, MA, 1974); and Wayne Hoffman and Ted Marmor, "The Politics of Public Assistance Reform: An Essay Review," *Social Service Review* 50 (March 1976), 11–23.

28. For an interesting argument concerning the importance of lobbying to democracy in the nineteenth century, see Margaret Susan Thompson, *The "Spider Web": Congress and Lobbying in the Age of Grant* (Ithaca, NY, 1985).

29. Indeed, a recent group of social scientists noted this interest by entitling a collection of essays *Bringing the State Back In.* See Peter B. Evans, Dietrich Rueschemeyer, and Theda Skocpol, eds., *Bringing the State Back In* (Cambridge, MA, 1985).

30. Quoted by Robert O. Keohane, "Associative American Development, 1776–1860: Economic Growth and Political Disintegration," in John G. Ruggie, ed., *The Antinomies of Interdependence* (New York, 1983), 84.

Introduction   31

31. For an excellent study of pluralism, see Andrew McFarland, *Power and Leadership in Pluralist Systems* (Palo Alto, 1969). For Marxist and neo-Marxist views of the state, see Martin Carnoy, *The State and Political Theory* (Princeton, 1984).

32. The liberal regime interpretation of the state is outlined in Stephen L. Elkin, "Pluralism in Its Place: State and Regime in Liberal Democracy," in *The Democratic State*, Roger Benjamin and Stephen L. Elkin, eds. (Lawrence, KS, 1985), 213–265. This view draws heavily from Charles Lindblom, *Politics and Markets* (New York, 1977), and Clarence Stone, "Systemic Power in Community Decision Making," *American Political Science Review* 74 (December 1980), 978–990.

33. Jim F. Heath, *Decade of Disillusionment: The Kennedy-Johnson Years* (Bloomington, 1975); Heath, *John F. Kennedy and the Business Community* (New York, 1969); and Hobart Rowan, *The Free Enterprisers: Kennedy, Johnson, and the Business Community* (New York, 1964).

34. Neil Gilbert, *Capitalism and the Welfare State* (New Haven, 1983), 140.

35. Thomas Byrne Edsall, *The New Politics of Inequality* (New York, 1984), traces the mobilization of the business community. A series of studies by the Urban Institute examines President Reagan's cuts in social programs.

PART ONE

Reconstructions of Policy Developments

W. ANDREW ACHENBAUM

Reconstructing the History of Federal Policies Toward the Aged Since 1920

FEDERAL policies toward the aged have reached an important crossroads in their development. Fifty years ago, Franklin Delano Roosevelt characterized the original Social Security Act as the "cornerstone in a structure which is being built but is by no means complete."[1] The description remains apt today: No other public-policy initiative can match Social Security's remarkable growth and demonstrable accomplishments in such a relatively short period of time.

Much as the New Deal architects anticipated, Social Security coverage has broadened and old-age benefits have increased. In 1940, only 222,000 Americans were eligible to receive federal retirement or survivors' benefits. The average worker got a check worth $22.60 a month; widows received even less. Now dispensing roughly $11 billion in benefits each month to one out of every four American households, Social Security (OASDHI) has become the government's largest domestic program. It provided 37% of the income available to elderly householders in 1981 and 46% of that available to older persons living alone. For blacks, Social Security constitutes an even greater percentage of income; the figures were 47% and 62%, respectively, that year.[2] The incidence of poverty among the old, which once far exceeded that for the population as a whole, now approximates the national average because of this safety net. Monthly Social Security checks clearly account for the success story: 30% of those aged 65 or over have incomes that fall below 150% of the poverty line; 75% of the elderly have incomes below $10,000 per year. Without Social Security, most older people would be in desperate financial straits.

In addition, the elderly receive essential medical coverage and social services—"entitlements" which Congress in 1965 grafted onto the Social Security structure by enacting Medicare, Medicaid, and the Older Americans Act. Medicare, which currently covers $50 billion of the costs for services incurred by the elderly per annum, has two parts. Part A is a hospital insurance plan, which provides coverage to Social Security beneficiaries and those collecting federal railroad retirement benefits. Part B, a voluntary and supplementary insurance plan, was intended to cover payments for physicians and surgeons as well as for diagnostic tests, ambulance services, prosthetic devices, and the rental of medical equipment that an elderly person might need. Medicaid was designed to offer relief to those aged and poor who could not possibly meet mounting medical bills. As a result of these initiatives, it is fair to say that the elderly enjoy more public coverage for their health-care needs than any other age group. Similarly, Title I of the Older Americans Act promised unprecedented public commitment to improve the quality of life for all senior citizens: the document presumed that it was Washington's duty to facilitate individuals' pursuit of "meaningful activities" and to have access to suitable housing and efficient community services. Once again, the elderly were given special consideration by tying a whole array of benefits to the Social Security umbrella.

Any effort to reconstruct the history of federal old-age policies must acknowledge, moreover, the indirect impact that Social Security has on a wide range of income-maintenance, health-care, and social-service programs for the elderly. Early-retirement provisions and benefit formulas used in most pension plans developed in the private sector were established in light of existing eligibility criteria under Social Security; each successive package of amendments that affects the federal income-maintenance program quickly changes rules in supplementary programs. Universality of coverage under Social Security, moreover, was hindered because federal and state public-employee pension programs were treated differently than coverage in the private sector; now that nearly all workers must contribute to Social Security, reforms in government-employee benefit structures are inevitable. Institutional arrangements for providing long-term-care programs for the elderly also reflect the impact of specific titles and funding triggers in the Medicare/Medicaid matrix: "medigap" programs fill holes in the existing continuum; the new "diagnostic related groups" program has already affected the length of older people's hospital stays; nursing-home regulations are designed to accommodate and conform to federal guidelines that affect hospital and Medicaid funding.

And yet, for all of Social Security's past achievements and present significance, there is a palpable undercurrent of uneasiness even among those who extoll OASDHI's vital role in enhancing the American way of life. There have been no easy votes in Congress since the enactment of the Supplementary Security Income program (1972).[3] Politicians ritualistically reaffirm their commitment to Social Security ideals as they assure beneficiaries that the program is sound. But there are sharp divisions among Democrats and Republicans, liberals and conservatives, and policymakers and pundits concerning older Americans' needs and what Washington can and should provide. Even the elderly disagree vehemently about the future course of federal old-age policies—as the repeated clashes over priorities waged by a septuagenarian president and octogenarian Representative Claude Pepper remind us.

Those interested in writing policy history therefore have a golden opportunity to get a handle on a major public-policy problem by applying the lessons of the past. A historian would quickly acknowledge, for instance, that the "crisis mentality" that pervades discussions of the nation's income-maintenance and health-care programs reached fever pitch in the 1980s, but the problems besetting America's old-age bulwarks did not erupt overnight. There is much talk, for instance, about how an acceleration in the aging of the population or the need to accommodate the present desires and future needs of the baby-boom generation impels us to cut programs. But fears of a "nation of elders in the making" and the specter of intergenerational conflict have disturbed federal policymakers for most of the century. In any event, long-term demographic trends already have fostered new social patterns and the rise of distinctive sets of personal attitudes and mass beliefs. Similarly, it is hardly newsworthy to note that many of the structural foundations and normative assumptions that gave coherence and vitality to initiatives in the public and private sectors prior to World War II have been eroded by fundamental changes in the political economy.

These same demographic and socioeconomic forces jeopardize the welfare state abroad: in fact, caring for the elderly consumes a greater percentage of the European GNP, and costs are skyrocketing there, too. But it is striking that leaders across the Atlantic rarely make the dire projections and indulge in the apocalyptic rhetoric that are commonplace here.[4] In part, the variation in response reflects differences in the respective political philosophies and processes. Europeans generally accept the legitimacy of state planning in addressing the welfare and employment needs of citizens over the course of their lives. In contrast, "welfare" and "employment" initiatives in the United States largely remain a patchwork quilt of programs. The pluralist, decentralized nature of our federal system reinforces leaders' unwillingness to develop an explicit national *aging* policy that melds the interests of all age groups into a social-welfare network designed to reinforce mutual responsibility.

"Shades of gray" color the nature and dynamics of American old-age policies at the national level. From the very beginning, federal policymakers have been loathe to make black-and-white choices. They opted instead for building on precedents that had been successful in the private sector and at the state and local levels. Hence, as the Committee on Economic Security drafted the scope and provisions of the original omnibus legislation that became the 1935 Social Security Act, it recognized that it was not the first to tackle the problem of old-age dependency. Since the colonial era, the family and local officials had been charged with caring for older people who no longer could fend for themselves. After the Civil War, churches, unions, ethnic societies, and fraternal organizations built private old-age homes and provided informal support groups. As Union veterans came of age, they and their dependents often qualified for pensions and sometimes were eligible for free medical care and housing. Increasingly after 1900, a growing number of private corporations—notably in transportation and heavy manufacturing sectors—provided retirement pensions. Insurance companies sold old-age annuities. Most large cities and counties provided nominal pensions for retired firefighters, police, and school teachers. Some states assisted their superannuated bureaucrats. The federal government inaugurated a retirement program for civil servants in 1920. After a few false starts, several states began in the 1920s to provide monthly assistance to those who met stringent age, residency, and financial requirements.

Far from vitiating traditional American preferences for self-reliance and voluntarism, and surely not unmindful of the importance of welfare capitalism and the perduring appeal of federalism (which gave enormous latitude to governments at the state and local levels), federal initiatives typically were designed to fill gaps in a modest and self-limiting way. Even in the depths of the Great Depression, which painfully exposed deficiencies in the prevailing piecemeal approach, radical reforms were eschewed in favor of longstanding principles and "Progressive" ideals. The architects of American social insurance rarely enunciated all the goals they hoped to achieve: they chose to proceed slowly, learning what they could accomplish by proceeding in a cautious manner. Theirs was a politics of pragmatic incrementalism. Policymakers adhered to a strategy of expanding existing programs in a flexible, step-by-step manner and then making modifications at the margins when flaws became untenable.

The politics of incrementalism no longer works as effectively as it did in the 1950s and 1960s. Yesterday's "sacred cows" for the elderly sometimes seem to be "golden calves" to a new generation. Critics across the political spectrum increasingly question whether old-age entitlements should be treated like sacrosanct rights and uncontrollable expenditures.[5] Plain speaking and decisive leadership might help to clarify current misunderstandings about the purposes of multifaceted programs like Social Security, but the historical record offers little hope for reforming federal policies in bold strokes. Attempts to wage a "war on poverty" (partly by liberalizing pensions and expanding OASDHI's scope) were not as misguided or counterproductive as critics charge, but even supporters must concede that they did not usher in a Great Society. It is also becoming harder and harder to believe that Reaganomics can rejuvenate the economy, streamline government, and protect the needy of any age, but the conservative assault on Social Security has forced liberals to rethink their positions.

Thus conditions are ripe for a new direction in federal aging policies. The political debate, however, will take place in a context that barely resembles the environment in which most existing programs were born. Before 1920, the elderly never engaged in collective action to deal with the social problems associated with growing old. A sprawling network of service providers, area agencies on aging, and senior-citizen interest groups now provides an effective advocacy forum within the broader context of the country's federated system.[6] The aged once engaged in traditional occupational pursuits, rarely at the cutting edge of change. Since the Great Depression, the status of older Americans has become a central issue in public-policy circles. More than ever, the economics of aging is vulnerable to federal budgetary constraints and the struggle of American industry to maintain its competitive advantages in a global market.

Americans in the past described the elderly as a homogeneous group with similar capabilities and common afflictions. Today, few deny that senior citizens are more diverse on every salient dimension than any other age group. Gerontologists sometimes distinguish between "the young old" (those who are healthy, comfortably fixed, and active) and "the old old" (those whose conditions and prospects confirm our worst fears of senescence). Policymakers and academics lately have stressed the need to bridge through federal initiatives what Stephen Crystal characterizes as the "two worlds of aging"—one for those who will enter later years with access to sufficient funds and services to live a fulfilling and healthful life, and another for those for whom old age will be a nightmare.[7] Yet even these dualities fail to capture the range along the continuum: many of today's elderly, contend consumer experts and advertising agencies, constitute an "invisible market."[8] Indeed, the variety of ways in which older Americans are making more out of less as they grapple with the finitude of life may be pointing the path to tomorrow. I am not prepared to claim that the elderly are at the cutting edge of societal developments, blazing the next frontier of America's evolution. But I am convinced that addressing the challenges and opportunities of an aging society, particularly as they are manifested in the shape of federal policies for the elderly, will play a key role in that transformation.

For this reason, it is important to understand how and why American old-age policies took the shape they did. If we are to achieve a synthetic understanding of the public-policy process in modern American society, we must use the lessons of the past as a guidepost to future trends. Probing the evolution of OASDHI and other programs for the aged provides a crucial vantage point for making sense of the whole pattern of policymaking in the United States.

Researchers can pick and choose among a wide assortment of paradigms to interpret the history of American old-age policies. In the past, historians and gerontologists borrowed heavily from the social sciences. They have formulated a set of "middle-range" hypotheses by adapting structuralist, functionalist, relativist, and pluralist constructs. Other investigators have designed conceptual frameworks that rest on a literary device—an apt metaphor, a central irony, a perennial paradox. Some scholars, to be sure, have disavowed any theoretical predilections or narrative device.

The study of old-age policies is still in its formative stages. Many scholars have made valuable contributions simply by hewing to the canons of their respective disciplines. (Indeed, we have much to gain simply by consolidating the reliable research that is already at our disposal.) As the first monographs and articles appeared, researchers became understandably self-conscious in reckoning the appropriate level and audience as they investigated the evolution of American old-age policies. Scholars readily acknowledged that it matters greatly whether a model deals with just this nation's experiences or generates cross-national comparisons, whether one is aspiring to write a broad synthesis or to produce a detailed case study, and whether the period under scrutiny consists of a year, a presidential administration, a decade of American history, or a time frame that highlights turning points in the development of public policies.

No single paradigm—or even consensus over research priorities and methodologies—yet dominates this field of inquiry. Nonetheless, historical gerontology, which barely existed a decade ago, has already been enlivened by criticisms of "mainstream interpretations" and attacks by Marxists, non-Marxists, and neo-Marxists against the New Left and New Right. Some authors write as if society were the sum of its institutions, studiously avoiding allusions to real people. To others, recounting the accomplishments and foibles of individual policymakers and the strengths and shortcomings of specific programs is far more important than comprehending "the big picture." Ideas count for nothing in some works; elsewhere, they constitute everything worth studying. Some investigators are interested in the centripetal forces that amalgamate various groups into concerted efforts to achieve a stated (or vaguely defined) political objective; others are preoccupied with the centrifugal forces that cause interests to clash and the best-laid plans to go awry.

One way to get a handle on the theoretical issues and conceptual choices at stake is to review the literature with two questions in mind: (1) What factors have affected the ongoing evolution of federal programs for the aged? (2) Do these factors also act as major catalysts of other changes in society? In my opinion, the "motor" that investigators claim moves society, and (by extension) has decisively influenced the shape of old-age policies at the national level, appears to be either economic, political, sociological, or intellectual in character. This motor, to be sure, rarely operates in a vacuum—it influences and is affected by other societal components. But ultimately a single force seems to be the causal agent that animates an investigator's analysis and remains so throughout the time frame under consideration. Let me amplify what I mean with a few illustrations.

There is a considerable body of literature that argues that the "modern welfare state"—of which programs for the elderly are plainly an important feature—is the result of economic growth.

"The logic of industrialism," in this view, has shaped and continues to dictate priorities. Welfare programs and bureaucracies that provide services to the elderly are the natural consequence of changing technological imperatives, rising standards of living, and shifting modes of production, capital formation, and consumption. With the maturation of an advanced-industrial economy, which has given rise to an unprecedented degree of prosperity and economic growth, society itself became more complex. There were increasing pressures to develop institutional arrangements that dealt with various constituencies by differentiating among their needs and providing services in a piecemeal manner. At the same time, however, these forces have unleashed a new set of unpleasant side effects, including forms of structural poverty (including a greater risk of old-age dependency) quite unlike that found in predominantly agrarian or preindustrial settings.[9]

Variations abound in economic reconstructions of the historical record. Some stress the cyclical nature of reformist impulses, prompted alternately on the economics of affluence (as was the case in the 1960s) or a severe economic downturn (as was the case in the 1930s). Harold Wilensky, among others, claimed that "economic level is the root cause of welfare-state development, but its effects are felt chiefly through demographic changes of the past century and the momentum of the programs themselves."[10] Note that in Wilensky's schema, an economic motor affects demographic shifts and influences policy choices, independent of a society's ideological commitments and political system.

Most classical Marxists also assume that the social relations of production determine the nature and dynamics of societal change. The welfare state in such interpretations is usually portrayed as an inevitable by-product of a capitalist state impelled by its overriding need (albeit manifested often in curious and contradictory ways) to protect, sustain, and advance capitalist economic structures. Helping the poor is, then, not the foremost objective of the welfare state. On the contrary: in their attempt to legitimize and effect their particular mode of accumulating capital, bourgeois societies created welfare measures to ensure "the continuous expansion of social investment and social consumption projects that in part or in whole indirectly increase productivity from the standpoint of monopoly capital."[11] From this perspective, it is beside the point that the specific needs of the elderly and the categorical benefits they derive vary from place to place and from historical moment to historical moment. Such variations in the final analysis are less salient than the inexorable similarities in strategies and objectives shared by all capitalist societies.

Rather than emphasizing economic issues exclusively in light of budgetary costs or in terms of some covert or overt cost-benefit analysis, a second set of interpretations argues that political forces led to the creation of social services and federal income-maintenance programs for less fortunate members of society, including the elderly. American historians used to contend that Washington's concern for the rights and needs of people at lower levels of the socioeconomic order was both a reflection and the result of its extending the franchise and increasing participation by those previously excluded from the democratic process.[12] Alternative formulations of this theme remain popular. To some, the civil-rights movement and war-on-poverty initiatives are a logical extension of commitments made to advance the Enlightened ideals that originally inspired the American and French revolutions. Similarly, the political fortunes of working-class movements and the ebb and flow of socialism in Western countries intrigue those who believe that efforts to promote equality have been percolating up from the grassroots level as the balance of power has shifted downward.[13]

A variation on this thesis seeks to describe and explain the rise of "interest-group liberalism" as an ongoing struggle by increasingly more sophisticated coalitions to gain more entitlements from governmental bodies. Underscoring the "pluralist" nature of contemporary democracies, proponents of this school of thought depict the scope and shape of the welfare state largely as the outcome of demands and constraints imposed by the need to reconcile conflicting interests among vocal and politically potent groups.[14] This line of reasoning has appealed to many students of the politics of aging, especially in the United States: the model offers a plausible way to account for the pressures that culminated in the enactment of the original Social Security Act (1935) and subsequently surmounted resistance to the passage of Medicare and the Older Americans Act in the wake of Lyndon Johnson's omnibus Great Society legislation.[15] Not only did these legislative landmarks embody the spirit of the age, but they affected the course of subsequent developments. Among other things, older men and women increasingly exercised their clout as a bona-fide interest group: their impact on government priorities depended not so much on whether they (or their advocates) were given a chance to present their case but on how well they competed against others in claiming an ever-growing share of the federal budget.

Neo-Marxists have offered subtle though divergent arguments about the ways capitalists have controlled governmental activities through their control of political power at the national level. Historians in the "corporate liberal" camp, for instance, debunk the pluralist interpretation by claiming that an elite increasingly after the turn of the century sanctioned welfare initiatives in a (seemingly desperate) attempt to save the state and rationalize the new urban-industrial order. Those with power basically forged an instrumental solution to longstanding systemic malfunctions, which reached crisis proportions in the depths of the Great Depression.[16] Others develop different strands of Marxist theory, suggesting that reforms did more than protect the vested interests of the ruling class; they also served to placate the forces of insurgency present in the lower classes. Thus some interpretations stress that providing old-age assistance defused the unrest fomented among the elderly by Townsendites and other radical activists.[17]

Still others claim that trends associated with the rise of the welfare state in Europe have pertinence to the American situation. To the extent that governments in most Western countries earmark an overwhelming proportion of their services and benefits to older citizens, they claim, the modern welfare state is above all a welfare state for the elderly. The current crisis of the welfare state therefore is at one and the same time a crisis emanating from the contradictory objectives of old-age policies.[18] This is a promising line of inquiry—one which obviously conjoins the interests of the historical gerontologists and public-policy analysts—but thus far the rhetoric of its proponents is more persuasive than their evidence. "No self-declared neo-Marxist theory of the capitalist state," according to Theda Skocpol, "has arrived at the point of taking state structures and party organizations *seriously enough.*"[19] Indeed, in order to appreciate the place of bureaucracies in the development of federal policies for the aged, it is necessary to read the intellectual successors of Max Weber, not just Karl Marx.

Few doubt that bureaucracies develop a momentum of their own. Studies of welfare programs for the elderly in this country and abroad, moreover, indicate that policymakers generally have operated in an arena with limited and narrowly defined options.[20] The institutionalization of categorical programs—policies that benefit certain segments of the population but not others—hence reflect not just political judgments but serve as a mirror into the norms and organization of society itself. Obviously, few choices that policymakers make are clear-cut; the range of options themselves typically

hews to a narrow band of gray shadings. Thus sociological interpretations of the evolution of old-age policies take particular delight in
seizing on the fuzziness of definitions of the meaning of the "welfare
state" and in exposing the acumen and biases that inhere in the
ways the boundaries of old-age policies have been delineated.

Once again, ideological predilections influence the story line. "No
government can afford to expand welfare services beyond a certain
limit without being punished by inflation, unemployment, or both,"
Claus Offe argued. "The margin of decision thus becomes so slight
in a capitalist society as to be barely visible."[21] In contrast, interpretations of American welfare history that stress reformers' humanitarian impulse point to a record of building on liberal precedents in
order to respond to the needs of the deserving, often making a point
of citing the elderly's limited financing and mounting health-care
costs as a way to justify additional entitlements.[22] From a social-
control perspective, however, the original enactment and subsequent expansion of OASDHI were shrewd but stingy attempts to
defuse political clamor and "regulate the poor."[23] Note how closely
these sociological arguments dovetail with political interpretations.
What sets them apart is their focus on forces that bind and divide
American society across ethnic, racial, and class lines; little emphasis is placed on party coalitions or voting patterns.[24]

Other political sociologists eschew the interplay of various segments of the population. Instead, they engage in an intensive exege-
sis of the mind-set and activities of a fairly small number of "elite"
actors. Thus Martha Derthick brilliantly traced how Social Security
managed to take shape very much as its creators intended between
1935 and 1972. Credit for OASDHI's success, in her view, belongs to
a small cadre of experts who shuttled from government posts to
academic and consulting positions and faithfully shepherded the
program through its formative years of development, making sure
that growth occurred in a politically feasible and manageable way.[25]
Others are less sanguine about the tight rein the insiders maintained. Carolyn Weaver fears that the inner circle lost sight of the
"insurance" features of the 1935 act in their eagerness to capitalize
on its potential as a "welfare" measure. Curiously enough, Jerry
Cates claims just the opposite: so obsessed were the experts with
preserving the equity component of OASI that they "insured inequality."[26] Now that Social Security's faithful servants no longer steer
the helm, the politics of Social Security reform, in Representative
Barber Conable's exquisite phrase, depends on "artful work." Yet, as
Paul Light implies in his study of the passage of the 1983 amend-

ments, the challenge facing policymakers in the 1980s is to adapt a program designed at a different time for a society that no longer exists—keeping in mind that few politicians can afford to promulgate an explicit intellectual rationale for what must be done.[27]

Because Americans are uncomfortable with ideologies and quick to point fingers at demagogues, dispassionate and disinterested "ideas" apparently did not count for much in defusing OASDHI's financing crisis. The anti-intellectualism of American political life that Richard Hofstadter illuminated two decades ago hardly seems worth mentioning because it is taken for granted in most interpretations of the evolution of old-age policies. This political fact of life, however, has a historiographic analog. Insofar as Marxists believe that modes of production shape all other dimensions of society, they tend to treat the development of policy-relevant value systems as a substructure without any autonomy of its own. Many non-Marxists subscribe to similar views. We are long past the time in which one can claim to produce "value-free" research, but many scholars contend that people's feelings, beliefs, and ways of structuring their community are highly integrated in "modern" society. As a consequence, few public-policy analysts have bothered to incorporate intellectual history and classical political theory into their models of economic, political, and social behavior.

This is a lamentable state of affairs, because traditional intellectual and political historians have provided us with a rich lode of monographs and articles that carefully delineate the power of ideas in the political arena. Much that Ellis Hawley tells us about the salience of "anti-statism" positions in the New Deal, after all, goes a long way to explaining some of the contours of the original Social Security Act.[28] And insofar as there is a cyclical pattern to the reformist impulse, as Arthur M. Schlesinger posited nearly fifty years ago, then surely there is much to be learned about the relationship between the power of ideas and the evolution of federal policy.

In recent years, in fact, students of American public policy have been treated to several path-breaking studies that suggest that the evolution of federal initiatives cannot be understood independently of their intellectual moorings. In *Shifting Involvements*, for instance, Albert Hirschman argues that the transformation of American social-welfare activities during the twentieth century conforms to a cyclical pattern of swinging from the pursuit of private ambitions to concerted public interests. The mainspring for this trend, Hirschman hypothesizes, is the disappointments that motivate both consumers and citizens to change preferences and actions as they become disenchanted with the diminishing pleasure they derive from specific types of experience alternately in the public and private spheres.[29] In *Habits of the Heart,* Robert Bellah and his colleagues appear to have rewritten de Tocqueville's critique of *individualisme* so that it resonates with contemporary sensibilities. Both neocapitalists and welfare liberals, according to the authors, agree that the purpose of government is to give individuals the means to pursue private ends—but these opportunities and freedoms have not provided even successful and ambitious middle-class Americans with genuine fulfillment.[30] Another pair of scholars starts from the premise that the union of democracy and capitalism has long dominated American public life. These pillars of "the American ethos" frequently conflict with each other, which has resulted in opposing policy prescriptions. On the basis of public-opinion-poll data and surveys of policymakers' views, however, it seems likely that Americans will continue to expect to receive their rights to entitlements under our form of welfare capitalism.[31]

Such studies provide an essential correction to models in which ideas are discounted and mass beliefs do not fit neatly into the trajectory of the driving "motor." In my judgment, however, the high level of abstraction and ambiguity embodied in the meanings of "capitalism," "democracy," "the public interest," and "individualism"— terms whose meanings shift over time—vitiates the influence of such pivotal tenets of nitty-gritty policy-making decisions. The policy elite, to be sure, appeals to such abstractions in their rhetoric. Yet a systematic review of the language used to institute and implement any significant old-age policy indicates that operational definitions and technical terms tend to reduce these overarching principles and values into more discrete, malleable components.[32]

What we need at this point, therefore, is an analytic construct that gives us a sense of the "big picture" as it describes and explains the evolution of old-age policies. Such a framework would incorporate insights from previous studies, embracing disparate and fluid economic, political, social, and cultural phenomena without giving undue weight to any single strand of the analysis. In addition, any worthwhile model must have a temporal perspective that too often is missing, understated, or mechanistically imposed in studies currently available.

We face three immediate historiographic challenges. First, we have not yet succeeded in placing the history of the elderly since 1920 into the context of the social history of the United States during the last half-century. The conceptual difficulty of this task is the mirror image of the intellectual problem encountered by those who initially tried to sketch out the history of aging in America. A decade ago, colonial and nineteenth-century historians had not yet figured out what was distinctive about the meanings and experiences of being old and growing older before the Great Depression. Much was known, however, about the history of the family, race relations, social mobility, and the impact of urbanization and industrialization on various ethnic and occupational groups. Thus most historians tried to "fit" the elderly into existing frameworks.[33] In contrast, the major institutions, events, and statistics about the aged in contemporary America are familiar, yet we still lack a sophisticated social history of the United States since the Great Depression.[34]

Second, we have not paid sufficient attention to the complexity of dynamics of old-age programs since World War II, making it quite difficult to integrate the fields of the so-called "new" social history and the "old-fashioned" concerns of political history. There has been a regrettable tendency to concentrate all historical interest in the formative years of a program and to write as if all subsequent developments flow naturally from initial presuppositions and operating procedures. Thus the brilliant social-control model offered by William Graebner in A History of Retirement affords us fascinating insights into the ways pension schemes in the public and private sectors from 1880 through 1936 were designed to regulate the labor force and remove superannuated workers in the name of efficiency. Yet Graebner never really grapples with the fact that the subsequent impact of "retirement" might have been redirected by the complexity and ambiguity of the historical process itself.[35] Part of the confusion arises from the misleading impression that social policies evolve in a vacuum. Graebner never tells us what the aged thought of programs, or how they adapted their working careers to make the best of their options. The elderly are treated homogeneously as conniving or unwitting pawns. Surely economists and sociologists have presented sufficient data to show us that older workers play a decisive role in adapting socioeconomic policies to achieve their own goals and preferences.[36]

Third, we still lack a handle on the interconnections between policy initiatives and the larger political economy that would allow us to formulate a societal interpretation of aging policies. Despite countless studies, academic experts and government officials are still unable to agree on the precise role of a major program like OASDHI on levels of savings and consumption, employment behavior, or even future federal deficits.[37] For this reason, I am not persuaded by the political economy of aging models posited by Carroll Estes, John Myles, or Laura Katz Olson, which argue that the self-destructive tendencies of all bureaucratic societies ominously set the stage for a "crisis" in the welfare state. The motif of "internal contradiction" implies that sooner or later all capitalist democracies will collapse—though probably not before a last-ditch effort to rectify the situation at the expense of the old and the poor.[38] Similarly (though for diametrically opposed reasons), the Marxists' *Schaderfreude*—joy at another's misfortune—complements the neoconservatives' fears that any redistributive policy perforce undermines the elegant efficiency of the private market. If analysts at both ends of the political spectrum are correct in contending that we are trapped in the "iron cage" of modernity's limited future, there is no need to wonder why pessimism runs deep.

There is an alternative metaphor for accounting for the current "crisis" in old-age policies. "The existence of conflicts or contradictory tendencies does not mean that the state must devour its own tail or collapse in total paralysis," Deborah Stone recently argued in *The Disabled State.* "States, too, can learn to walk with crutches and braces."[39] Just as the state hobbles along, so too policymakers manage to muddle through.

The present status of old-age policies, in my view, reflects past mistakes as well as astute insights which were executed in a volatile and complex societal environment. They result from compromises forged long ago for different purposes; their creators would hardly be surprised that their initiatives must be readjusted to conform to prevailing trends and future possibilities. Changes in the status quo are forged in the nation's vital but ephemeral center: an arena where logic is grudgingly appreciated and consistency rarely valued. Particularly in the United States, where the stigma of "welfare" confounds political action and spills over into the body politic, it is the norm rather than the exception to tinker with existing programs and contemplate reforms on an incremental basis.[40] Significant alterations are possible: if the times are good, the elderly will benefit; if the economy sours, the old cannot expect to receive special entitlements. For better and for worse, however, America's policy elite tries to lead an informed electorate by persuading them that any changes in the status quo arise out of longstanding practices and conform to current circumstances and foreseeable trends.[41]

It is for this reason that I think a developmental model makes the most sense. Scholars (myself included) have had modest success in applying a "modernization" model in reconstructing the history of old-age policies in America and Europe. We have gone beyond original formulations that opted for mono-causal linkages between demographic shifts and the rise of urbanization/industrialization/bureaucratization, etc., to explain changes over time to create more supple models that should lead us to the societal interpretations I am urging. At their best, modernization models increase the likelihood that researchers will identify interdependencies in the political economy, recognize differential rates of societal change and the autonomous nature of many institutions, and be sensitive to pivotal dysfunctions in attitudes, behavior, and policy.[42] But criticisms of existing modernization have been so damning—it is no less easy to avoid teleology and determinism using this construct than it is in formulating a neo-Marxist schema—that it might be better at this stage of our discussion to move to alternative formulations. Some investigators, for instance, are presently exploring ways to think of America as an "aging" society, mindful of the dangers of making too facile use of an analogy that equates societal development with the stages of an individual's life course.[43] Such a model would conjoin the policy history of the aged with educational and socialization issues that are paramount in writing a policy history of children and youth and with the employment and family-related issues that are central to the policy concerns of the middle-aged.

The ultimate value of a developmental model is that it helps us grasp how past decisions affect future options. America's current old-age programs, after all, did not emerge full blown. They grew out of the richness and contrarieties in our nation's evolution. They result from past policies—not just at the federal level but in the private sector and at the grassroots level—and they have been shaped by the unexpected and often counterproductive consequences of well-intentioned ideas. American old-age programs demonstrate that in the policymaking arena artful rhetoric and technocratic legerdemain often count for more than candor or social experimentation. Hence future policies will doubtless be intimately linked to national conditions overall, but their precise shape is impossible to predict. Where we go from here depends in large measure on how well we build on past successes, learn from our mistakes, and adapt to ever-changing conditions. By broadening our focus from the reconstruction of old-age policy-making to policies for all age groups, we should be able to grasp the "big picture" that affects *all* policies—not just those for any single age group. And if we can accomplish that task, then efforts at theory building in the fledgling field of policy history will be enhanced by the possibility of transferring middle-level generalizations from this narrow field of inquiry to other areas of the policy realm.

NOTES

1. "Presidential Statement Signing the Social Security Act," reprinted in *The Report of the Committee on Economic Security of 1935*, 50th Anniversary edition (Washington, D.C.: National Conference on Social Welfare, 1985), 145.

2. U.S. Senate, Special Committee on Aging, *Developments in Aging, 1983* (Washington, D.C.: Government Printing Office, 1984), 18; *Social Security Bulletin* 47 (July 1984), 40–41, 57.

3. SSI provides more than two million Americans who do not qualify for OASDHI benefits a minimal level of assistance.

4. Peter N. Stearns, "Contemporary Social Security in Comparative Perspective: What Kind of Crisis?" in U.S. Senate Special Committee on Aging, *Fifty Years of Social Security*, serial 99–C (Washington, D.C.: Government Printing Office, 1985), 71—87.

5. Peter Ferrera, *The Inherent Contradiction* (San Francisco: Cato Press, 1981); James Fallows, "Entitlements," *Atlantic Monthly*, November 1982, 52–53; Robert Kuttner, *The Economic Illusion* (Boston: Houghton Mifflin, 1984).

6. William P. Browne and Laura Katz Olson, eds., *Aging and Public Policy* (Westport: Greenwood Press, 1983); Jack L. Walker, "The Origins and Maintenance of Interest Groups in America," *American Political Science Review* 77 (April 1983), 390–406.

7. Stephen Crystal, *America's Old Age Crisis* (New York: Basic Books, 1982).

8. Rena Bartos, "Over 49: The Invisible Consumer Market," *Harvard Business Review* 58 (January–February 1980), 140–148.

9. Clark Kerr et al., *Industrialism and Industrial Man*, rev. ed. (New York: Oxford University Press, 1964); F. L. Pryor, *Public Expenditures in Communist and Capitalist Nations* (Homewood, IL: Richard D. Irwin, 1968).

10. Harold L. Wilensky, *The Welfare State and Equality* (Berkeley: University of California Press, 1975), 47.

11. James O'Connor, *The Fiscal Crisis of the State* (New York: St. Martin's Press, 1973), 24.

12. Daniel Boorstin, *The Genius of American Politics* (Chicago: University of Chicago Press, 1953); Richard Hofstadter, *The Age of Reform* (New York: Vintage Books, 1955).

13. Seymour Martin Lipset, *Political Man* (Garden City, NY: Doubleday, 1960); C. Hewitt, "The Effect of Political Democracy and Social Democracy on Equality in Industrial Societies," *American Sociological Review* 42 (June 1977), 45–464.

14. David B. Truman, *The Governmental Process* (New York: Alfred A. Knopf, 1951); Theodore Lowi, *The End of Liberalism* (New York: W. W. Norton, 1968).

15. Henry J. Pratt, *The Gray Lobby* (Chicago: University of Chicago Press, 1976); Robert B. Hudson and Robert H. Binstock, "Political Systems and Aging," in *Handbook of Aging and the Social Sciences*, Robert H. Binstock and Ethel Shanas, eds. (New York: Van Nostrand Reinhold, 1976), 369–401.

16. James Weinstein, *The Corporate Ideal in the Liberal State: 1900– 1918* (Boston: Beacon Press, 1968); Ronald Radosh, "The Myth of the New Deal," in *A New History of Leviathan: Essays on the Rise of the Corporate State*, Ronald Radosh and Murray Rothbard, eds. (New York: E. P. Dutton, 1972), 146–187.

17. Jill S. Quadagno, "Welfare Capitalism and the Social Security Act of 1935," *American Sociological Review* 49 (Fall 1984), 632–649. In general, see Nicos Poulantzis, *State, Power, Socialism* (London: NLB, 1978).

18. Anne-Marie Guillemard, ed., *Old Age and the Welfare State* (Beverly Hills: Sage, 1983).

19. Theda Skocpol, "Political Responses to Capitalist Crises: Neo-Marxist Theories of the State and the Case of the New Deal," *Politics and Society* 10 (1980), 199–200.

20. For more on this general point, see Hugh Heclo, *Modern Social Politics in Britain and Sweden* (New Haven: Yale University Press, 1974); Aaron Wildavsky, *Speaking Truth to Power* (Boston: Little, Brown, 1979).

21. Claus Offe, "Advanced Capitalism and the Welfare State," *Politics and Society* 2 (Summer 1972), 479–488.

22. Arthur J. Altmeyer, *The Formative Years of Social Security* (Madison: University of Wisconsin Press, 1963); Theodore Marmor, *The Politics of Medicare* (Chicago: Aldine, 1973).

23. Frances Fox Piven and Richard A. Cloward, *Regulating the Poor* (New York: Vintage, 1971); Walter I. Trattner, ed., *Social Welfare or Social Control?* (Knoxville: University of Tennessee Press, 1983).

24. See, by way of contrast, Jerome M. Clubb, William H. Flanigan, and Nancy Zingale, *Partisan Realignment: Voters, Parties and Government in American History* (Beverly Hills: Sage, 1980).

25. Martha Derthick, *Policymaking in Social Security* (Washington, D.C.: The Brookings Institution, 1979).

26. Carolyn Weaver, *The Crisis in Social Security* (Durham, NC: Duke University Policy Studies, 1982); Jerry Cates, *Insuring Inequality* (Ann Arbor: University of Michigan Press, 1983).

27. Paul Light, *Artful Work* (New York: Random House, 1985).

28. See Ellis Hawley, "Social Policy and the Liberal State in Twentieth-Century America," in this volume.

29. Albert O. Hirschman, *Shifting Involvements* (Princeton: Princeton University Press, 1982).

30. Robert N. Bellah et al., *Habits of the Heart* (Berkeley: University of California Press, 1985).

31. Herbert McClosky and John Zaller, *The American Ethos* (Cambridge, MA: Harvard University Press, 1985).

32. Murray Edelman, *Words That Succeed, Policies That Fail* (New York: Academic Press, 1977); Harold R. Johnson et al., *American Values and the Elderly* (Ann Arbor: Institute of Gerontology, 1979).

33. See, for instance, David Hackett Fischer, *Growing Old in America*

(New York: Oxford University Press, 1977); W. Andrew Achenbaum, *Old Age in the New Land* (Baltimore: Johns Hopkins University Press, 1978); and Carole Haber, *Beyond Sixty-Five* (New York: Cambridge University Press, 1983).

34. Two possible models are Morton Keller, *Affairs of State* (Cambridge, MA: Harvard University Press, 1977), and Morris Janowitz, *The Last Half-Century* (Chicago: University of Chicago Press, 1978).

35. William Graebner, *A History of Retirement* (New Haven: Yale University Press, 1980).

36. James Schulz, *The Economics of Retirement*, 3d edition (Belmont, CA: Wadsworth, 1985); Herbert Parnes, ed., *Work and Retirement* (Cambridge, MA: MIT Press, 1981); Robert C. Atchley, *Social Forces of Later Life*, 4th edition (Belmont, CA: Wadsworth, 1985); and Gary S. Fields and Olivia S. Mitchell, *Retirement, Pensions and Social Security* (Cambridge, MA: MIT Press, 1985).

37. Henry J. Aaron, *The Economic Effects of Social Security* (Washington, D.C.: The Brookings Institution, 1982).

38. Carroll Estes, *The Aging Enterprise* (San Francisco: Jossey-Bass, 1979); John Myles, *The Old-Age Welfare State* (Boston: Little, Brown, 1984); Laura Katz Olson, *The Political Economy of Aging* (New York: Columbia University Press, 1982).

39. Deborah A. Stone, *The Disabled State* (Philadelphia: Temple University Press, 1984), 189.

40. James A. Patterson, *America's Struggle Against Poverty, 1900–1980* (Cambridge, MA: Harvard University Press, 1981).

41. I elaborate this thesis in my Twentieth-Century Fund report, *Social Security: Visions and Revisions.*

42. W. Andrew Achenbaum, *Shades of Gray* (Boston: Little, Brown, 1983), 182–185; Peter Flora and Arnold J. Heidenheimer, eds., *The Development of Welfare States in Europe and America* (New Brunswick: Transaction Books, 1981).

43. See, for instance, my "Images and the Myth of America as an Aging Society" and essays by Alan Pifer, H. R. Moody, and John and Matilda Riley in the spring 1986 issue of *Daedalus.*

BRIAN BALOGH

Securing Support: The Emergence of the Social Security Board as a Political Actor, 1935–1939

IN the past fifteen years, historians of twentieth-century American politics have discovered the significance of large-scale organizations. In their accounts of the Progressive Era and its antecedents, Robert Wiebe, Robert Cuff, Samuel Hays, and most recently Stephen Skowronek have focused on bureaucratization, the quest for efficiency, and the growth of the administrative state.[1] Ellis Hawley has reanalyzed the 1920s in a similar vein.[2] It was Louis Galambos who identified this trend and in it saw the basis for a new conceptual framework, which he called the "organizational synthesis."[3] This synthesis has been instrumental in explaining one of the most dramatic transformations in the history of American politics—framed at one end by an era of torchlight parades and high voter participation directed toward achieving legislated solutions, and at the other by open-ended legislation that often marked the beginning rather than the resolution of political struggles.[4]

I want to thank the Department of History at Johns Hopkins University for its financial support in the writing of this essay. I owe a special debt to Professor Louis Galambos for his critical readings of this essay in draft form, and to the assistance of the staff of the National Archives, particularly Dr. Aloha South.

It is ironic that having shifted the locus of politics, historians have been slow to follow it into its new haunts. They have explained the social and economic causes behind the transformation—usually in terms of interdependence—and they have meticulously traced the course of the legislation that brought these organizations to life. But when it came to looking at the organizations themselves, stock descriptions—usually drawn from Weberian models which left little room for politics, or, conversely, social control models leading to the inevitable "capture" of agencies—were the rules.[5]

Fortunately, there are signs that historians are discovering the independent political agendas buried in bureaucratic policymaking. This trend is best represented by the recent work of Samuel Hays. In his essay on the historical development of regulation Hays writes: "We need to observe the actors in that regulatory process more directly and to focus on the people involved in it, their perspectives and choices, the web of public and private institutions surrounding them, and the relationship between administrative choice and the larger public ideology and choice."[6]

My own study of the Social Security Board follows Hays's lead and focuses on this agency's formative years. These are crucial years for most agencies and they provide an excellent opportunity to examine its political development and influence. It is in the early years that agencies must feel their way toward the resolution of contradictions purposely left ambiguous in their enabling legislation. Not only are these decisions political, they are often volatile, being precisely the issues that more representative bodies chose not to touch at the time legislation was passed. The political skills developed by a new agency may well determine whether it survives or perishes. They inevitably influence the shape of the policy that emerges. Finally, examining politics in an agency's formative years is an important step toward developing a more dynamic conception of administrative politics. Many of the images we rely upon today are drawn from the political-science literature. While illuminating, it is important to remember that their emphasis on expert decision-making limited to a few actors operating behind closed doors is based upon the political scientists' observations of established institutions.[7] This does not necessarily explain how these organizations became established institutions or the political skills that were required to get there.

The case of the Social Security Board (SSB) is instructive. The SSB developed a variety of skills—in particular, in the area of public relations—that do not fit into the insulated style of politics normally associated with administrative agencies. The SSB used its political arsenal to establish a consensus for the least familiar but most hotly debated title of the Social Security Act—the title commonly called social insurance today. Ultimately, the SSB was successful in establishing a style of policymaking that Martha Derthick has characterized as "constricted consensus."[8] But before 1939, Derthick acknowledges that "the need to get the program securely established was still the first priority of executive planners."[9]

It is to the crucial transitional period—framed by broadly arrayed public pressure that led to a legislative compromise on the one end, and the far more restricted and directed debate at the other—that we now turn.

THE LEGISLATION

The Social Security Act, which was signed into law by President Roosevelt on August 14, 1935, established three major programs: grants to states for Old Age Assistance (OAA) administered by the states and supervised by the federal government; compulsory old age insurance, entitled Old Age Benefits (OAB), to be administered by the federal government; and Unemployment Compensation (UC) administered by the states and supervised by the federal government.[10] OAA provided matching federal funds (up to $15 a month) for persons sixty-five or older, effective as soon as state plans were approved. OAB called for taxes at the rate of 2%—shared by covered employees and employers—to begin January 1, 1937; regular benefits to those retiring at age sixty-five were not to be paid out until January 1942.[11] Unemployment Compensation established a federal tax on employers of 1% of earned wages (rising to 3% by January 1938) effective January 1, 1936.[12] Employers could, however, claim a credit of up to 90% of that amount (the remaining 10% was to fund the cost of administration) for taxes paid to state UC programs.

In the words of the president of the American Association for Social Security, Abraham Epstein:

> The Act embodies all three possible philosophies of government: (1) The principle of Federal grants-in-aid to States; that is, "we'll help you finance a State plan if you'll set it up in such a way as to meet our requirements," (2) A Federal-State tax-offset scheme, which is to say, "we'll levy taxes to finance the undertaking, but we'll remit them in any State which

levies similar taxes of its own," and (3) A completely national plan; that is, "we'll levy the taxes and conduct the whole enterprise."[13]

Thus the Social Security Act was flexible legislation that offered something to local-control traditionalists who favored the grant-in-aid approach and immediate, though limited, benefits to the aged. But it also provided a federally administered alternative—OAB—that was self-financing and promised a permanent solution to the problem of aged dependency at little cost to the federal government.

ORGANIZATION

The Social Security Act established a three-member bipartisan board, appointed by the President with the advice and consent of the state. As chairman, the President appointed the Republican ex-governor of Vermont John Winant. The two Democratic appointments were Arthur Altmeyer and Vincent Miles. Miles was a lawyer from Arkansas who had been that state's representative on the Democratic National Committee; Altmeyer was a seasoned state and federal administrator.[14]

Altmeyer was relentless in his efforts to establish firmly the OAB insurance approach as the cornerstone of American social-welfare programs. That the current Social Security Administration is housed in the Altmeyer Building is just one indication of the dominant role he played. Altmeyer epitomized the cautious strategy pursued by the SSB: he was a stickler for detail, sensitive to pressure from key political actors, and always willing to defer a confrontation that he risked losing, only to return to the matter when the situation appeared to be more advantageous. Describing his managerial style to an interviewer in 1966, Altmeyer confided:

> I have a very methodical mind, I think a good mind . . . but not a flashy mind, and I think a conservative mind in weighing the pros and cons and probably leaning a little bit to the conservative side when it comes to an administrative decision.[15]

One reason for Altmeyer's caution was his explicit desire to build a lasting institution. In his words:

I think it was necessary to establish the SSB as a more or less disembodied institution whose head couldn't be chopped off because of personalities involved in some decision. So that fitted into my notion of conservatism and desire not to stick my neck out too far.[16]

The board selected Frank Bane, director of the American Public Welfare Association, as its executive director. Bane was the key figure in negotiating OAA and UC plans with the states. He had built his career as a state welfare administrator in Virginia and Tennessee and referred to himself as a "walking delegate for the states."[17]

That key SSB staff had already experienced the give-and-take of legislative compromise contributed to their flexibility as administrators. Two of the three board members (Winant and Altmeyer), Executive Director Bane, the SSB's counsel, the directors of two operating bureaus, and Altmeyer's influential assistant, Wilbur Cohen, had all participated in drafting the original bill. They were familiar not only with the final legislation as it emerged from Congress but also with the history of the legislation and the balancing of interests that shaped the final act. If one of Altmeyer's favorite quotations (from John R. Commons) was true, and administration really was legislation in action, many of the SSB's administrators joined that action after a running start.

The board members and its executive director also capitalized on one of the most important aspects of the SSB's organizational structures: the fact that one board was responsible for administering the three different philosophies of social welfare incorporated in the Social Security Act.[18] Specifically, this meant that conflicts between the OAA and the OAB approach could be resolved within the SSB, rather than debated publicly between agencies.[19]

Another distinctive organizational trait of the SSB—its relative independence from Executive Branch supervision—created both disadvantages and advantages for the board. On the one hand, the SSB was unencumbered by interference from a cabinet-level secretary.[20] On the other hand, the board's independent status exposed it to direct pressure from Congress. Because the Social Security Act exempted lawyers and "experts" from the civil-service appointment process, the SSB was flooded with congressional referrals in the winter of 1935–36.[21] Fortunately, from the SSB's point of view, many of its key personnel were already in place.[22] While Altmeyer paints a picture of steadfast resistance to patronage requests, it appears that the SSB grew more flexible on this issue in order to smooth over differences with key congressmen.[23]

Several features of the SSB's early organization and staffing stand out. They clearly set a pattern for its future actions. That its executives were talented, but cautious and politically sensitive, was an important factor in the SSB's success. Altmeyer, in particular, was a guiding force in the first five years. Key personnel were also experienced in the art of compromise and realpolitik. They were particularly sensitive to potential conflicts with the states and Congress. They knew how to take advantage of the strengths that the SSB's organizational structure offered, and through limited tactical retreats were able to gloss over its disadvantages. Fitting into the existing political milieu was crucial to them: their survival as an organization and their ambitions to establish a lasting institution depended on it.

HOLDING THE LINE: SUPERVISING OLD-AGE ASSISTANCE IN THE STATES

Although the SSB favored the insurance approach (OAB) to meeting the needs of the elderly, it could not ignore pressure for quick results. Regular OAB benefits were not scheduled to begin until 1942, but by approving state OAA plans, the SSB could provide an immediate response to the demands of the elderly. Consequently, the SSB's top priority in its first six months of operations was approving the state proposals.

OAA was, however, the program with the least amount of federal statutory control. Legally the SSB's hands were tied in the crucial areas of personnel selection and in establishing eligibility criteria. Although the legislation required that the SSB approve a plan of administration for every state, the law explicitly prevented the SSB from prescribing provisions that had to be followed in regard to "selection, tenure of office and composition of personnel."[24] The law also limited the SSB's discretion insofar as it contained virtually no definition of need, thus leaving this important criterion to the states.[25]

The law thus created a tricky political problem for the board. Despite its desire to get benefits into the hands of needy elderly persons as quickly as possible, the SSB feared that inadequate controls over personnel would lead to scandals that might shake the foundations of the permanent institution it sought to build. The SSB was also concerned that in the absence of a clear federal definition of need, states might submit plans that waived any demonstration of it; in other words, plans that might come dangerously close to the Townsend concept of aid to everybody over 60—regardless of need.[26] Maintaining this fine line between pensions as a right and pensions based on need was crucial to the SSB. Years later, Altmeyer was quite forthcoming about the issue:

> If the SSB had approved state laws which specified the pay-
> ment of a uniform amount to all persons over 65 regardless of
> need, it is quite likely that it would have fanned the flames of
> the Townsend movement, which was a factor in the 1936
> elections and reached its peak of intensity during the 1938
> congressional elections. The final result might very well have
> been to scrap the old age insurance system before it ever went
> into operation.[27]

Consequently, the SSB moved cautiously to achieve through administration of the law what it had lost when the law was written. Well aware of Congress's concern that OAA be locally administered, the SSB went out of its way in all of its public statements to insist that it had no desire to influence state plans. Behind the scenes, however, the SSB began to orchestrate its interpretation of the law. Bane put it this way:

> We began to suggest—I underscore suggest—to the states as
> they developed their plans that it would be a good idea for them
> to have merit systems and so on. We could not enforce them at
> that time. It was not in the act. In fact, the act specifically
> provided that we couldn't dictate their personnel standards.[28]

McKinley and Frase—observers of the SSB's first two years of administration who wrote a "capture and record" account of their observations—called this technique "a policy of persuasion, teaching and friendly leadership."[29] Whenever there was a potential problem with a state plan, Bane was sent to negotiate. He was constantly on the road, talking to governors and pushing the board's view of Social Security.[30]

The SSB also strengthened its hand by providing "technical assistance" to developing state administrations.[31] According to Bane:

We used to have little task forces to send out. If they [the states] were writing a statute, we would send some of the people from the general counsel's office. If they were setting up an accounting system, we would send someone from our accounting outfit. . . . And I did a lot of roaming around myself, promoting the kind of setup which we would want, particularly in connection with the state legislatures if they were considering acts.[32]

The SSB did not confine itself to systems; it also intervened in the actual personnel selection process. Ewan Clague, who eventually became the SSB's director of research and statistics, described how he influenced the selection of particular personnel: "I sent out my regional representatives to talk to some university in the community and find out if there weren't some professor who would like to take time off to work in this field. Then we urged appointment at state level."[33] Clague claimed that he was successful in securing positions for many of these professors, who in turn recruited their students.[34]

The SSB also applied pressure indirectly. It worked closely with groups like the National Civil Service Reform League and the American Public Welfare Association, who in turn lobbied state legislatures.[35] Thus when Bane left the SSB to become the director of the Council of State Governments, he could still be very helpful in his new position.[36]

The SSB thus sought to shape state policy while avoiding conflicts but was eventually forced to hold hearings and suspend grants in three states: Illinois in July 1937, Oklahoma in February 1938, and Ohio in October 1938. These drastic steps came, however, only after months of negotiation and (in the board's view) empty promises by the states.[37]

In Illinois, the SSB delayed intervention because it did not want to be charged with playing politics during the primary campaign that pitted Governor Hoerner against the regular Democratic organization.[38] When the SSB finally did take action, Illinois was quick to offer promises that it would clean up its administration. The SSB was equally quick to accept. Both sides in the dispute apparently feared they were suffering from bad publicity.[39] Louis Resnick, the SSB's director of informational services, wrote to Frank Bane that "the Board is receiving the brunt of public criticism and condemnation because of its suspension of grants to the State for old-age assistance."[40] Resnick went on to propose that in the future comparable situations be anticipated "by a carefully handled informational program to prepare the public for the possibility of a suspension of funds."[41]

Subsequently, in handling the Oklahoma and Ohio situations, the SSB showed an increased awareness of the importance of public relations.[42] As McKinley and Frase recognized: "The field staff and the Board must have knowledge of the political topography of the states if they expect to steer a successful course."[43] Their prescription called for:

> . . . negotiation, compromise, aversion of the eyes, and occasional cracking down. . . . [A] good administrator will have to be prepared to accept and apply them when the situation indicates. In this sense, politics and administration will have to march hand in hand.[44]

By pursuing this strategy, the SSB hoped to eliminate potential problems before the state plans were even submitted. The technical assistance it provided was one means for assuring this outcome. Where states threatened to establish potentially dangerous precedents, high-level negotiation and indirect pressure on state legislatures were also important. Although largely successful, these techniques did not always work. Where public reports of corruption threatened to tarnish the SSB's reputation, it distanced itself from the charges by holding hearings and suspending grants. Here, public relations became increasingly important. Without winning this battle, it was virtually impossible for the board to employ the only direct control it had over state OAA programs—cutting off funds.

PROMOTING OLD-AGE BENEFITS: SELLING INSURANCE

Although the SSB sought to dampen enthusiasm for more radical pension proposals by getting benefits in the hands of the elderly as quickly as possible, its greatest concern was in establishing a permanent alternative to government-funded pensions. As we have seen, the Social Security Act incorporated several different philosophies in addressing the problem of providing security to the aged. The SSB strongly favored the compulsory-contribution approach embodied in OAB.

Analysis of the SSB's organizational and political requirements suggests at least three reasons for this preference. First, of all the titles established under the act, OAB was the only one that was directly administered by the federal government. Thus most of the SSB's personnel were assigned to this program and responsibility for successful administration rested squarely on the SSB. More significantly, the program offered unlimited opportunities for agency expansion.

But the SSB's emphasis on OAB seems to have involved more than the desire for potential agency expansion. OAB offered a managed solution to the problem of aged dependency. OAB was not likely to suffer from runaway costs in the foreseeable future because the insurance principle required contributions from both employers and employees. The federal government contributed nothing out of general revenues (as opposed to OAA, where the federal government matched state contributions).

It was not just potentially high costs that were managed by the insurance approach. The concept provided built-in restraints to political demands by establishing the principle that what you get back depends on what you put in. As J. Douglas Brown, a consultant to the Committee for Economic Security (CES) who helped draft OAB legislation, put it:

> Less tangible, but even more important [than controlling costs] in terms of morals and motivation in a democratic country, was the fear that a steadily increasing proportion of aged people on needs-test assistance would lead to frustration, bitterness and resultant repercussions. The welling emotionalism that supported the Townsend movement was all too evident.[45]

Brown felt that OAB provided "a more constructive program" that would "limit the assistance approach to its appropriate residual level of protection."[46]

That "appropriate residual level," Brown's euphemism for the poor, suggests a third reason behind the SSB's policy choice. The board was too politically savvy to attempt to build a lasting institution on a foundation supported only by the poor. "It was a dictum of program excutives," writes Martha Derthick, that

> "a program for the poor is a poor program.". . . They assumed that the poor in the United States are despised by themselves and by others, and that a government program designed for

their benefit would be despised too. Hence the ideal program for old age security should benefit everyone, poor and non-poor. Benefitting all classes, it would have the support of all classes.[47]

Thus, organizational imperatives (OAB was the only program directly administered by the SSB), the need to manage political and fiscal conflict, and considerations of future political support pushed the SSB toward its preference for OAB.

But administrators' predilections hardly translated directly into broad-based support. When the SSB began pushing the insurance concept, support for the program—a political untouchable today!—was not yet clearly defined. Unlike OAA, which had been debated for years, OAB was a relatively new idea introduced by a small group of economists; there was no existing mass support for the compulsory insurance approach.[48] Perhaps due to the relative newness of the idea and undoubtedly due to the complexity of the program itself, the public had little understanding of the differences between OAA and OAB.[49] In fact, even those who designed the public-opinion surveys appear to have confused these two concepts; their surveys are thus not helpful.[50] Nor was organized support from interest groups particularly strong.[51] Even organized labor did not take a major interest in Social Security.[52]

In addition to the problem of poorly defined support, OAB faced some immediate political threats. Questions about the Social Security Act's constitutionality clouded many of the SSB's actions until the Supreme Court rendered a favorable decision in May 1937.[53] Meanwhile, the board was saddled with the difficulty of administering an unusually large program. The organization deviated from the more traditional federal-state relationship, involved the creation of gigantic reserve funds, and posed an administrative challenge—that of assigning numbers and initiating accounts for 30 million employees—of unprecedented scale. The legislation also required that taxes begin five years before regular benefits—never a politically popular sequence.[54] As Edwin Witte, the executive director of the CES, put it, "For nearly two years after the Social Security Act became law, serious doubts continued to exist about its ever coming into full operation."[55] Witte cited among other factors the "[p]olitical opposition to the legislation that became much stronger than it had been before its passage, coming both from radical groups and from commercial insurance and other business interests."[56]

The SSB responded to these challenges by promoting a set of images that linked the OAB approach to what were perceived to be basic American values. It emphasized the insurance aspects of the program and its concomitant stress on self-sufficiency; it side-stepped the compulsory aspects of OAB. It also suggested that with the eventual expansion of OAB, there would one day be no need for OAA.[57]

The board approved the assignment of Social Security numbers with trepidation. At board meetings, Altmeyer expressed the point of view that the major challenge of the SSB was demonstrating that OAB was a simple program that could be easily administered.[58] Yet board meeting after board meeting deferred decisions on method and timing.[59] By May 1936, the board decided to postpone assignment of numbers until after the election in order to avoid potential political embarrassment.[60] With time running out, the board, which had hoped that the U.S. Employment Service would handle this unpleasant task, was becoming desperate. The unofficial minutes of the September 5, 1936, board meeting report noted: "Mr. Altmeyer thinks if we can farm this thing out, it will be all right, but if not, we are sunk."[61]

It was FDR who finally bailed out the SSB. He leaned on the Post Office, which agreed under pressure to handle the job.[62] The SSB wasted little time in instructing its field staff that the Post Office "has complete charge of assigning benefit account numbers and we have very little to do with it."[63]

It was an election year, and with the administration under attack from the Townsendites and other advocates of pension plans, it was impossible to avoid all criticism. Initially the board pursued an official policy of ignoring criticism, but eventually it did respond and indeed grew increasingly adept at turning such criticism to its advantage. Alf Landon's attack on OAB in September 1936 provides one of the earliest examples of this. Landon charged that the Social Security Act was "a glaring example of bungling and waste" that would encourage "federal snooping."[64] There was as well a Republican-sponsored, anti-Social Security payroll-stuffing campaign. In response, Chairman Winant resigned his position on the board in order to be free to defend the Act. Under Acting Chairman Altmeyer, the SSB launched its own massive publicity campaign defending OAB.[65] The SSB distributed millions of pamphlets and a newsreel entitled *We the People*, produced under contract to the SSB. It worked closely with organized labor for the first time during this campaign.

With the landslide election behind it and assignment of numbers under way, the organization systematized its use of publicity. What had originally been justified as a one-time response to distortion of the program by critics continued as a routine function. Informational Services organized a speaker's bureau that sent "experts" to communities across the nation to discuss the benefits of OAB.[66] These speakers promoted the SSB's philosophy of social insurance. They were also an important means of conveying public opinion back to the Washington headquarters.

Gradually, this aspect of the board's political efforts gathered steam. Informational Services added full-time motion picture and radio scriptwriters and promoters to its staff and produced more movies and a series of "real-life dramas" dealing with a "typical" American family in a "typically" American town in order to explain OAB.[67] As late as 1940, "promotion of further understanding of the insurance approach to the problem of security" was still Informational Services' top objective.[68] But included among the past year's techniques for spreading the word was the "development of a new labor information technique, designed to multiply channels of information to organized labor groups" and an "expanded service to labor groups and to the Board in consideration and reporting of problems and complaints."[69] Director of Informational Services Max Stern explained that "[i]nstead of telling all of the story to all of the people at once, our major job is becoming increasingly one of intensive and specialized informational effort."[70]

While routinized public-relations efforts brought the SSB's view of social insurance to millions of Americans, such constant public exposure had its drawbacks. A problem arose, for example, when in April 1937 Informational Services issued a routine press release on the number of wage earners contributing to OAB. Senator Vandenberg, who was engaged in a running battle with Frances Perkins on her estimates of the number of unemployed workers in the nation, used the SSB's figures to undercut publicly Perkins's estimates.[71] This was not, of course, the kind of response to public relations that the SSB sought.

From its inception the board tried to respond to criticism without appearing to be too heavy-handed or political in its activities. As early as March 1936, the board, at the suggestion of Chairman Winant, decided that the regional offices would be used to respond to local criticism of the program.[72] Altmeyer, in a May 4, 1936, interview, was quite candid in explaining how the regional manager could get the publicity job done while avoiding charges of propaganda:

They [regional managers] have the knowledge and personality to do effective public relations work. This is urgently needed. Other government agencies, by confining their attention to the regular publicity channels and personnel, have made a mistake which the board does not want to repeat. . . . Were the board to rely upon the regional informational service representative, it would lay itself open to the charge of propaganda. This is not true of the regional manager, who speaks directly for the board.[73]

Anxious to take advantage of this method of meeting its publicity needs, the SSB opened several regional offices before there was much else to do.[74]

While holding the line with OAA, the SSB actively and aggressively promoted OAB. The board first sought to demonstrate that, like private insurance, OAB could be prudently administered: it successfully avoided the controversial issue of assigning numbers, first, by delaying the inevitable until after the election, and, second, by forcing the job on another agency. It reached out to a broader public through techniques ranging from movies to local representatives and relied upon its widespread organization to report back on public opinion. It sought to establish an interest-group clientele in organized labor. Again, these activities initially grew out of the defensive response to the Republican attack on Social Security, but they soon blossomed into a routinized function within Informational Services. Sensitive to accusations of distributing propaganda and playing politics, the SSB publicly characterized its efforts as responding to misleading criticism or as simply providing information. The SSB adapted its regional administrative structure to meet its public-relations needs, and all the while worked hard to cultivate its ties with Congress.

ADJUSTING TO CRITICISM: AMENDING THE FACT
The SSB's increased flexibility regarding patronage has already been mentioned. But the SSB had more to offer congressmen than jobs for their constituents. After some initial hesitation, the SSB began, for instance, to provide technical assistance in drafting legislation.[75] The board also drafted responses to congressional constituents who questioned aspects of the Act and prepared a number of speeches for friendly congressmen.[76]

As opposition to aspects of the Act mounted—not only from those advocating universal pensions but also from conservatives who feared the buildup of large reserves—the SSB realized that certain modifications to the legislation had to be made, and that it must ask Congress for these amendments. In fact, the SSB's operating bureaus had been submitting proposed amendments to the board since late 1936.

A November 1936 memo from Eleanor Dulles in Research and Statistics is representative of the proposed amendments that were circulating within the SSB. This proposal called for OAB benefits to be advanced, for coverage to be broadened, and for reimbursement to states for OAA to be increased.[77] This particular memorandum makes it clear how sensitive the SSB staff was to public criticism of the Act; the staff viewed its control of legislative amendments as essential to establishing OAB on a permanent basis. As Dulles pointed out:

> The time has come when all serious criticism must be taken into account. . . . [P]ublic sentiment and expert opinion both seem at this time to be tending toward old-age pensions in limited amounts, which will be available to a large proportion of the aged as a matter of right. . . . [T]he dangers inherent in a large and unpredictable change in the plan offer a real threat to stability.[78]

Dulles went on to warn that although there was some justification for a "waiting" policy to "avoid stirring up doubts long enough to get the machinery in operation," the dangers of losing control of change outweighed this problem; she advocated immediate revisions. The board, however, continued to defend the Act in public and discuss the timing of potential changes at its meetings.[79]

In January 1937, capitalizing on increased public criticism of the reserves, Senator Vandenberg held hearings on this issue and sought to force the SSB's hand. When Vandenberg suggested that an advisory council of experts be established to recommend changes in the legislation, Altmeyer went along with the idea.[80] His letter to the President reveals a great deal about the SSB's fundamental strategy for dealing with this sort of opposition. He pointed out that the proposed amendments to the Act were likely to become a "very hot partisan issue."[81] After citing the mounting pressure for change, Altmeyer continued:

As a matter of fact, I think it is possible not only to offset these attacks on the Social Security Act, but really to utilize them to advance a socially desirable program, fully in accord with present fundamental principles underlying the Social Security Act and within our financial capacity.[82]

Altmeyer proved to be a perceptive prognosticator. With the aid of his staff, he played an essential role in shaping the favorable outcome he had predicted. Together they made good use of the Advisory Council (appointed by the SSB in conjunction with the Vandenberg subcommittee), which was chaired by J. Douglas Brown and included representatives from labor and business.[83] As Martha Derthick has written:

[T]he Advisory Council became for the SSA's executives a convenient mechanism of "cooptation" in Selznick's classic definition, "the process of absorbing new elements into the leadership or policy-determining structure of an organization as a means of averting threats to its stability or existence."[84]

Besides the SSB's direct role in the selection of the council members, the key to its influence over the council appears to have been the role played by the SSB's staff—the same staff that served the council.[85]

The SSB also had improved its relations with Congress by developing a legislative specialist in 1937, a role admirably filled by Wilbur Cohen. Cohen understood politicians and the political process. He was intimately familiar with the program itself and the SSB's objectives and was a pragmatist who knew when to compromise.[86] With his help the SSB carefully orchestrated its positions at congressional hearings by providing friendly expert witnesses and by drafting questions to be used by friendly congressmen while questioning critics of the program.[87]

This effort was particularly important because the SSB faced an increasingly independent and conservative Congress in 1939.[88] It is thus no surprise that Congress did not accept the entire legislative package proposed by the SSB. In fact, it went against the recommendation of both the SSB and the council in eliminating the 1% tax increase schedule for January 1940, thus further reducing the size of the reserves. But it did adopt the SSB's central compromise regarding the speed-up and liberalization of benefits and concomitant reduction of the size of reserve funds.[89]

The SSB was thus able to maneuver between opposition from both the left and the right, use its co-opted Advisory Council, and exploit its improved relations with Congress to expand benefits provided under the favored insurance program. The fact that the 1939 amendments—by moving away from a fully funded reserve and toward a pay-as-you-go system—made the insurance analogy far less plausible did not prevent the SSB from increasing its emphasis on this important symbol:

> As the links between tax payments and benefits grew more and more tenuous, the program became less and less like insurance, and the less like insurance it became, the more its executive leaders insisted that that was what it was.[90]

Most significantly, the debate revolved around how to reform OAB, not the choice between OAA and OAB. The SSB had weathered the storm from Townsendites and other advocates of universal pensions without a means test. Its promotional activities were instrumental in shifting the context of the debate from pensions versus insurance to a more technical discussion of the reserve required to fund insurance and the rate at which those insurance benefits should be paid out. The SSB had nurtured interest groups, like labor, who favored employment-based benefits (OAB) over benefits accessible to those without work histories (OAA). It had eliminated some of the most poignant examples of poverty by the rapid distribution of means-tested OAA through the states.

CONCLUSIONS

This brief analysis of the SSB's entry into politics suggests several conclusions. With acronyms increasingly replacing surnames as history's protagonists, it will not suffice to treat these complex organizations merely as politically passive vehicles. We must chart their political development and attempt to measure the breadth of their influence on the policies they administer. As my account of the SSB's first five years shows, the agency was an important political actor; it developed political skills and exercised them in order to establish a permanent place for itself and its programs.

Not all New Deal agencies developed these skills. In his case study of the Farm Security Administration (FSA), Sidney Baldwin describes an agency that, initially, enjoyed freedom from congressional oversight and other restraints. Although this allowed the agency to experiment and improvise:

> This very freedom. . .was a politically costly luxury, for it liberated the leaders of the FSA from having to adhere to a carefully specified path of Congressional consent. It also freed them from the requirement of having to defend themselves frequently in Congress and thus building acceptable justifications for practices which challenged conventional ways and which overstepped the bounds. Consequently, the political muscles of the FSA became flabby.[91]

The price paid by the FSA for its political naïveté was organizational obsolescence.

Not so in the SSB's case. Political considerations were influential in shaping its objectives—particularly its preference for OAB as opposed to OAA—and its political skills were essential for realizing these objectives. Negotiating skills and sensitivity to the local political landscape helped the SSB hold the line with OAA programs administered by the states; its institutionalized public-relations efforts and ability to convert criticism into program expansion won acceptance for the preferred, but relatively unknown, OAB alternative.

It is possible to discern a general pattern in the SSB's actions. At first, the agency's leaders felt that it was crucial to maintain its image as an objective, apolitical administrator. It sought to gain influence by providing technical assistance; its role in formulating state OAA plans and providing staff to the Advisory Council is a good example of this. But confronted with the task of promoting a relatively unknown program, the SSB found that it could not ignore public relations. The organization distanced itself from potentially controversial issues, used political attacks to launch its own promotional activities, and adapted its regional organization to serve its public-relations needs. Finally, the SSB realized that promoting a popular symbol—in this case the symbolism of insurance—was far more important to garnering popular acceptance than rigid adherence to the programmatic details that supported such symbols. Even as the 1939 amendments undermined the basis for the SSB's insurance analogy, the SSB relied on it more heavily.

The early years of Social Security illustrate a broader pattern that has become one of the most common in American politics. The first phase—conflicting interests hammering out a legislative compromise that is ambiguous enough to satisfy all—has been amply documented. It is the second phase of this pattern—the administrative promotion of selected portions of that compromise—that warrants closer study by historians. I have argued that the initial years of a new program are a particularly fruitful period for such research. In the SSB's case it offered insight into the integral links between institutional development and that institution's policy predilections.

The SSB took the route that offered the least political resistance and the largest amount of agency control. In the two-tier system of OAB and OAA, it tilted toward the program that promised middle-class support, low federal costs, and exclusive administrative control. It sold this program to the public in terms that fit into its perception of basic American values—individualism and self-sufficiency. It assiduously avoided the political onus associated with income redistribution. It substituted carefully managed programs for radical proposals. It used demands by conservatives for smaller reserves to speed up the payout of OAB benefits to the middle-class constituency it hoped to build.

The SSB's preference for the OAB approach has left a lasting mark on social-welfare programs in America. Subsequent program expansions (such as disability benefits and health insurance) have been built around the compulsory insurance principle. Once established as an institution, the SSB was increasingly able to define issues regarding social-welfare policy in its own terms. It reshaped in significant ways the very political environment to which it had originally adapted out of fear for its own existence. There can be little doubt that this ensured its survival.

But it would be a mistake to conclude from this that the course of welfare policy was dictated solely by the bureaucrats. A fruitful area for further study lies in tracing the relationship between administrative agencies and congressional entrepreneurs. It may be that the policy process I have described for Social Security is precisely the technique policy-oriented congressmen used to distance themselves from short-term controversies while hitching their wagons to policies and constituencies with real staying power.

NOTES

1. Robert H. Wiebe, *The Search for Order, 1877–1920* (New York: Hill and Wang, 1967); Robert D. Cuff, *The War Industries Board: Business-Government During World War I* (Baltimore: The Johns Hopkins University Press, 1973); Samuel P. Hays, *Conservation and the Gospel of Effi-*

ciency: The Progressive Conservation Movement, 1890–1920 (New York: Atheneum, 1969); Stephen Skowronek, *Building a New American State: The Expansion of National Administrative Capacities, 1877–1920* (Cambridge: Cambridge University Press, 1982).

2. For example, see "Secretary Hoover and the Changing Framework of New Era Historiography," in Ellis W. Hawley, ed.; *Herbert Hoover as Secretary of Commerce* (Iowa City: University of Iowa Press, 1981); and "The Commerce Secretariat, and the Vision of an Associative State," *The Journal of American History* 61 (1974), 116–140.

3. Louis Galambos, "The Emerging Organizational Synthesis in Modern American History," *Business History Review* 46, no. 1 (Autumn 1970), 279–290.

4. Mark L. Kornbluh's dissertation in progress, "From Participatory to Administrative Politics: A Social Analysis of American Political Behavior, 1880–1920" (The Johns Hopkins University), describes participatory politics at its peak and charts its decline. An excellent summary of the transition from participatory to bureaucratic politics can be found in Richard L. McCormick's "The Discovery that Business Corrupts Politics: A Reappraisal of the Origins of Progressivism," *The American Historical Review* 86 (1981), 247–274.

5. Gabriel Kolko's *Railroads and Regulation, 1877–1916* (New York: W. W. Norton, 1965) and *The Triumph of Conservatism: A Reinterpretation of American History, 1900–1916* (New York: The Free Press, 1963) are good examples of the concentration upon legislation that created central organizations. Kolko's work is also a good example of that legislation leading to "captured" agencies. Robert Wiebe, on the other hand, relies on a far more Weberian model of bureaucratic behavior (*The Search for Order*).

6. Samuel P. Hays, "Political Choice in Regulatory Administration," in Thomas K. McGraw, ed., *Regulation in Perspective: Historical Essays* (Cambridge, MA: Harvard University Press, 1981), 126. History informed by "supply-side" organizational theory has pushed the discovery of bureaucratic political agendas to its extreme. Carolyn Weaver's *The Crisis in Social Security: Economic and Political Origins* (Durham, NC: Duke University Press, 1982) is a pertinent example of this. By failing to consider the political, ideological, and organizational context in which bureaucracies operate—as Hays calls for—Weaver oversimplifies the motivations behind the SSB's entry into politics.

7. See, for example, Francis E. Rourke, *Bureaucracy, Politics, and Public Policy* (Boston: Little, Brown, 1969).

8. Martha Derthick, *Policymaking for Social Security* (Washington, D.C.: The Brookings Institution, 1979), 23.

9. Ibid., 272.

10. The Federal Social Security Act [Public, No. 271–74th Congress]. Title I established OAA; OAB was established by titles II and VIII; UC, by titles III and IX. Other programs established by the Act were: Aid to Dependent Children (title IV); maternal and child welfare programs (title V); grants for state public-health facilities (title VI); and Aid to the Blind (title X).

11. Taxes were to be paid on the first $3,000 of earned income. These taxes were to be held in a reserve fund that was to be invested in federal securities bearing an interest rate of 3% per annum. Taxes were scheduled to increase at

regular intervals (the first increase to 3% effective in 1940), rising to 6% by January 1, 1949. Many employees were excluded from coverage; the largest excluded groups were agricultural and self-employed employees.

12. The same groups of employees were excluded from coverage as under OAB. In addition, only employers with eight or more employees were required to participate.

13. Abraham Epstein, "Our Social Insecurity Act," *Harpers Magazine*, vol. 172 (December 1935), 61.

14. Before being appointed as chairman of the Committee for Economic Security's technical board, Altmeyer had been an assistant secretary of labor and prior to that served both as chief statistician and as secretary of the Wisconsin Industrial Commission.

15. Columbia Oral History Collection (hereafter COHC) (Columbia University, New York), interview with Arthur Altmeyer (1965), 190.

16. Ibid.

17. COHC interview with Frank Bane (1965), 38.

18. The skeleton of the organization consisted of the following operating bureaus: unemployment compensation, federal old-age benefits, and public assistance. The service bureaus included: information services, general counsel, research and statistics, accounts and audits, and business management.

19. Despite the absence of public debate, there was, as might be expected, interbureau rivalry within the SSB. For instance, in October 1936 Jane Hoey, director of the Bureau of Public Assistance, articulated the tension between the OAA approach and the insurance approach, pointing out in a memo to Frank Bane the difficulty of coordinating the two policies and suggesting that the federal government abandon the direct administration of OAB in favor of grants-in-aid. This proposal did not get very far with the board. See Hoey to Bane, October 15, 1936, in "Amendments" file, box 5, "Records of the Chairman of the Board, 1935–1942" (Record Group 47, National Archives, Washington, D.C.).

20. Such encumbrances were not merely theoretical. Soon after the 1939 reorganization that placed the SSB under Federal Security Administrator McNutt, McNutt tried to get political mileage out of an investigation he launched into the assignment of Social Security numbers. See the column by Drew Pearson and Robert Allen, September 19, 1939, in "Press" file, box 38, "Records of the Chairman."

21. Review of "Representatives" file, boxes 15 and 16, and review of "Senate" file, boxes 17 and 18, in "Records of the Chairman."

22. COHC interview with Bane, 74.

23. For Altmeyer's position, see Arthur J. Altmeyer, *The Formative Years of Social Security* (Madison: University of Wisconsin Press, 1966), 51. Counsel Thomas Eliot and observers McKinley and Frase saw flexibility on this issue; see Charles McKinley and Robert W. Frase, *Launching Social Security: A Capture-And-Record Account, 1935–1937* (Madison: University of Wisconsin Press, 1970), 387, 426, 483, 484; COHC interview with Thomas Eliot (1965), 64.

24. Edwin E. Witte, *The Development of the Social Security Act* (Madison: University of Wisconsin Press, 1962), 145.

25. Paul H. Douglas, *Social Security in the United States* (New York: McGraw Hill, 1936), 110.

26. Townsend had proposed paying two hundred dollars a month to every person 60 or over, provided that they retire and spend the money during the course of the month. For a detailed account of the Townsend movement, see Abraham Holtzman, *The Townsend Movement: A Political Study* (New York: Bookman Associates, 1963). For a critical evaluation of the projected economic impact of the Townsend plan, see *Twentieth-Century Fund's The Townsend Crusade: An Impartial Review of the Townsend Movement and the Probable Effects of the Townsend Plan* (New York: Twentieth-Century Fund, 1936).

27. Altmeyer, *Formative Years*, 61.

28. COHC interview with Bane, 90.

29. McKinley and Frase, *Launching Social Security*, 473.

30. Ibid., 19, 386; for a good example of Bane's travels and speaking engagements, see "Informal Notes of Board Meetings," in Social Security Administration: Commissioner's Office (accession #47–79–56, National Archives, Suitland, MD), April 28, 1936. For the board's discussion of Bane's ongoing negotiations in Kansas and Ohio, see Informal Notes, January 31, 1936; February 4, 1936; February 11, 1936; and February 17, 1936.

31. Robert T. Lansdale, Elizabeth Long, Agnes Leisy, and Bryon T. Hipple, *The Administration of Old Age Assistance* (Chicago: Public Administration Service, 1939), 14.

32. COHC interview with Bane, 92.

33. Ibid., interview with Ewan Clague (1965), 118.

34. Ibid.

35. Altmeyer to Bane, December 23, 1936, in "memoranda-Bane" file, box 62, "Records of the Chairman"; COHC interview with Bane, 30.

36. COHC interview with Bane, 118.

37. See "Illinois," "Oklahoma," and "Ohio" files in boxes 108, 112, and 113, respectively, in "Records of the Chairman."

38. McKinley and Frase, *Launching Social Security*, 183.

39. Bureau of Public Assistance to the Executive Director, September 30, 1937, Louis Resnick to Frank Bane, August 10, 1937, in "Illinois" file, box 108, "Records of the Chairman."

40. Resnick to Bane, August 10, 1937.

41. Ibid.

42. Bureau of Public Assistance to Executive Director, December 22, 1937, in "Ohio" file, box 112, "Records of the Chairman"; Beullah Amidon, "Sooners in Security," *Survey Graphic* 27 (April 1938), 203–207.

43. McKinley and Frase, *Launching Social Security*, 488.

44. Ibid.

45. J. Douglas Brown, *An American Philosophy of Social Security: Evolution and Issues* (Princeton: Princeton University Press, 1972), 56.

46. Ibid.

47. Derthick, *Policymaking for Social Security*, 217.

48. Brown, *An American Philosophy of Social Security*, 8; and Edwin E. Witte, "Organized Labor and Social Security," in Milton Derber and Edwin Young, eds., *Labor and the New Deal* (Madison: University of Wisconsin Press, 1957), 257.

49. Michael E. Schiltz, *Public Attitudes Toward Social Security: 1935–1965* (Washington, D.C.: U.S. Government Printing Office, 1970), 29.

50. Ibid., 34.

51. McKinley and Frase, *Launching Social Security*, 483.

52. Witte, "Organized Labor and Social Security," 271.

53. Concern about UC's and OAB's constitutionality was a major consideration in drafting legislation to create both of these titles. In its administration of these programs, the SSB pressed the Justice Department for an early court test (see Altmeyer to Roosevelt, November 10, 1936, in "Technical Amendments" file, box 5, "Records of the Chairman") and prepared an economic brief that may have helped in obtaining the favorable court decision (see COHC interview with Eliot, 68).

54. Lump sum "death benefits" were paid out starting January 1937, but the volume of these was very low.

55. Witte, "Organized Labor and Social Security," 255.

56. Ibid., 256.

57. Frank Bane cited his own and other SSB administrators' statements, claiming that OAA would "fade away" as one of their greatest mistakes. COHC interview with Bane, 120.

58. Informal Notes, July 24, 1936.

59. Review of Informal Notes, January 1936–November 1936.

60. Informal Notes, May 5, 1936.

61. Ibid., September 5, 1936.

62. Ibid., September 23, 1936.

63. Minutes from the October 22, 1936, Executive Staff Meeting, in "Executive Staff Meeting" file, box 67, "Records of the Chairman."

64. Alfred Landon speech, September 26, 1936, in *Vital Speeches of the Day*, vol. III.

65. McKinley and Frase, *Launching Social Security*, 357, 358.

66. "Field Notes," May 29, 1937, in "Statements on Personnel Policy" file, box 33, "Records of the Chairman."

67. "Informational Services Plans in Progress and in Retrospect (*Confidential*)," updated [appears to be mid-1937] in "Informational Services" file, box 37, "Records of the Chairman."

68. "Bureau of Informational Services Statement of Objectives and Program," June 1940, separate report, box 37, "Records of the Chairman."

69. Ibid.

70. Ibid.

71. Altmeyer to Bane, April 26, 1937, in "Press" file, box 38, "Records of the Chairman."

72. Informal Notes, March 10, 1936.

73. McKinley and Frase, *Launching Social Security*, 107.

74. Informal Notes, March 27, June 29, 1936.

75. Informal Notes, February 20, 1936; Assistant Counsel Calhoun to Altmeyer, February 14, 1938, in "Amendments" file, box 5, "Records of the Chairman."

76. For examples of responses drafted for congressmen, see "Unemployment Compensation" file, box 7, "Records of the Chairman." For an example of speech preparation, see the SSB's correspondence with Ways and Means Chairman Doughton; "Analysis of Pension Plans," September 27, 1938; Altmeyer to Doughton, October 17, 1938; and Altmeyer to Doughton, October 25, 1938, in "Pension Plans" file, box 92, "Records of the Chairman."

77. Dulles to Bane (*Confidential*), November 9, 1936, in "Amendments" file, box 5, "Records of the Chairman."

78. Ibid.

79. "Unofficial Minutes for Board Meeting," February 6, 1937, in "Amendments" file, box 7, in "Records of the Chairman."

80. Altmeyer, *Formative Years*, 89.

81. Altmeyer to the president, September 11, 1937, in "Amendments" file, box 5, "Records of the Chairman."

82. Ibid.

83. Comparison of Altmeyer's letter to the "Final Report of the Advisory Council on Social Security" (76th Congress, first session, Senate Document no. 4).

84. Derthick, *Policymaking for Social Security*, 90; Derthick cites Selznick's *TVA*, 13.

85. Although asserting that his advisory council was "independent," Brown attributed the centerpiece of the proposed changes in 1939 to SSB staff:

> It was an idea from the staff that we would do two or three things at once. We would get benefits up faster by using the average [wage], regardless of how long contributions had been made; two, we would hold down the reserve by getting benefits paid out; third, we would make the system viable politically. In other words, we'd get insurance benefits out faster and better, over against old age assistance. [COHC, interview with J. Douglas Brown (1965), 48]

86. Derthick, *Policymaking for Social Security*, 54.

87. See "Questions on the Federal Old-Age Insurance System" [questions directed at critic of the program, John Flynn], in "Protests and Criticisms" file, box 7, "Records of the Chairman"; see letters to friendly economists requesting that they testify at the February 1939 Ways and Means hearings, in "List of Economists and Research Agencies" file, box 37, "Records of the Chairman."

88. See James T. Patterson, *Congressional Conservatism and the New Deal* (Lexington: University of Kentucky Press, 1967), 288–324.

89. Social Security Act Amendments of 1939 (76th Congress, first session, in House Report no. 728).

90. Derthick, *Policymaking for Social Security*, 224, 225.

91. Sidney Baldwin, *Poverty and Politics: The Rise and Decline of the Farm Security Administration* (Chapel Hill: University of North Carolina Press, 1968), 9.

JUDITH SEALANDER

Moving Painfully and Uncertainly: Policy Formation and "Women's Issues," 1940–1980

IN 1904, Sarah Platt Decker, newly elected president of the General Federation of Women's Clubs, announced to her members: "Ladies, you have chosen me to be your leader. Well, I have an important piece of news to give you. Dante is dead; he has been dead for several centuries, and I think it is time we dropped the study of his *Inferno* and turned our attention to our own."[1]

Decker was not the first to make such a suggestion. Instead, she participated in a long tradition of female efforts to change social customs and public policies that hindered improvements in the status of women. Throughout the nineteenth and twentieth centuries, established public and private institutions responded to pressures exerted by those who had in fact turned their attention to the "*Inferno*" of women's issues.

The nature of those responses provokes questions interesting to students of the policy-making process. What factors have influenced the male leaderships of major public and private organizations to seek women advisers and make "women's issues" concerns that required policies? What roles have these women advisers been allowed to play? Are generalizations about the nature of the policy-making process itself apparent from an examination of the techniques by which mid-twentieth-century government and philanthropic organizations made their "women's" policies?

This essay obviously cannot do justice to the large question of policy-making and women's issues for all American institutions or all time periods. Rather, it attempts to pose questions about ways policies have been made or not made through the use of a much more narrowed focus: an analysis of the histories of three advisory bodies—two created by the federal government and one funded by private philanthropy between 1940 and 1980.

These bodies, the Women's Advisory Committee to the War Manpower Commission, 1942–45, John F. Kennedy's President's Commission on the Status of Women, 1961–63, and the National Women's Employment Project, 1977–79, spanned a forty-year period, granting chronological perspective. Moreover, their histories, while recent, reflected debates about proper roles for women which had raged since the nineteenth century. And they asked the same question that had dominated many of those debates: What policies should society adopt to provide expanded opportunity for women?

All three bodies were appointed to give policy advice on women's issues. But in no circumstance did actual institutional policy reflect wholesale acceptance of the counsel given. In the case of the Women's Advisory Committee, in fact, actual policy usually contradicted suggested policy. These bodies merit study not because they were able in all cases to make major contributions to policymaking. Rather, they merit study precisely because they reveal, through their failures as well as their successes, the tangled web of factors that determined the degree of genuine attention and respect accorded women's issues and women advisers and that shaped not just advice but eventual policies. Moreover, their histories prompt possible generalizations about policy-making within mainstream American institutions in the mid-twentieth century.

The Women's Advisory Committee to the World War II War Manpower Commission was an organization which pleased no one. Its history illustrates the severe limits imposed on even very moderate women's-rights advocates when the male superiors to whom they reported had no commitment to equality for women. For years before 1941, women federal bureaucrats, especially at the U.S. Department of Labor, had warned that any major war would require the labor of millions of additional women workers. Few policymakers, even within the Labor Department, paid attention.[2] Of course, within a year, the enormous labor requirements of war production had begun to exhaust the supply of available men; by September 1942, some 14 million women were at work, over three million more than had been employed before Pearl Harbor. Some one million formerly unemployed women had found new jobs; more than two million new women workers had further swelled the labor force.[3]

Many individuals and groups pressed federal war planners to allow women official participation in policy matters affecting women's employment. Mary Anderson, director of the Women's Bureau within the Labor Department, unsuccessfully lobbied members of the Office of Production Management and its National Labor Supply Committee to appoint women to their staffs. By February 1942, both had been dissolved as the new War Manpower Commission consolidated federal responsibility for labor mobilization. When Paul McNutt, head of the new commission, searched for candidates for his Management-Labor Policy Committee, Anderson and allies in women's organizations pressed again to gain one or two seats for women. Margaret Hickey, president of the National Federation of Business and Professional Women, summarized the lobbying effort when she urged quick recognition of the important roles women would have to play. "In a war for survival of their homes," she said, "women's place is in the war."[4] The all-male Management-Labor Policy Committee rejected the idea of women as equal colleagues; some members threatened to resign if any woman received an appointment to the committee. McNutt, himself hostile to the idea of a full-fledged voting membership for a woman, offered instead to appoint an advisory committee.[5] Margaret Hickey, who, as president of an important women's professional organization, had worried publicly that a women's advisory body without voting rights would have limited effectiveness, ironically became head of the Women's Advisory Committee and saw close-hand her prophecy fulfilled.

The Women's Advisory Committee held its first meeting in September 1942 and its last in March 1945. Its thirteen women members included women's organization leaders, women prominent in education, journalism, and business, as well as representatives of the AFL, the CIO, and the National Farmers' Union.[6]

Despite the prominence of many of its members and the symbolic backing of the academic, business, and labor organizations of which many members still served as paid officials, the Women's Advisory Committee was a failure. Its history illustrates the impossible position facing women who served as tokens within organizations whose leaders were not really interested in their policy advice and who had firm prejudices about women's abilities.

McNutt's administrative order establishing the Women's Advisory Committee stated that it should initiate studies and the formulation of policies, as well as consider those referred by the chairman. [It] is authorized to consider and recommend to the chairman of the War Manpower Commission matters of major policy concerning the activities of the Commission, particularly as they affect women.[7]

However, the Advisory Committee never received an independent budget. The absence of a technical staff or research assistance made it impossible for it effectively to "initiate . . . the formulation of policies." In fact, members themselves received no pay, only travel expenses to monthly meetings in Washington. Given their numerous other responsibilities, not all members attended most meetings. In reality, a core group of five women, Hickey overwhelmingly the most important among them, did much of the work. Some of the advisers took only a slightly disguised tongue-in-cheek attitude about their appointments, even in 1942, wondering to colleagues if there was a "real place for such a group."[8]

The place for the group was clearly on the sidelines. When Advisory Committee policy recommendations clashed with those of McNutt, they usually disappeared, never to surface publicly as War Manpower Commission pamphlets or memos, usually to remain in typescript form in committee minutes or papers, sometimes to appear in a haphazard way as the text for a speech given by Margaret Hickey or as material given to the occasional reporter who interviewed one of the committee members.

Three controversies illustrate the situation. Throughout the war the Advisory Committee urged greater attention be paid to training and guidance of women workers. In September 1945, Hickey returned from a trip to England and a series of interviews with Labour Minister M. E. Bevin to report "British emphasis on guidance and counseling is much stronger than ours."[9] In America, the Advisory Committee argued, higher rates of turnover and absenteeism for women war workers, compared to men, could be countered if employers followed the British example. Instead, most plants provided neither comprehensive training nor serious counseling for new women workers. Many companies which employed counselors for their women workers chose socially prominent women, often friends of company executives. The recommendations of the Advisory Committee were available on request, but with no overt encouragement from the War Manpower Commission and no general policy in place, few companies established the kinds of training and counseling programs the Advisory Committee suggested.[10]

Part-time work proved to be another issue about which the Advisory Committee suggested sensible policies, which commission leaders largely ignored. Advisory Committee memos urged that women with children of school age be allowed to work different, perhaps shorter, shifts, with beginning and ending hours adjusted to school hours. The committee argued that women should be allowed to split shifts and share jobs, speculating that if such a plan became widely used mothers and older women could form a more efficiently used reserve from which additional labor could be drawn. Such a system would cause less social disruption and less pressure on already overcrowded housing than would an effort to recruit workers from outside war-work areas. Part-time workers, if not engaged in job-sharing, could relieve full-time workers, and give them an occasional full weekend for rest. Again, the War Manpower Commission did little to persuade employers to make the necessary adjustments in plant organization. Part-time programs were never popular with industry in the United States.[11]

Day care for the children of women war workers provides a final illustration of a controversial issue for which the Advisory Committee "formulated policy," only to find it ignored. The Lanham Act, passed in 1942, enabled federal officials to establish and partially fund such child-care centers, but the effort was poorly organized. By 1943, at least six major government agencies had begun some kind of day-care program.[12] The emphasis in most cases was on temporary emergency care. The Advisory Committee correctly argued that the need for national coordination was urgent. One agency should take charge of the program, providing seed monies for facilities that should be developed as community projects, not under the auspices of individual employers.[13]

In May 1943, Kaiser Shipbuilding received an appropriation of a million-and-a-half dollars from the Maritime Commission to set up nurseries and child-care centers in its plants. The Advisory Committee, confronted with a direct challenge to its advice to set up day-care centers through community and not company auspices, sent a strongly worded protest to Chairman McNutt. He told them, however, the money had been allocated and could not be withdrawn. Interestingly, the Kaiser day-care experiment, like several other such wartime ventures, was not a success. In April 1944, Saidie Orr Dunbar, a past president of the General Federation of

Women's Clubs and a member of the Advisory Committee, visited the Kaiser centers, reported they were badly underutilized and concluded that workers associated day care with company charity, implying that if programs had been centrally coordinated and planned with communities women might not have felt any stigma leaving their children.[14]

Advisory Committee policy recommendations on day care, as on all other issues, were vague, filled instead with rhetoric about "community pride" and "woman's full potential."[15] Had Hickey been allowed a research staff, her committee's reports would probably have been more detailed. Still, they often made good sense. Taken seriously, the committee could have helped McNutt better supervise womanpower as well as manpower recruitment and service. But it advised a commission which was no more diligent in securing equal rights and optimum conditions for women war workers than it was eager to allow its women advisers dignity and equality. In fact, commission members let it be known that "there was concern about a developing attitude of miltancy" which was "unnecessarily feminist" among its Women's Advisory Committee.[16] Far from being "unnecessarily feminist," Advisory Committee members, to a woman, all social and political moderates, had soft-pedaled "feminist" issues such as equal pay.

Margaret Hickey, who had accurately prophesized the powerless role her Advisory Committee would play, repeated her performance when, at war's end, a radio interviewer asked her to predict women's postwar roles. She said:

> Well, women's greatest progressive strides are invariably made in time of war rather than in time of peace. . . . When the war is over the tide may recede somewhat. But undoubtedly there will be a net gain. . . . I think the American people are moving painfully and uncertainly toward new ideas, but I do not think they grasp the full significance of the changes that are taking place today and of the greater changes to come.[17]

Margaret Hickey was certainly right that greater changes were to come. Increasingly, one postwar role for women was that of working wife. Within a decade and a half, by 1960, the number of married women at work exceeded the number of single women for the first time in American history. Three out of five women workers were wives. Moreover, the average woman worker was older, by 1960, in her forties rather than in her twenties, a break again from statistics which had characterized prewar decades.[18] Although significantly better educated, the average woman worker in the postwar period had not entered the middle class by virtue of higher job status or better wages. Instead, she had entered it when she combined her wages with her husband's, and the flood of wives into the labor force led to spectacular increases in average family earnings during the years 1947–63.[19]

Not only had women's employment patterns changed since World War II, so apparently had marriage expectations. Divorce rates skyrocketed along with birth rates. Finally, the actions of a few hinted of future changes in expectations of proper public and political roles for women. Some women emerged as social-protest leaders: refusing to sit in the back of buses, demanding that the bomb be banned.[20] These developments, as Hickey had predicted, did not immediately alter popular images of a female retreat to the suburbs, and certainly the Eisenhower administration did not place the changing status of American women high on its agenda of issues demanding attention.

Initial statements by some Kennedy administration appointees seemed to confirm a conclusion that not only the American people but its leaders as well were as yet unwilling to grasp the full significance of postwar changes. Under-Secretary of Labor James O'Connel argued, for instance:

> When a woman comes to be viewed first as a source of manpower, second as a mother, then I think we are losing much that supposedly separates us from the Communist world. The highest calling of a woman's sex is the home.[21]

But other officials took, at first privately, a less traditional line. United States Labor Department officials like Esther Peterson, assistant secretary for Labor Standards, saw a critical need for well-educated workers to cope with a highly technological workplace. But would the government, as it had before World War II, fail to anticipate that women would have to compose part of that better-trained workplace? Were government policies that still said that the highest calling of a woman was the home contributing to the problem?

Not only did President John Kennedy receive pressure from his own bureaucratic appointees to reconsider federal policy, but trade unionists, prominent politicians, and church officials urged him to undertake a formal government consideration of women's status. Kennedy further expressed interest in government "white papers" issued by the Bureaus of the Census and Labor Standards, discussing the rise of the two-income middle-class family and projecting even further economic and social change for American women. Esther Peterson, a woman with White House entree, and Eleanor Roosevelt, widely respected as an advocate for women's issues and influential in liberal Democratic circles, strongly urged the creation of a presidential commission composed of prominent Americans.[22] In a memo explaining the need for a commission, Esther Peterson wrote, "The increasing participation of women in all aspects of our national life has occurred so rapidly that society and the economy have lagged in fully accepting and adjusting to women's changing activities. By focusing on some of the changes . . . the Commission can help foster understanding and acceptance of those activities."[23] Thus motivated, John Kennedy established in December 1961 his President's Commission on the Status of Women.

The twenty-six members of the commission received orders to submit a written report to the President by 1963, evaluating the economic, political, and social status of American women. Committees appointed by the commission investigated a diverse range of topics and took pains to define its work as a complete review of women's status in America. Separate committees met to discuss education, taxes, and civil and political rights for women, but the best-attended and most significant committees were the ones on labor law and female employment.

Leaders of women's organizations, women trade unionists, and women educators participated. The presidents or past presidents of the National Council of Jewish Women, the National Council of Catholic Women, the National Council of Negro Women, and the National Council of Churches sat on the commission. So did a female executive of the Electrical and Machine Workers, AFL-CIO, and the president of Radcliffe College. Esther Peterson assumed leadership of the commission after the death of the commission's chair, Eleanor Roosevelt, in 1962. But the President's Commission was not exclusively female. If the commission included prominent women, it also included powerful men. Members of Congress, union leaders, businessmen, and five cabinet members joined the commission. There is no question that the members of the Kennedy Commission, as a group, were able to tap resources and gain attention for policy recommendations more easily because Kennedy chose a mixed-sex group of advisers.[24]

Paul McNutt only reluctantly established the Women's Advisory Committee, then imposed second-class status on its members, denying them voting rights and even, on occasion, basic courtesy. John Kennedy, however, in establishing his advisory group, treated his women experts very differently. The commission gathered at the White House on October 11, 1963, for instance, to submit its final report. White House protocol officers had grouped members of the commission for official photos. When President Kennedy entered the room, he noticed that males filled the entire first row, the row of course most apparent to the cameras. Without saying a word, he motioned to Senator Maurine Neuberger and Congresswoman Edith Green to move into the front row.[25]

President Kennedy wanted not only to spotlight high-level women officials like Neuberger and Green, he also wished to assure that the federal government was a "showcase for equal opportunity for women in employment."[26] Therefore, he instructed John Macy, commission member and chair of the Civil Service Commission, as part of the work of the commission, to review all possible inequities in federal hiring and promotion practices. Macy and fellow commission member Attorney General Robert Kennedy headed a subcommittee investigation which discovered that, rather than being a showcase, the federal government permitted its agencies to designate a preferred sex when filling jobs, that half such requests for positions above the four lowest grades were for men only, and that 94% of job openings at the three highest federal civil-service grades were designated for men only. In 1934, Attorney General Homer Cummings had reviewed this practice and found it legal. In 1962, Attorney General Robert Kennedy reviewed his predecessor's decision, judged it to be a misreading of an 1872 statute, and reversed it.[27] In truth, few women received appointments to "front row" positions in the Kennedy administration as a result of the commission-instigated civil-service reforms. There was, however, a marked increase in the number of women who entered the federal civil service. Macy argued in a 1964 interview that the changes meant that women would have the chance to participate at all levels, that, in time, they would have many chances to move into front rows.[28]

The fact that powerful government officials like Macy and Robert Kennedy, not to mention John Kennedy himself, sat with women colleagues meant that commission members, in some instances, actually instituted changes potentially beneficial to women. The women who worked within the system as members of the Kennedy Commission were colleagues with men who did not worry publicly that they might be unnecessarily feminist. The commission's final report urged an extensive series of court tests based on equal protection guarantees of the Fifth and Fourteenth Amendments of laws and practices that discriminated against women. It recommended that the Federal Fair Labor Standards Act should be extended to cover areas such as hotels, restaurants, and laundries, where large numbers of women labored without its benefits. Women workers, moreover, should be paid maternity leave or comparable insurance benefits. States should follow the federal example and adopt equal-pay legislation for women. Discriminatory educational, union, and employer practices that restricted female access to promotions and higher paid jobs should be eliminated through stricter laws. Legislation, moreover, should protect the right of all workers, male and female, to join unions and bargain collectively.[29] During the next decade, many of these policy recommendations would be embodied in laws and executive orders that included the Equal Pay Act, Title VII of the Civil Rights Act, Title IX of the Education Acts Amendment, and Executive Order 11246, mandating the beginning of federal affirmative-action programs.

But the President's Commission on the Status of Women, while responding to the "greater changes" Margaret Hickey had reported, was still a mainstream organization, inside and not outside the system. The commission members, all female, who tried to bring up topics deemed too controversial, found themselves just as frozen out as had the hapless women advisers to Paul McNutt.

While willing to open new ground with discussions of maternity leave or Social Security payments to housewives, the commission refused, for instance, to comment in print publicly on birth control and abortion law. At least one commission member, Oregon Senator Maurine Neuberger, tried unsuccessfully to get the commission to favor a liberalized abortion policy. She did not even succeed in producing a printed transcript of committee discussions about abortion policy. As she later commented:

> It was too new an idea. It wasn't Kennedy, Catholicism, or anything; it was just one of those ideas that people had to finally come to believe in. Anyway, actually, the people in the Administration were protecting the Administration by urging us not to do it. And it came up . . . but, you see, we were a Commission that had to go through the Labor Department and GSA [General Services Administration] to get things printed. They wouldn't print it if they didn't want to. He [Labor Secre-

tary Willard Wirtz] would have had to okay the printing of the material.[30]

By 1977, fewer topics seemed taboo for private or public mainstream organizations. In fact, rather than resisting women advisers, philanthropies, as well as government, funded some of them. The Rockefeller Foundation, which saw the change in women's roles and status as a topic demanding attention, launched the National Women's Employment Project in 1977 with a $25,000 start-up grant. Other philanthropies, such as the Ms. Foundation, soon also contributed. Since the early 1970s, several local organizations of women clerical workers had sprung up independently in widely separated cities. In their grant applications to the Rockefeller Family Fund, the leaders of six of these organizations proposed to create a national umbrella organization, the National Women's Employment Project, to set policy for its member groups.[31] Member organizations of the National Women's Employment Project—Women Employed in Chicago, 9 to 5 in Boston, Dayton Women Working, Cleveland Women Working, Women Organized for Employment in San Francisco, and Women Office Workers in New York—agreed to a goal, "To see that bureaucracy works."[32] That goal would certainly have earned the approval of members of either the Women's Advisory Committee or the President's Commission on the Status of Women. The NWEP defined bureaucracy broadly, to include private as well as public sectors. It set itself two tasks: first, to review federal policies which affected woman clerical workers, and, second, to compile a study of an industry whose "bureaucratic policies" were "notoriously unfair" to women workers. Interestingly, in attempting these tasks, the NWEP warily viewed government bureaucracy as a source of both good and evil. Agencies such as the Office of Federal Contract Compliance, the Wage and Hour Division of the Department of Labor, and the Equal Employment Opportunity Commission had to be monitored, pressured to remember the needs of women.[33]

Nevertheless, the group sought government help as it began an investigation of that "notorious" industry, banking. By late 1979, local member organizations had produced reports on the major banks in their communities. Banks, as holders of federal deposits, had the status of federal contractors required to fulfill federal affirmative-action guidelines. Federal agents, responding to NWEP requests or the specific requests of local member groups, often agreed that banks openly discriminated against women employees. For instance, U.S.

Department of Labor contract compliance investigators charged Third National Bank of Dayton, Ohio, with "a pattern of discrimination against its minority and women employees" and in initial review documents assessed nearly one million dollars in back pay for 110 employees who had "suffered the effects of past discrimination."[34]

At first glance, the National Women's Employment Project, while funded by private philanthropy, bore resemblances to the Women's Advisory Committee or the President's Commission. Its members issued policy recommendations to male-led, mainstream government organizations.[35] Like members of the President's Commission, leaders of the National Women's Employment Project found sympathetic male allies in government, especially in the U.S. Office of Contract Compliance, men who were convinced that the time had arrived for government to exercise an activist role in ending discrimination against women. But like members of the commission and, far more strongly, the members of the Women's Advisory Committee, leaders of the National Women's Employment Project also experienced the limits of government and philanthropic activism. By late 1979, "working woman" was not quite so fashionable a buzzword with foundations. The National Women's Employment Project, which, in its banking studies, had openly attacked many aspects of American corporate structure, found foundation support, usually linked to corporate support, gone. As early as 1978, Ellen Cassedy, president of the NWEP board, began sending plaintive memos, listing the philanthropies which had turned her down. A postscript scrawled at the bottom of one memo telescoped her frustration:

> PS: I just had a dream that I went out to lunch with Susan Beresford (of the Ford Foundation). When I took the check up to the cash register, the bill was $65. I was alarmed because I didn't have that much, so I asked Susan if she might help out. She said she was really sorry, but she just couldn't. What could this possibly mean??? I think I need either a vacation or a grant.[36]

In the end, the National Women's Employment Project turned to a different part of the mainstream, the union movement, for help. It was a move that marked a victory for the project's leaders, especially those in Boston and New York, who had for over a year been urging that "we begin to think more seriously about the unions." In 1979, the project ceased to exist formally and became instead, under the new name, "Working Women," a project of the National Association of Office Workers. In 1981, Working Women and the Service Employees International Union formed District 925, specifically to organize office workers.[37]

Do these three case studies merit generalizations about women's issues, male-led organizations, and policy-making processes? One seems to be that mainstream male-led organizations have, in the postwar period, considered women's issues if pressed to do so by women's organizations or women lobbyists. However, they have made actual efforts to remedy inequity and have treated their women colleagues with respect only if additionally pressured by groups and individuals not identified exclusively with women's causes. Moreover, women's issues had to be vital to the self-interest of the male-led organizations, crucial to the success of their plans, for them to be given a high priority.

Thus, the National Federation of Business and Professional Women lobbied successfully for the creation of both the Women's Advisory Committee and the President's Commission on the Status of Women. But Paul McNutt felt free to ignore and humiliate his women advisers, while John Kennedy did not. An important factor explaining this different reaction was the fact that Kennedy received advice not only from women's-issues advocates but also from men, generally outsiders to women's policy concerns but people he trusted, like Robert Kennedy. And these men strongly urged him to set up a body to review the status of women in America and formulate a new agenda of programs and policies for women's issues. Moreover, John Kennedy himself read reports which argued that postwar economic and social roles for women had to be studied by any leader wishing to guide American society.

Yet, even though Kennedy's commission was a body whose policy recommendations earned far more serious scrutiny than had those of the Women's Advisory Committee, it still counseled an administration that did not see women's issues as central to its objectives and its self-interest, an administration ready to abolish discriminatory civil-service rules but not ready to appoint a significant number of high-level women officials.

The history of the National Women's Employment Project also illustrates the crucial role of such self-interest. Abandoned by major philanthropies whose corporate sponsors could not always see their self-interest served by equal pay and equal status for women, the National Women's Employment Project dissolved. However, as

Working Women it reemerged, allied with a union movement that had begun to see the advocacy of women's issues as being in its self-interest.

In the seventies, unions had experienced their greatest gains among teachers, health care, and other public-sector workers, with the result that union percentages of women members rose, and surveys began to indicate that among workers not in unions, women were more interested in organizing than were men.[38]

Of course, one could persuasively argue that Paul McNutt or John Kennedy should also have seen women's issues directly involving self-interest. But these three case studies suggest that the self-interest must not only exist but be perceived. If it is not, advocates of equity for women seem to policymakers to be "unnecessarily feminist."

The fact that such individuals sought to create policies that were not "unnecessarily feminist" in the forties while their successors in ensuing decades sought to create policies that would best make the federal government a "showpiece" of equal opportunity for women illustrates an even more important generalization about women's issues and the policy-making process. In the recent past many public- and private-sector policies in this area acted as mirrors rather than as generators of social change.

During World War II policymakers assured the American public that the war emergency would create only temporary changes in traditional roles for women. It took two decades, millions of wives in the labor force, and the dramatically increased importance of the woman-dominated white-collar economic sector for policymakers to begin during the Kennedy administration to demand equal pay and equal opportunity for women. It was only against a backdrop of even further social, economic, and political change that philanthropies and unions turned from exclusion to embrace women's issues.

Policies for the "women's issues" considered here—policies about legal equality, equal pay, or abortion availability for women, for instance—reflected rather than led contemporary public opinion. The social climate of a particular era, and not policymakers themselves, seems to have been the key in determining agenda for policy-making.

Such a pattern of response rather than leadership may have been peculiar to policy-making on women's issues during the postwar period. That, however, is unlikely. If anything, those setting policies would seem to have had less interference from a relatively unmobilized, largely nonunionized group of women workers, say, than from a highly mobilized group of bankers or generals. Why would women's-issues policy-making closely reflect the current social climate as well as the perceived political and economic influence of the subject group, while banking or military policy did not? These case studies, then, suggest the criteria which in the postwar era have been necessary before mainstream organizations have taken women's issues seriously. They also suggest a broader generalization about the policy-making process itself. Not just the American people but their policymakers as well moved "painfully and uncertainly toward new ideas." Not just the American people but their policymakers as well had trouble "grasping the full significance of the changes that are taking place . . . and of the greater changes to come." In the area of women's issues at least, mainstream public and private organizational policies were not Machiavellian, not even particularly directive. Rather they straggled in the rear, along a path of social change already cut by the emerging women's movement, by new economic roles for women, and by changes in the American social and political climate.

NOTES

1. Quoted in Sherna Gluck, ed., *From Parlor to Prison: Five American Suffragists Talk About Their Lives, An Oral History* (New York: Vintage, 1976), 13.

2. Judith Sealander, *As Minority Becomes Majority: Federal Reaction to the Phenomenon of Women in the Work Force, 1920–1963* (Westport, CT: Greenwood Press, 1983).

3. " 'Womanpower': An Appraisal by the Women's Advisory Committee" (typescript), 1–4, RG211, The Records of the Women's Advisory Committee to the War Manpower Commission, National Archives, Washington, D.C. (hereafter WAC, NA).

4. Margaret Hickey, Speech Transcript, "Women's Role Today and Tomorrow (undated)," typed copy in WAC, NA.

5. For a history of the War Manpower Commission, see George Flynn, *The Mess in Washington: Manpower Mobilization in World War II* (Westport, CT: Greenwood Press, 1979).

6. A list of WAC members included Eleanor Park of New York City, assistant to the manager of Industrial Relations, Union Carbide and Carbon Corporation (active alternate); Blanche Ralston of Coahoma, Mississippi, former regional director of the Professional and Services Division of the Work Projects Administration; Ruth Allen, University of Texas, San Antonio, Texas (did not serve full term of office); Mrs. Harris T. Baldwin of Washington, D.C., former vice-president of the League of Women Voters; Dorothy J. Bellanca of New York City, vice-president of the Amalgamated Clothing Workers of America; Bess Bloodworth of New York City, vice-president and a director of the National Women's Trade Union League (ac-

tive alternate); Saidie Orr Dunbar of Portland, Oregon, executive secretary of the Oregon Tuberculosis Association and past president of the General Federation of Women's Clubs; Gladys Talbott Edwards of Denver, director of education for the National Farmers Union; Dr. Esther Cole Franklin, associate in social studies, American Association of University Women, Washington, D.C. (did not serve full term of office); Beatrice Blackmar Gould of Philadelphia, co-editor of the *Ladies Home Journal*; Margaret A. Hickey of St. Louis, lawyer and business executive; Mrs. Lowell Fletcher Hobart of Cincinnati, past national president of the American Legion Auxiliary; Jenny Matyas of San Francisco, vice-president of the International Ladies' Garment Workers' Union. Names given in minutes of Women's Advisory Committee (typescript), January 17, 1945, in records, WAC, NA.

7. Administrative order no. 22, August 31, 1942, Point 4, Entry 139, copy in WAC, NA.

8. Women's Bureau *Bulletin No. 244*, 36.

9. Press release, Women's Advisory Committee, Washington, September 20, 1945, WAC, NA.

10. "History of the Women's Advisory Committee, War Manpower Commissions" typescript, marked "Revised, July 1945," 8–12, WAC, NA.

11. "History of the Women's Advisory Committee," 11–13, Women's Bureau *Bulletin No. 244*, 26.

12. The Office of Defense Health and Welfare Services (WMC), the U.S. Office of Education, the Children's Bureau, the Federal Works Agency, the Office of Civilian Defense, and the Works Project Administration.

13. "Recommendation of the Women's Advising Committee: A Summary," April 30, 1944, Entry 36, WAC, NA.

14. Women's Bureau *Bulletin No. 244*, 30–31.

15. See "Recommendation of the Women's Advisory Committee."

16. Women's Bureau *Bulletin No. 244*, 40–42.

17. Margaret Hickey, interview transcript, marked "Cincinnati, February, 1945," Item 35, WAC, NA.

18. See "Working Wives," *The Wall Street Journal*, October 30, 1963; U.S. Department of Labor, Bureau of Labor Statistics, *Handbook of Labor Statistics, 1920–1971* (Washington, D.C.: Government Printing Office, 1972), 30–51; Eli Ginzberg, "Paycheck and Apron—Revolution in Women Power," *Industrial Relations* 7 (May 1968), 193–203.

19. In 1940, two-fifths of all working women had at least a high-school education, and by 1960 more than three-fifths had high-school diplomas. See "Educational Attainment of Women in the Labor Force," Women's Bureau Special Pamphlet, Press Release File, August 1960, Records of the Women's Bureau, National Archives, Washington, D.C. (hereafter WB, NA); "Working Wives," *The Wall Street Journal*, October 30, 1963.

20. For a discussion of the status of women during this period, see Milton Cantor and Bruce Laurie, *Class, Sex, and the Woman Worker* (Westport, CT: Greenwood Press, 1977), and William Chafe, *The American Woman: Her Changing Social, Economic, and Political Roles, 1920–1970* (New York: Oxford University Press, 1972).

21. Address by James O'Connel, press release, June 3, 1960, typescript, Press Release File, WB, NA.

22. See "Materials: Minutes of Meetings, October 24, 1960–January 19,

1962," The President's Commission on the Status of Women (The John F. Kennedy Presidential Library, Boston, MA) (hereafter PCSW, KL). Cynthia Harrison argues that Peterson, a long-time and influential Kennedy adviser on labor issues, acted as the catalyst that prompted the establishment of the commission. Peterson, in effect, differed from other presidential "spokespersons" for women's interests by focusing on a commission and equal-pay legislation rather than appointments for women to government posts. See Cynthia Harrison, "A 'New Frontier' for Women: The Public Policy of the Kennedy Administration," *Journal of American History* 67 (December 1980), 630–646.

23. Memorandum from Esther Peterson to members of the President's Commission, "Background Information," PCSW Document no. 62–25, PI, PCSW, KL.

24. *Members of the President's Commission on the Status of Women:* Mrs. Eleanor Roosevelt, Chair; Dr. Richard A. Lester, Professor of Economics, Princeton University, Vice Chair; Mrs. Esther Peterson, Assistant Secretary of Labor, Exccecutive Vice Chair; Attorney General Robert F. Kennedy; Secretary of Agriculture Orville L. Freeman; Secretary of Commerce Luther H. Hodges; Secretary of Labor Arthur J. Goldberg; Secretary of Health, Education and Welfare Abraham A. Ribicoff; Chair, U.S. Civil Service Commission, John W. Macy, Jr.; Senator George D. Aiken, Republican, of Vermont; Senator Maurine B. Neuberger, Democrat, of Oregon; Representative Edith Green, Democrat, of Oregon; Representative Jessica M. Weis, Republican, of New York; Mrs. Ellen Boddy, civic leader, rancher, Henrietta, Texas; Dr. Mary I. Bunting, President, Radcliffe College, Cambridge, Massachusetts; Mrs. Mary R. Callahan, member, Executive Board, International Union of Electrical, Radio and Machine Workers, AFL-CIO; Dr. Henry David, president, New School for Social Research, New York City; Miss Dorothy Height, president, National Council of Negro Women; Mrs. Margaret Hickey, contributing editor, *Ladies Home Journal;* Mrs. Viola H. Hymes, national president, National Council for Jewish Women; Edgar F. Kaiser, industrialist; Miss Margaret J. Mealey, executive director, National Council of Catholic Women; Miss Marguerite Rawalt, president, National Federation of Business and Professional Women's Clubs; William F. Schnitzler, secretary-treasurer, AFL-CIO; Dr. Caroline Ware, sociologist, historian for UNESCO; Dr. Cynthia C. Wedel, co-chairman of the National Council of Churches' Committee on the Cooperation of Men and Women in Church and Society (PCSW Document 5, February 8, 1962, PCSW, KL).

25. The incident is recounted in Oral History Transcripts, Oral History of John Macy (May 23, 1964), 60, PCSW, KL.

26. Kennedy, quoted in ibid., 58.

27. Ibid., 58–59.

28. Ibid.

29. Margaret Mead, ed., *American Women: The Report of the President's Commission on the Status of Women* (New York: Scribners, 1965), 20–73, 181.

30. Oral History Transcripts, Oral History of Maurine Neuberger (February 12, 1970), 15, PCSW, KL.

31. These funds were administered by the Rockefeller-funded Youth Project. Minutes of NWEP meeting, October 8, 1977, Chicago, "N.W.E.P. Memos

and Correspondence," box 4, no. 1. The Records of Dayton Women Working, Department of Archives and Special Collections, Wright State University Library, Dayton, Ohio (hereafter DWW, WSU).

32. Memo to NWEP board from Heleny Cook, April 13, 1977, "N.W.E.P. Memos and Correspondence," box 4, no. 2, DWW, WSU.

33. Letter from Ellen Cassedy to Angie Austin, May 22, 1978, box 4, no. 2, DWW, WSU.

34. Notes: "Banking Industry Research: Evidence Compiled by Dayton Women Working and Cleveland Women Working," 1979, p. 3, box 3, no. 15, DWW, WSU.

35. In 1978, President Jimmy Carter appointed Eleanor Holmes Norton to head the EEOC. Nevertheless, men headed most agencies which the NWEP dealt with. Moreover, men headed the local branches of even most EEOC offices and were the investigators and officials local member groups petitioned. Ellen Cassedy to Angie Austin, May 22, 1978, box 4, no. 2, DWW, WSU.

36. Ellen Cassedy memo to NWEP Groups, Carol, Karen, June 23, 1978, box 4, no. 2, DWW, WSU.

37. Memo, Ellen Cassedy to NWEP board, "Future of N.W.E.P.," May 10, 1979, box 4, no. 2, DWW, WSU; Steve Askin, "Female Rights Spell Trouble for Bosses," In These Times, July 27–August 9, 1983, 11.

38. Ibid.

PART TWO

The Historical and Institutional Contexts of Policy-making

MORTON KELLER

Social Policy in Nineteenth-Century America

A NY discussion of social policy—or indeed of any kind of public policy—in
the history of the United States must begin nowadays by considering
the character of the American state. The latest turn in the wheel of
academic fashion has made the state a major object of concern. Before turning to the character of social policy (and social policymaking) in nineteenth-century America, it is appropriate to examine the
underlying ideological (and hence intellectual) basis of this current
interest in the concept of an American state.

Not too long ago, academic discussion of American public policy
was dominated by buzzphrases such as "liberal capitalism," "corporate liberalism," and "social control"—formulations designed to underline the point that "the executive of the modern state" was best
seen (in the classic Marx-Engels formulation) as "a committee for
managing the common affairs of the whole bourgeoisie." But the
weight of historical evidence against so reductionist a view of the
actual workings of American politics and government has made this
a less than satisfactory mode of interpretation.[1]

In consequence, another line of analysis has recently come into
favor. This view stresses the autonomy of the state as a social institution in its own right, linked to but not necessarily a simple hand-
maiden of predominant material forces. The "Austro-Marxist" theo-

reticians of the early twentieth century, Karl Renner in particular, pioneered in developing the argument that the state had a largely independent role in organizing and changing the economic system and the social structure. Gramsci developed still further the variable relation between state and society; and Althusser distinguished between the determining force of the modes of production and the occasional dominance of institutions such as the state. ("In other words, the material determined, except where it did not," is one unkind commentator's characterization of this aperçu.)[2]

The "idea of the state as the institution of political rule" is hardly a Marxist creation. It was central to the long and rich "continental European tradition of political thought about authority." But the bulk of historical and theoretical writing about Anglo-American politics and government has rested on the assumption that these are "stateless" societies, with no historical or legal tradition of an autonomous, dominant state structure. It is only as the twentieth century draws to a close and decades of regulation, welfare, and warfare, ever-larger bureaucracies, ever-greater government taxation and expenditure, and ever more active and assertive economic and social policymaking have become a conspicuous part of the Anglo-American experience that "bringing the state back in" has come to be an attractive intellectual enterprise.[3]

But the place of the state in the history of American politics and government is still matter for controversy. It is (or at least it should be) an occasion for the reawakening of a long-term battle of the books. One side of this ongoing historiographical debate rests on a pluralist tradition of analysis that emphasizes American exceptionalism— those aspects of the American experience that distinguish it from its European counterparts—and on diverse interests operating within a distinctive, commonly shared, for want of a better word, "liberal" sociocultural setting. The other is a tradition (primarily though not exclusively Marxist in its intellectual origins) that sees American experience in terms of forces and institutions (classes and class conflict; the evolution of market capitalism; now the state) that transcend national distinctions and differences.[4]

Of course in practice these traditions often overlap. American pluralist-exceptionalists are hardly indifferent to conflicts between (some, certain) workers and (some, certain) employers, or to changes in modes of production or the role and relative power of government. Similarly, those working in the Marxist tradition make distinctions among workers, farmers, capitalists, and professionals that are at times hard to distinguish from a pluralist view of American society.

Nevertheless, the tension between these two strands of historical, sociological, and political-science analysis persists. And just as the application of the Euro-Marxist concept of class has fostered decades-long controversy over its utility to the American scene, so does (or so should) the application of the Euro-Marxist concept of the state be viewed not as a self-evident basis for analysis but as a concept whose utility is subject to debate.

What is the box score of the contest to date? At least for the earlier period of American history, the exceptionalists so far have tended to prevail. Attempts to view colonial America in terms of the social structure of ancien régime Europe have not succeeded very well. It would seem that the sociocultural wine of the Old World underwent a sea change more often than it traveled well. Neither the distinctive independent-farmer social structure of white colonial America nor black slavery find ready analogues in the contemporaneous European social setting of aristocrats and peasants.

Nor do the Anglicization of American elites in the mid-eighteenth century or the rise of a self-conscious urban artisanry, subjects of recent historiographical attention, significantly alter things. Just over the horizon lay a revolution, and a new government, that in large part was the work of those elites. While they drew on the language and ideas of the European Enlightenment, the home-grown character of what they were up to remains the predominant feature of the literature on the Revolution and on the intentions of the Founders. Similarly, recent efforts to read European-like class struggle into the domestic conflicts of the Revolutionary and post-Revolutionary eras have not yet led to significant recasting of the view that the American and French revolutions are more to be contrasted than compared.[5]

Perhaps the most influential attempt to put the early American political and governmental experience into a larger, Western context is the argument that the Revolution and the new nation were informed by a political philosophy of Republicanism with deep European antecedents.[6] But once again, unique American realities tend to overwhelm European analogies. Indeed, those realities appear to lead inexorably in the early nineteenth century toward a "state structure"—that is, forms of government, of politics, of law, and of public policy—that diverges increasingly from its contemporaneous European counterparts.

Karl Marx thought that the United States was the first (and at the time the only) modern state, because it was there that bourgeois, laissez-faire liberalism was most strongly entrenched. But the more we learn about the "liberal" Europe of the mid-nineteenth century, which presumably provided Marx with a model of the prototypical bourgeois state, the more we realize how tenuous was laissez-faire liberalism on the Continent—and how far beyond a European bourgeois dimension was the liberalism of nineteenth-century America.[7]

The parliaments of the mid-nineteenth-century European states were increasingly dominated by lawyers, manufacturers, bankers, journalists, and professors—the shock troops of Liberalism—as the nineteenth century progressed. But these bodies coexisted far more readily with constitutional monarchy (the form of government of every major west European state before 1871) and with a still-vigorous aristocracy and gentry than with mass democracy. And aristocrats—the old ruling class—still controlled the premierships, the military, the diplomatic apparatus, and the higher bureaucracy of the European polities.

These inheritors of the ancien régime, more than bankers and businessmen (and still less "public opinion"), set the tone of the foreign policies—and the frequent wars—of the mid-nineteenth-century European nation-states. (There were five major conflicts in the West between 1854 and 1871: the Crimean, Austrian-Prussian, Danish-Prussian, Franco-Prussian, and American Civil wars. Merely to list them is to underline how very different from the others was our Civil War.)

True, we can see in nineteenth-century Europe the rise of political parties (Liberal, Catholic, peasant, Socialist) seeking mass memberships, a development that at least superficially echoes the American experience of the time. (British Whigs become Liberals coterminously with the transformation of American Whigs into Republicans.) The liberal political press of major European cities (the *Daily Telegraph* in London, *Le Temps* and *Le Figaro* in Paris, the *Neue Freie Presse* in Vienna) is analogous to Horace Greeley's *Tribune* and Henry Raymond's *Times* in New York. And a growing agitation for voting and representation rights is evident in England and later the Continent, as it was in Jacksonian America. To ignore the links between Jacksonian democracy and the impulses behind the revolutions of 1830 and 1848 and the Reform Act of 1832, the political scientist William B. Munro observed, "disregards the essential unity of American and European history."

But looked at more closely, the tenor of public life in the mid-nineteenth-century United States was strikingly different from its European counterparts. Take the major item on the European liberal (and radical) social-reform agenda of the time: the extension of repre-

sentative government and political democracy. The Chartist movement of 1839–42 in its scale and intensity (and lack of immediate
results) was England's 1848. The Great Charter consisted of six demands: manhood suffrage, voting by ballot, equal electoral districts,
payment of members of Parliament, annual parliaments, and the
abolition of property qualifications for candidates: all long and solidly ensconced in the American political system. The struggle for
expanded (male) suffrage would rage through much of Europe until
well into the twentieth century; in America by the 1870s universal
white male suffrage had been in place for almost half a century,
black voting had attained at least constitutional affirmation, and
women could vote in two territories. When Munro observed that
"Lord John Russell and Sir Robert Peel [the authors of many of the
political reform measures of early nineteenth-century England] were
the Sam Adams and Andrew Jackson of British politics," his quick
addendum—"in somewhat more chaste editions"—hardly bridges
the vast difference of context that separates these pairs.[8]

Nineteenth-century American public policy was the product of a
relatively democratic political system operating in a social framework defined by an egalitarian cultural nationalism, powerful traditions of localism and individualism, and the varied, particularistic
economic demands of a sprawling, developing country. Certainly
this social scene had "liberal" and "bourgeois" aspects, but these
were far indeed from the contemporary European-Marxist context.

That difference is strikingly evident in the contrasting nineteenth-
century American and European experience in the realm of what
social scientists call "state-building." As Walter Dean Burnham has
observed, "The chief distinguishing characteristic of the American
political system before 1861 is that *there was no state.*"[9] The predominant American trend down to the 1860s was for less, not more, government; the rise of bourgeois liberalism in Europe made not for a weaker
but a stronger national state. The mid-Victorian compromise of
Queen and parties (the age of Disraeli and Gladstone) that quieted the
British polity in the mid-nineteenth century; the comparable mix of
new bourgeois and old aristocratic and monarchical elements in the
Second Empire of France's Louis Napoleon; the powerful drives to
"unification" (that is, to expanded hegemony) by Cavour of Piedmont
and Bismarck of Prussia—all of these were examples of state-building
that had no real American counterpart.

It is in this context that we may now try to characterize mid-
nineteenth-century American public policy. The consequences for
social policy, such as it was, were not unlike those for economic

policy, such as it was. In both cases James Willard Hurst's metaphor of "the release of energy" still serves, as does Theodore Lowi's designation of "distributive" policy, in which the goal was to parcel out benefits as widely as possible rather than to apply resources to some grand raison d'état.[10]

Hand in hand with the thrust for the "creative destruction" of economic privilege came a demand for the elimination of traditional forms of social control: an established church, hierarchical titles and modes of behavior, privileged institutions. But given the character of the American polity, this did not take the form of national policies instituted by enlightened bureaucrats à la Bismarck, and certainly did not see the rise of proto-socialist or proto-social democratic political parties. Rather, social policy was implemented primarily on the state and local level, and through an intense—and intensely decentralized—political party system, which in European terms hardly added up to a state at all.

Thus early and mid-nineteenth-century American law, uniquely in its time, became at the hands of lawyers, judges, and legislators an important instrument for the expression and implementation of social as well as economic change: a dramatic contrast with its traditional European (and English) character as a relatively passive conservator of precedent and tradition. As in the economic realm, the major thrust of early nineteenth-century American legal innovation was in the direction of way-clearing, tending to free individuals to do what they might, seeking to make the common law accord with the predominant realities of life and thought in the new nation.

This is evident in family law, where by mid-century the rules governing marriage and divorce were freer and looser in the United States than anywhere else in the Western world. It may be seen as well in criminal law, which attained a comparable notoriety for its attention to the rights of the accused. If First Amendment freedoms figured little in the constitutional law of the time, this was because what remained in the way of formal government restrictions on freedom of speech, press, and religion was being cleared away by the state legislatures.[11]

Comparably distinctive was the relationship in America between social policy and party politics. Social reform in late eighteenth- and early nineteenth-century Europe was the product of two distinct (though mutually influencing) sources: an elite tradition of humanitarian concern, with both Enlightenment and evangelical strands, and a more socially diverse tradition of egalitarianism, part of the developing history of the Western Left.

Much of early American social reform stemmed from similar sources. Founding Fathers influenced by the Enlightenment such as Franklin and Jefferson; evangelical, Quaker, and (as their party declined) Federalist advocates of antislavery and other causes: these were the progenitors of what would be a continuing tradition of elite/ genteel American reformism, the American equivalent of the European *gentilhomme* reformer. So too were figures such as the British-born Frances Wright and Robert Dale Owen, and the American-born Thomas Skidmore: American counterparts of the prototypical late eighteenth- and early nineteenth-century English and European radicals celebrated by E. P. Thompson and E. J. Hobsbawm.

But as we have seen, much of the agenda of the early and mid-nineteenth-century European Left was already law or custom in the United States. The American political spectrum had shifted so that a European liberal was roughly equivalent to (though probably to the right of) an American conservative such as John Quincy Adams. This is why I find unconvincing recent attempts to read importance into the supposed rise of an American working class in early nineteenth-century New York City. The instances of a working-class consciousness manifesting itself—the General Trades Union of the 1830s, the "uprising" of 1850—pale into insignificance when set against the persisting overlap in the social views of artisans, small employers, and laborers, the constant and complex intermix of evangelicalism, nativism, antiblack racism, and economic radicalism, and the enormous attractive pull of major party politics.[12]

The social reality of class no less than the social reality of the state was vitiated by other, more particular and varied determinants of social identity—ethnocultural, regional, political—when precisely the opposite was happening in Europe. The consequences for the determination and application of nineteenth-century American social policy were so different from their European analogues that to try to explain them in terms of the workings of an American state— or in terms of class—is to distort rather than to clarify.

"The discovery of the asylum"—a burst of proposals for and the construction of penitentiaries, almshouses, orphan asylums, and reformatories during the early nineteenth century—has been called an American "revolution in social practice." Its purposes, observes David Rothman, were "to promote the stability of the society" but also to rehabilitate the inmates of these institutions and, beyond that, to establish a pattern of proper social organization for the society at large.[13]

Certainly there was a coterminous development of similar institutions elsewhere in the West. But there is no gainsaying the fact that the building of asylums in early nineteenth-century America stemmed from an awareness of social problems, a search for their causes, and schemes for their alleviation whose sources were far more varied and complex than elsewhere.

It is reductionist to see in this phase of American social policy—perhaps the most substantial of the time—primarily an effort at social control in the current usage of that term. The asylum movement had more diverse social purposes, and a larger social base, than that. The rise of the American common school (yet another form of asylum, but surely fed by both a desire for social control and a desire for expanded opportunity); reform of the penal code to lessen the weight of imprisonment for debt, and even in a few states the abolition of capital punishment; movements for world peace, temperance, and against slavery—these coincided in time, purpose, and *dramatis personae* with the asylum movement. Together they constituted a uniquely American effort to create an institutional framework for the good society, as (it was widely assumed) the Constitution and the development of democratic politics had done and were doing for the good polity.

Of course all of these social causes had their European (and particularly their English) analogues, and were bound up with a Protestant evangelicalism and a desire for social control born of the new industrial, post–French Revolution society of the West that were hardly limited to the United States. But it was in America that these efforts most readily found a place in popular politics; that social reform first found a popular as well as an elite footing; that the dual purposes of social control and social democracy first appeared in all of their intertwined complexity.

The character—and the consequences—of a distinctively American approach to social policy may be seen as well in the rise (and fall) of the politics of temperance and nativism. It is true that, as contemporary historiographic fashion has it, these causes were fed by the social anxieties bred by industrialism, immigration, and social change. But they also had an appeal to elements of the population not so directly caught up in such developments—Maine prohibitionists, border state Know-Nothings—who subsumed them into the concerns of an active (increasingly, a hyperactive) popular political culture.

One accompaniment of the early nineteenth-century democratization of American politics (and of American life) was a more open field for new ideas about social organization. There was a notable (indeed, a unique) readiness to turn to popular politics as a proper outlet for broad and varied policy purposes. The Anti-Masons of the late 1820s and early 1830s, a political party whose ostensible major purpose was opposition to the Masons and other secret societies, were the first of a series of special-purpose parties, seeking liquor prohibition, or constraints on immigrants or Catholics, or—ultimately—the end of slavery.[14]

The effort to end black slavery and the Southern defense of that institution was the most evocative example of the tensions and ambiguities peculiar to early and mid-nineteenth-century American social policy. The same rich, even fierce American traditions of localism, individualism, freedom, and voluntarism fed both the Northern antislavery/abolitionist movement and the Southern proslavery/secessionist response. Southerners came to see in the preservation of slavery and the creation of the Confederacy the application of basic American values: freedom and voluntarism (for whites), individualism and local self-determination. If the American Everyman could create his own church, school, corporation, political party, and lifestyle, then why could he not own black slaves (conveniently denied a place in the human family) or create his own nation? By the same token, more and more northerners came to see the preservation of the Union and (for a growing but lesser number) the ending of human slavery as essential to the perpetuation of that same American experiment in liberty and self-government.

A comparative examination of the evolution of the British and American antislavery movements reveals the distinctive context (so far from a contextual world defined by class or the state!) in which this most portentous of nineteenth-century American social policies was played out. We may start with the baseline of 1807, when the abolition of the British slave trade became law and a similar end to the slave trade (after the twenty-year waiting period prescribed by the Constitution) was passed by Congress. At first the two movements followed parallel lines: elite/evangelical reformers of a similar stripe were behind the formation of the London Anti-Slavery Society (1823) and of the American Anti-Slavery Society (1832).

But then the two diverge. Leading English evangelicals (most were Anglicans), in close conjunction with their friends, relatives, and associates in the political and governmental Establishment, secured a sweeping Emancipation Act ending slavery in the Empire in 1833, only a decade after the founding of the Anti-Slavery Society. But the thirty-five years between 1830 and the Thirteenth Amendment ending slavery in 1865 saw deep schisms along ideological and religious lines within the American antislavery movement, the rise of a powerful popular politics of antislavery (and of proslavery), a protracted, complex, increasingly bitter struggle over the issue waged in Congress, the courts, public opinion, and most of all electoral politics, and of course the fighting of a massive and bloody Civil War before this peculiar institution finally was ended.

In the British case, everything about the political system conspired to make resolution of the slavery issue relatively easy. The colonial slaveholders had no direct parliamentary representation (although their British backers did). No significant differences of social, political, or economic identification divided supporters of emancipation or separated them from potential opponents. Most of all, the relatively closed nature of the system made possible an expedient resolution of the issue. It was precisely because the American polity was a far more democratic and participatory one that the slavery issue in the United States was so much more dramatic and profound, so much more difficult to resolve through state policy.[15]

On the face of it, the Civil War might have seemed to mark the injection into American public life of the power and apparatus of the modern nation-state and the implementation of national social policies on a scale hitherto unknown. The end of slavery and the passage of legal, legislative, and constitutional props to black citizenship, a "peace policy" toward Indians, and the beginnings of national support for education through the Morrill Land Grant College Act were among the forays into new realms of social policy that came with the conflict.

The war experience itself gave a new cachet to planning, to the organized power of the state. There was much talk—and some evidence—of a postwar generation ready to use state instruments to help attain the good society. The American Social Science Association, modeled on an English prototype, came into being in 1865. Its chief goals were inquiry and policy formulation in education, "Sanitary Reform," "Social Economy," and jurisprudence. John Stuart Mill assured the members of the association in 1870: "reason and right feeling on any public subject has a better chance of being favorably listened to, and of finding the national mind open to comprehend it, than at any previous time in American history."[16]

But the failure of Reconstruction underlined the fact that in the nineteenth-century United States it was exceedingly difficult to link social policy-making with the national government. Whatever constraint the outcome of the Civil War put on states' rights, it did not extend to social policy, which continued to be regarded as the peculiar province of the states in the American federal system. If anything, this principle was reinforced, both in theory and practice. The police power of the states to legislate for the safety, morals, health (and, a significant late nineteenth-century addition, the welfare) of their people was solidly reinforced by the courts; indeed it served as the great rationale for economic and social regulation by the states.

So it was the several commonwealths, and not the national government, that became the major source of the late nineteenth-century American public-policy response to the social problems of industrialism. This contrasts dramatically with Wilhelmine Germany, late Victorian England, and the France of the Third Republic, where the beginnings of social policymaking in the realms of welfare, labor, and economic regulation are distinctly national.

What is more, the social policy-making impulse stemmed not so much from a developing elite of reform intellectuals, planners, bureaucrats, and the like, but rather from the intensely organizational, participatory, machine-led political party system of the time. Thus urban social welfare (aside from private charity) and public works alike were the products not of planners but of politicians: the boss-controlled, graft-ridden, vote-getting apparatus of urban political machines. Similarly, the only major federal social-welfare program of the late nineteenth century was an intensely political—even partisan—one: the pension system for Union veterans and their dependents.[17]

The pre-1900 American social-policy response to the problems generated by the twin forces of industrialism and urbanism has been called the product of a "state of courts and parties." But it may be questioned whether so varied, decentralized, and responsive rather than initiatory a structure of politics and government may be called a "state"—any more than the mass of American laborers, so divided by ethnicity, religion, region, and culture, may usefully be called a "class."

Still, there were intimations of something more going on as well, and scholars have found in this period the beginnings of the more familiar, modern, bureaucratic-administrative state. William Brock holds that the late nineteenth-century rise of state boards of charities and public health, bureaus of labor statistics, and railroad commissions marks "the beginning of the epoch in which we now live," one of public investigation and responsibility. Stephen Skowronek argues that in the movements for civil-service reform, army reorganization, and federal railroad regulation were the seeds of a new American state with a national administrative capacity.[18]

But these activities were far from the realm of the issues that most concerned Americans: housing and living conditions, education, social welfare, race relations. In themselves they reveal how far from a modern administrative state was the late nineteenth-century American polity. The politicos let the civil service grow not because they were impelled by a desire for administrative efficiency, but because corporations and other business interests were replacing officeholders as the major source of party patronage, and because the politics of placeholding cost more than it was worth in disappointed office seekers. To increase the efficiency of a minute army policing Indians in the west hardly affected major American issues or interests. And shifting railroad regulation from the parties to the courts better served the interests of the parties than of the railroads (or of the American "state"), as later developments amply proved.

Social policy in the early twentieth-century United States—the social policy of the Progressive Era—may best be seen as the American variant of an impulse that was evident in much of the Western world. Once again, a comparative view is useful in sharpening our sense of just how full (or how empty) was the glass of American social policy.

Jan Romein and Norman Stone have shown how widespread in the West was a new consciousness of social problems and new modes of inquiry, policy formation, and political mobilization, around the turn of the century. Enlightened elites and experts; print media fostering a better (or at least more broadly) informed public opinion; political systems more responsive not only to the demands of particular interest groups but to more broadly based policy demands as well; most of all, a substantial increase in the legislative and administrative apparatus of welfare and other social policy—these were the distinctive attributes of turn-of-the-century public policy-making both in America and in much of western Europe. But just as nineteenth-century government based on social and economic liberalism—Ferdinand Lassalle's "night-watchman state"—meant one thing in Europe and quite another in America, so too did what has been called the "social state" of the early twentieth century.[19]

After 1900, by common agreement, a sea change is evident in American public life. The anxieties that came with mature capitalism—fear of the power of large corporations, the belief that an industrial work force would be subject to the lure of radical or socialist appeals, a heightened concern over immigrant masses clustered in large cities and industrial towns—are credited with feeding the stream of political, social, and economic policy-making that made up the progressive movement.[20]

On the face of it, something very similar was going on in turn-of-the-century Europe. Under the chancellorship of Caprivi, Germany in the early 1890s undertook "a new course" of labor reform. Italy's Crispi spoke of a "new life"; British Liberals formulated their Newcastle Programme of social reform.

After 1900 this impulse became much stronger. "Technocratic" governments based on center-left political alliances sought to use the power of the state to eliminate social evils. Conspicuous in this movement were the British Liberals, in power after 1906, led by Asquith, Lloyd George, and Churchill, who enacted major health insurance and unemployment legislation; Clemenceau's Radical ministry in France from 1906 to 1909; Giolitti's "long ministry" in Italy; the Bulow-block of Radical Liberals, National Liberals, and Conservatives in Germany. Everywhere, stronger government machines were created, expanding their activities in education, postal services, health, urban affairs, and social welfare. Taxes and bureaucracies rose sharply: British public servants increased from 153,000 in 1901 to 644,000 in 1911; French from 451,000 to 699,000; German from 907,000 to 1,159,000. Senior civil servants and politician-administrators dictating public policy rose to prominence: Robert Morant in British education, Gustave Monod in French education, Lloyd George and Churchill in British labor and welfare policy, Arthur Fontaine in French labor reform.

The major components of this turn-of-the-century European social reform were enlightened (or more intelligently self-interested) conservatives, increasingly important cadres of experts and intellectuals, and a popular left-liberalism ranging from reform-minded centrists to socialists. Most of all, it reflected the growing salience of class politics in European society. Norman Stone concludes, "After 1890, class-war made the basis of politics in Europe."[21]

Can much the same be said of American progressivism? Were its political, economic, social, and intellectual sources similar? Did the nineteenth century "state" of courts and parties give way, as recent literature argues it did, to a new kind of American state with "national administrative capacities"? Can we speak meaningfully of an early twentieth-century American public policy dominated by autonomous servants of the state and/or corporate interests? Was there, in sum, a substantial convergence of American with European statemaking in the realm of social policy? Or did the distinctive, exceptional character of the American politics and government continue to prevail?[22]

We may first determine just what the major American national social-policy agenda was and how it compared with its European counterparts. In Britain, and to a lesser extent in other European countries, two topics were of primary importance: welfare and labor measures—health insurance, accident and unemployment compensation—and (as in the cases of the British Education Act of 1902 and the Briand law of 1905) the relationship of church and state. The context in which early twentieth-century European social policy emerged was one of increasing class conflict, reflected in major, continuous strikes—in railroads, coal, steel, the docks; a rising Socialist political presence (the new British Labour Party, the powerful German Social Democrats); and, in counterpoint, the growing presence of the political Right, drawing in some cases on anti-Semitism, in all cases on the increase in xenophobic nationalism and militarism (fed both by old aristocratic elites and radical Right rabble-rousing) that characterized pre-1914 Europe.

So to delineate the European picture is in effect to underline its contrast with the United States. Both in substance and in context, the American situation was very different. True, large strikes, socialism—the "class issue"—were of concern in American public life as well. But the agenda of public policy continued to be shaped not by sophisticated (or atavistic) conservatives, or liberal social reformers, or labor spokesmen, but by a party system more responsive to ethnocultural than to class demands, by a structure of government still intensely federal (in which the states had all but complete say in major areas of social concern), and by a legal system in which constitutional restraints on the active state still had substantial weight.

While national welfare policy—in areas such as workmen's compensation, social insurance, child labor—languished, the American social agenda of the early twentieth century came increasingly to be dominated by issues with nineteenth-century roots but with a new salience in an urban-industrial age: prohibition and immigration restriction. And it was the Eighteenth Amendment and the Volstead Act, and the quota and national-origins system of immigration restriction, that in terms of their impact on American life may be said to have been the most important achievements—the jewels in the crown—of national American social policy in the early twentieth century.

A distinctive legacy, but hardly the achievements of a modernizing, autonomous state. Nor did these policies necessarily foretell the course of American social policy as the twentieth century continued to unfold. In those laboratories of social experimentation, the states, much of the social welfare policy that bore fruit in the New Deal and later was germinating during the first two decades of the twentieth century. And the infrastructure of modernity—near-universal secondary education, a road system that allowed the automobile to work its revolution in American life-styles—was being built under the auspices of the existing state-local party-politics polity.

Of course, it is true as well that in books and periodicals, in the law schools, universities, and social-science disciplines, the expertise, programs, and mind-set of the post-1930 welfare-administrative state was taking form. And the great national and international events of the past half century—the Great Depression, World War II, and the Cold War—would provide the setting for the rise of institutions, policies, taxation and expenditure, and personnel that together might fairly be said to fulfill anyone's definition of a purposeful national administrative state. But the relationship of modern American government to the statelessness that predominated through so much of our past is a topic in itself.

NOTES

1. Examples of this genre include Gabriel Kolko, *The Triumph of Conservatism* (Glencoe, IL, 1963); James Weinstein, The *Corporate Ideal in the Liberal State* (Boston, 1966); David F. Noble, *America by Design* (New York, 1977); and R. Jeffrey Lustig, *Corporate Liberalism: The Origins of Modern American Political Theory, 1890–1920* (Berkeley and Los Angeles, 1982).

2. Kenneth Dyson, *The State Tradition in Western Europe* (Oxford, 1980), 235. See also Theda Skocpol, "Bringing the State Back In: Strategies of Analysis in Current Research," in Peter B. Evans et al., *Bringing the State Back In* (Cambridge, England, 1985), 3–37.

3. Dyson, *State Tradition in Western Europe*, vii–viii.

4. The classic statements of the liberal-pluralist exceptionalist view are those of Louis Hartz, Daniel Boorstin, Oscar Handlin, and Richard Hofstadter; the socialist-nonexceptionalist tradition is embodied in the work of Barrington Moore, Gabriel Kolko, and, more recently, historians such as Edward Pessen, Michael Katz, and Sean Wilentz.

5. Edmund S. Morgan, *American Slavery and American Freedom* (Williamsburg, 1980); on Anglicization, John R. Murrin, "Anglicizing an American Colony" (Ph.D. dissertation, Yale University, 1966); Gary B. Nash, *The Urban Crucible: Social Change, Political Consciousness, and the Origins of the American Revolution* (Cambridge, MA, 1979).

6. On Republicanism, see J. G. A. Pocock, *The Machiavellian Moment: Florentine Political Thought and the Atlantic Republican Tradition* (Prince-

ton, 1975); Robert E. Shalhope, "Republicanism and Early American Historiography," *WMQ*, 3d ser., 39 (1982), 334–356; Joyce Appleby, *Capitalism and a New Social Order: The Republican Vision of the 1790s* (New York, 1984).

7. This discussion draws on W. E. Mosse, *Liberal Europe: The Age of Bourgeois Realism, 1848–1875* (London, 1974); E. J. Hobsbawm, *The Age of Revolution: Europe, 1789–1848* (London, 1962) and *The Age of Capital, 1848–1875* (London, 1975); William L. Langer, *Political and Social Upheaval, 1832–1852* (New York, 1969); Theodore S. Hamerow, *The Birth of a New Europe: State and Society in the Nineteenth Century* (Chapel Hill, NC, 1983). See also Raymond Grew, "The Nineteenth-Century European State," in Charles Bright and Susan Harding, eds., *Statemaking and Social Movements* (Ann Arbor, 1984), 83–120; Arno J. Mayer, *The Persistence of the Old Regime: Europe to the Great War* (New York, 1981).

8. William B. Munro, *The Invisible Government* (New York, 1928), 74.

9. Burnham quoted by Robert O. Keohane, "Associative American Development, 1776–1860: Economic Growth and Political Disintegration," in John G. Ruggie, ed., *The Antinomies of Interdependence* (New York, 1983), 84.

10. James W. Hurst, *Law and the Conditions of Freedom in Nineteenth-Century America* (Madison, 1956); Theodore J. Lowi, "American Business, Public Policy, Case-Studies, and Political Theory," *World Politics* 16 (1964), 677–715. See also Richard L. McCormick, "The Party Period and Public Policy: An Explanatory Hypothesis," *Journal of American History* 66 (1979), 279–298.

11. Hurst, *Conditions of Freedom*; Lawrence J. Friedman, *A History of American Law* (New York, 1973); Michael Grossberg, *American Family Law in the Nineteenth Century* (Chapel Hill, NC, 1986). The work of Morton Horwitz and others proceeds from a more Marxist-inspired view of the nature of the early nineteenth-century American economy. But it accepts the Hurstian perception of American law of the time as instrumentalist and way-clearing.

12. Sean Wilentz, *Chants Democratic: New York City and the Rise of the American Working Class, 1788–1850* (New York, 1984); Amy Bridges, *City in the Republic: Antebellum New York and the Origins of Machine Politics* (Cambridge, England, 1984). See also Ira Katznelson, "Working-Class Formation and the State: Nineteenth-Century England in American Perspective," in Evans et al., *Bringing the State Back In*, 257–284; and Charles C. Bright, "The State in the United States during the Nineteenth Century," in Bright and Harding, eds., *Statemaking*, 121–158.

13. David J. Rothman, *The Discovery of the Asylum: Social Order and Disorder in the New Republic* (Boston, 1971).

14. The best survey of these subjects is still Alice F. Tyler's *Freedom's Ferment* (Minneapolis, 1944; paperback, 1962). For a model study of their political context, see Ronald P. Formisano, *The Transformation of Political Culture: Massachusetts Parties, 1790s–1840s* (New York, 1983).

15. William E. Nelson, *The Roots of American Bureaucracy, 1830–1900* (Cambridge, MA, 1982), chap. 2; David Turley, "Moral Suasion, Community Action and the Problem of Power: Reflections on American Abolitionists and Government, 1830–1861," in Rhodri Jeffrys-Jones and Bruce Col-

lins, eds., *The Growth of Federal Power in American History* (DeKalb, IL, 1983), 25–35; Reginald Coupland, *The British Anti-Slavery Movement* (London, 1933); Betty Fladeland, *Men and Brothers: Anglo-American Antislavery Cooperation* (Urbana, IL, 1972).

16. Morton Keller, *Affairs of State: Public Life in Late Nineteenth-Century America* (Cambridge, MA, 1977), 123. See also Leonard P. Curry, *Blueprint for Modern America: Nonmilitary Legislation of the First Civil War Congress* (Nashville, 1968).

17. Keller, *Affairs of State*, passim. But see Robert Harrison, "The 'Weakened Spring of Government' Revisited: The Growth of Federal Power in the Late Nineteenth Century," in Jeffrys-Jones and Collins, eds., *Growth of Federal Power*, 62–75.

18. Stephen Skowronek, *Building a New American State: The Expansion of National Administrative Capacities, 1877–1920* (Cambridge, England, 1982); William R. Brock, *Investigation and Responsibility: Public Responsibility in the United States, 1865–1900* (Cambridge, England, 1984).

19. Jan Romein, *The Watershed of Two Eras: Europe in 1900* (1967; Middletown, CT, 1978); Norman Stone, *Europe Transformed, 1878–1919* (London, 1983).

20. See Robert H. Wiebe, *The Search for Order, 1877–1920* (New York, 1967), and the historiographical discussion in Daniel T. Rodgers, "In Search of Progressivism," *Reviews in American History* (December 1982), 113–132.

21. Stone, *Europe Transformed*, part II.

22. Cf. Skowronek, *New American State*; Morton Keller, "Anglo-American Politics, 1900–1930, in Anglo-American Perspective: A Case Study in Comparative History," *Comparative Studies in Society and History* 22 (1980), 458–477; Theda Skocpol and John Ikenberry, "The Political Formation of the American Welfare State in Historical and Comparative Perspective," *Comparative Social Research* 6 (1983), 87–148; Ann S. Orloff and Theda Skocpol, "Why Not Equal Protection? Explaining the Politics of Public Social Spending in Britain and the United States, 1880–1920" (typescript).

ELLIS W. HAWLEY

Social Policy and the Liberal State in Twentieth-Century America

THE distinguishing feature of liberal democracies, it has been said, is the divi-
sion of labor between the market and the popularly controlled or
democratic state.[1] The latter has functions to perform in maintaining social order, resolving social conflicts, and providing social services; and it has policy decisions to make concerning the way in
which it performs these functions. But its role in the social sphere is
a limited one. Major social decisions, including many of those concerning such matters as work organization, industrial location, compensation for labor, choice of industrial technology, and styles of
consumption, are made through private exchange relations, which
means that the level of social well-being is in significant part dependent on market transactions. And for the state's officials, whose
success and tenure depend upon sustaining certain levels of social
well-being, what happens in the market may be of greater importance than the social-policy choices made in the public sector.

If this be the case, the regimes of both nineteenth- and twentieth-
century America qualify as liberal democracies. Yet clearly, the latter, the twentieth-century liberal state, has developed features that
distinguish it from as well as link it to the former. Three of these are
immediately noticeable. It has, for one thing, a larger assignment of
social tasks. While the division of labor between market and state

remains, the line marking out their respective spheres is not where it once was. It has, for another, a different division of the governmental tasks as between its federal component and government at the state and local levels. More of the social ordering, provisioning, and conflict resolution is performed at the national level through federal agencies exercising federal powers. And it has, for a third, a significantly different set of institutions through which policy decisions are made and implemented. America's nineteenth-century liberal state was one of courts and parties.[2] Its twentieth-century state is one in which a bureaucracy of administrative agencies has come to play a major role, not only in implementing policy decisions but in making them; and as part of this new institutional growth, it has developed a complex of bureaucratized pressure groups, scientized intelligence agencies, and corporatized public-private relationships having no real counterpart in its nineteenth-century predecessor.

It is with the development and workings of this latter-day state, moreover, that studies of federal social policy in the twentieth century have been, and I think should be, centrally concerned. One question has had to do with the state's expansion in the social sphere. What, in other words, have been the social and political dynamics behind its assumption of new social tasks and the accompanying change in its division of labor with the market? Why and how has this taken place? Another question concerns the formation and workings of its new instrumentalities for policy-making and implementation. Why have these taken the form that they have, and what explains the striking and persistent differences between the American variant of them and the variants found in other twentieth-century liberal democracies? And still other questions concern inputs and outputs and the changes in these over time. Who has had access and leverage, who has supplied the ideological raw materials and social intelligence, and what have been the characteristics and consequences of the decisions made and the programs undertaken?

On all of these matters there has been a growing body of scholarship, accompanied by much debate, some false starts and dead ends, and what seem to be promising steps toward fuller understanding and more satisfying explication. The time has come for some assessment of where we have been, where we stand, and where we might go in this regard. And what follows is intended as a very modest contribution to this. In particular, it seeks to provide a general overview of the search for explanation and to offer some thoughts about the current fit between theory and evidence.

I will begin, then, with the broadest and most general of these questions. Why did the American state take on new social tasks? Where did the demand for this come from, and what was it that allowed this demand to be at least partially satisfied? Why did the limited social sphere of the nineteenth-century state become the larger and more complex sphere characteristic of the state in the twentieth century?

The American case of this development has been difficult to fit into some of the models used to explain it elsewhere. America as it entered the twentieth century had no heritage of monarchical bureaucracy of the kind that built some modern states. Nor did it have or ever develop a strong socialist movement of the kind that had to be accommodated or co-opted in various other nations. What it did share, however, with most other cases was a set of market-produced economic and social changes generating discontents and problems for which new forms of state-building became potential responses. Increasingly, as the nineteenth century drew to a close, the market was selecting technologies, locations, structures, and growth patterns that led to widespread questioning of its capacity to hold society together and secure needed forms of social cooperation. There was talk of market-produced trust, labor, urban, educational, developmental, and destabilization "problems," which seemed to be growing worse rather than correcting themselves through further market transactions. And there were those capable of being persuaded that both their lot and social well-being in general could be improved by having governmental agencies shoulder some of the social decision-making being done by the market. If the potential here was somewhat less than in other cases, it was nevertheless a real one.[3]

What America also shared with most other cases, although again perhaps to a lesser degree, were developments altering older perceptions about government's limited capacity to perform such tasks.[4] While its civil service remained stunted and of such a character as to raise strong objections to enlarging the state's social sphere, the America that entered the twentieth century was developing in its private sector a new administrative class. It was a class being equipped with new organizational and planning skills tied into new informational and communication systems. It was a class, moreover, imbued with great optimism about what could be accomplished through the intelligent application of scientific knowledge and methods, particularly if the intelligence included a "human relations" component. And whether validly or not, it was a class that could see itself and be seen by others as having the qualities needed to enhance a liberal government's task-performing capacity. Its development as a resource upon which an expanded state could draw, provided it devised proper mechanisms for doing so, added to the potential for governmental expansion.[5]

There was, then, from the late nineteenth century on, a potential for enlarging the American state's role in the social sphere. On this most students of the subject seem to agree. But potentials of course need not be realized; and what we still need to explain is why and how this particular potential was at least partially realized. What were the dynamic elements in American politics that tapped the potential and succeeded in translating it into the kind of state building that produced America's twentieth-century state? On this there has been much disagreement, both on just what these elements were and on the extent to which they differed from the elements performing this function elsewhere.

The explanation that long dominated historical writing on the subject and is still embedded in much of it has stressed the impact of wavelike reform movements in breaking through the barriers to governmental expansion, securing social legislation, and building the institutional machinery through which the state has sought to alter the social output of the market. These movements are seen as originating in periodic swings of the national mood from self-centeredness to concerns about social justice, swings that are said to have been particularly characteristic of the American middle class, and swings that have allowed reformist politicians to unite "progressives" of all classes and put through programs purporting to achieve greater justice in the social order. In a "progressive history" version, the results are judged to have been beneficial, helping to bring about higher levels of social well-being by creating something closer to the size and kind of public sector called for by demographic and economic change. In a rival but less common "conservative" version, they are judged to have been detrimental in this regard. But in both the translation of potential governmental expansion into actual governmental expansion has been the work of reform movements that have appeared on one side of oscillating shifts in the public mood.[6]

Such an explanation, however, has turned out in the face of continuing research to have left far too much unexplained. Such shifts in mood have occurred; they can be documented; and one can make a plausible case that they have occurred at relatively regular intervals and have, if some adjustments are made for externalities, tended to form a self-perpetuating cycle.[7] But the inadequacy of the explanation has become apparent as researchers have gotten below the political rhetoric accepted by its formulators and begun to scrutinize more closely the "movements" involved, the intervals between them, and the particular innovations in using state power to modify the play of market forces. Under close scrutiny, the "movements" have tended to dissolve into a multitude of interest groups using competing forms of "public interest" rhetoric and opportunistically bargaining with each other for measures to solve or alleviate some of their "problems."[8] Under similar examination, the intervals have ceased to be periods of "rest" and inactivity in the production of the modern state.[9] And when studied in detail, the innovations in using state power to alter the market's social output seemed to involve myriad quests for security, status, preservation, market power, tax-financed "pork," and improved business performance, as well as concerns about social justice.[10] Seemingly, the notion of a movement-built social-liberal state left more unexplained than explained.

A second answer to this question of how potential governmental expansion was translated into actuality, one that emerged in conjunction with the criticism of "progressive history" and the movement into historical studies of constructs from political science and sociology, has been that stressing the formation and behavior of interest groups and modernizing elites. A new world of interest groups, it is argued, arose from the associability of those affected by market-produced social transformation and the opportunities opened up by improvements in education, communication, and organizational tools. It was these newly formed groups that tapped the potential for new state action and through bargaining and compromise, among themselves and with government officials, joined in aggregative coalitions to support specific measures. They were assisted in doing this by a new breed of "political brokers" and by new technical and intellectual elites who helped to design the measures, offered themselves as the instruments through which particular interests could be reconciled with the public interest, and thus sought to create a social order in which their expertise and wisdom would be more highly valued. And the result, particularly at times when the barriers to governmental expansion were weakened by heightened problem consciousness, a sense of national crisis, or faith in the problem-solving capacity of a strong political leader, was political force capable of achieving innovative breakthroughs that gave the state enlarged social tasks and new kinds of machinery for performing them.[11]

Once the breakthroughs were achieved and gained legitimacy, moreover, they tended to be institutionalized in ways that gave them a capacity for further expansion and development, at least of an incremental sort. A new complex of interest groups arose from clients, beneficiaries, and sponsors. This became intertwined with administrative, planning, and legislative units in ways that produced "iron triangles" and "symbiotic unions," "captive" bureaus and associations, and mechanisms of corporatist consultation and power sharing. And from the process came the power not only to defend innovations but also to develop, bargain for, and implement expansionist and auxiliary schemes.

Such a formulation seemed to explain much that the notion of wavelike movements arising out of shifts in the popular mood could not explain. It gained wide acceptance; and it became and has continued to be the answer in a second kind of "progressive history" engaged in debate with a "conservative" rival. In the former the interest groups, modernizing elites, and new political brokers became agents of social progress, engaged in exchange relations, having their own version of the market's "unseen hand" and producing similarly beneficial results in liberal state-building. In the latter they became the elements that had broken down the checks and balances established by wiser men, made the government a source of unearned economic rewards and consequent economic foolishness, and thus kept the level of social well-being below what it might have been.[12]

Still, it was difficult to explain the whole of the new American state's social interventions in terms of potentials realized through interest-group formation, power, and interaction. There were innovations that did not seem to fit, innovations, it seemed, that could not be accounted for without bringing in other sources of power. And coming into their own in the 1960s were critics who charged that most of the explanation amounted to a "mystification" that was being used to mask the real purposes of the state's social interventions and the real social and political forces responsible for them. The real beneficiaries had been neither society as a whole nor the members of newly formed interest groups but rather a capitalist class that because of such intervention had been able to cope with its manpower and competitive problems, keep the potential for true social progress from being realized, and thus retain its social privileges. This had also, some went on to argue, been the real intent; and the real statebuilding power, the one that had shaped political culture, ideology, agendas, associations, and procedures so that interest-group activity had led to this end, had been class power. The outcome was best understood as class weaponry in an ongoing struggle characteristic of all capitalist societies, America included. If there was an American exceptionalism, it lay more in the sophistication with which the

American ruling class had waged the struggle than in the absence of class structure and conflict.[13]

The search for this class power in the historical record, however, has in general been a disappointing and unsuccessful one. One could find a continuing structure of privileges and inequalities, some evidence that the state's social interventions had helped to reduce pressures for ending these, and individual examples of sophisticated privilege holders who had seen these interventions as their saviors and worked to promote and shape them. But the evidence offered to show that such "corporate liberals" spoke for and exercised the power of a class and in this capacity had designed and built the twentieth-century state as a class instrumentality remained thin and unpersuasive. There was too much evidence suggesting that other privilege holders had not agreed with or supported their designs and that the bulk of such class power as existed had on a number of occasions been arrayed against but failed to prevent an enlargement of the state's social sphere. There was also the persisting inability of the explanation's proponents to locate and specify control mechanisms that seemed capable of imposing class will on public-policy output. And to suppose, as some did, that these evidential problems stemmed from the feigning of opposition for tactical purposes or the cleverness with which the exercise of power was concealed led to notions of conspiracy that rested upon unbelievable premises.[14]

Under close scrutiny, then, the "corporate liberal" explanation has not fared well. The debate over it, however, did bring out major weaknesses in the competing "interest group" explanation; and one result has been the rise of another line of inquiry, one that has seemed to me considerably more promising. This has been the search for at least part of the explanation in the autonomous behavior of those in charge of the nation's political institutions and organs. It has involved a shift away from the notion of democratic government as a neutral executor for forces arising in the society, be they movements, interest-group aggregations, class power, or historical logic; has recognized that the forces for tapping and realizing state-building potentials can arise through autonomous political action undertaken by those with political problems to solve; and has concentrated on recovering such behavior from the historical record and making it part of a more satisfying explanation.[15] In a sense, those involved have been moving back toward the idea that "history is past politics" and that the greatest illuminator of state-building is political history, although the more usual claim is that political and social history must be combined if the twentieth-century liberal state is to be understood.

One of the most promising insights to come out of this perspective on the matter has been that concerning the "regime imperatives" of liberal democratic systems and the problems these pose for the officials in charge of public-sector resources. Given the division of labor between market and state, it is argued, such officials have been beholden both to those making political choices and those making economic ones. Their survival, political credits, capacity to manage, and ability to leave their marks on political life have depended not only on maintaining political bases but upon doing so in ways that allowed a property-based market to perform the tasks still assigned to it. In a sense, those making the most important economic choices, particularly potential investors and economic developers, have functioned as something approaching a second constituency. Their dissatisfaction, as reflected in altered expectations and decisions based on them, could mean less public-sector resources and weaker political bases. And this need to satisfy dual constituencies has worked to produce the curious mixture of social welfare and business promotion activities that has characterized liberal democratic states in the twentieth century. The former has grown out of a need to maintain political bases and a willingness to use them for projects of social betterment or protection; the latter out of a need to secure satisfactory market performance and make the political projects palatable to those whose economic decisions mattered when it came to attaining this goal.[16]

In the American case, where the weakness of both the anticapitalist left and the antidemocratic right has left officials or potential officials without realistic alternatives, this explanation seems to work especially well. It helps to explain the policy "ambivalences" and "inconsistencies," particularly the alternate wooing and lambasting of business, that have been noted in such presidencies as those of Woodrow Wilson, the two Roosevelts, and John F. Kennedy. It helps to explain the coexistence of redistributive, anticorporate, and citizen entitlement programs with measures to sustain and expand a market-produced corporate society, the "taming" of each to allow this coexistence, and the political energy expended in insisting that the two are or could be made complementary. It may help to explain the arrangements under which implementation of public projects for altering the market's social output has been entrusted to business administrators and organizations or the persisting efforts to bring representatives of the two constituencies together in corporative councils and other consensus-building bodies. And its recognition that skillful politics attuned to changing perceptions and concerns in each constituency can at times enhance the autonomy of officials and thus create discretionary power open to influence by "idea men" claiming social expertise seems to provide a way of explaining much in the American experience that has been left unexplained by movement, interest-group, and ruling-class models.

In any event, the shift of focus back to governmental institutions and officials whose output can be analyzed in terms of regime forms, cultural and structural constraints, political problem solving, and the openings that appeared for discretionary action and expert prescription would seem to be a quite promising development in the continued effort to understand how the expanded social sphere of America's twentieth-century state came into being. One cannot of course ignore what was happening in the society as well as the state. Much of the potential for state-building has to be explained there, and at times parts of the state have lost their autonomy and become appendages of social forces. But formulations in which the state is viewed as a mere extension of cyclical swings, interest-group interaction, social organization, or ongoing class struggle have not held up well. And the indications are that a more satisfactory answer can be had if pride of place in the story is given to state institutions as they are operated by public officials.[17]

A focus on state and political frameworks and on the sense of the state among political participants can also help to explain why America's efforts to alter the social output of the market have produced arrangements and instrumentalities differing from those found in other liberal democracies. Here again efforts have been made to explain this by focusing on the peculiarities of America's class structure, social geography, ethnic composition, or interest-group population. And again one cannot ignore the persisting differences in the society as well as the state. But the most satisfying and persuasive explanations in recent years have come from inquiries highlighting historically inherited but changing state frameworks and the activities and evaluation processes taking place within them.

The differences to be explained here, as brought out in the comparative literature, are essentially six in number. One has been the underdevelopment and incoherence, comparatively speaking, of America's policy-planning apparatus in the social sphere. Its twentieth-century state, in other words, has failed to develop regularized institutions for generating a national plan and making this part of the policy and administrative process. A second has been the similar underdevelopment of formalized corporative mechanisms working to produce and implement "social contracts" or to shield rationalizers from "irresponsible" interest-group pressures. Such machinery has appeared in particular sectors and programs and more broadly on an emergency or ad hoc basis but has not been generalized and formalized to the extent found elsewhere. A third has been the American state's comparatively heavy reliance on quasi-privatist machinery for welfare provision and evaluation and particularly on a form of this developed by businessmen and professionals as opposed to labor unions, churches, or other kinds of associated endeavor. In this respect, one can see it as more privatized or businesslike. A fourth has been the comparatively heavy reliance of the American state on the machinery of subnational units, not only to implement federal social policy but to adapt it to local standards and operate local programs. This has remained a distinguishing feature despite the remarkable expansion in federal tasks and the use of federal power. And a fifth has been the comparatively large component of patronage politics to which the American thrusts toward meritocracy, programmatic action, and citizen entitlements have continued to accommodate themselves. An earned share in the altered social output has continued to depend, somewhat more than elsewhere, on being part of a successful patronage organization.[18]

Finally, there has been the less comprehensive coverage of the American version of national welfare benefits. It has remained without programs that have become standard elsewhere, has been on the whole less standardized, and has retained a sharper bifurcation between such "earned" benefits as "social security" and an "unearned" category designated as "welfare." So marked have these features been that some analysts have categorized America as having a "positive" state but not a welfare one. And among students of the subject, there has been growing skepticism about the view that this "incompleteness" is of a transitory nature and will disappear as a "welfare laggard" catches up. Its history suggests a distinguishing feature that, like the others noted here, has had and may continue to have considerable staying power.[19]

Some of these differences, as noted before, are clearly related to and may be partially explained by American exceptionalism in its social power structure, discontents, and ideals. But my sense of these is that they can easily be exaggerated and that much of the explanation has to be sought and can probably be found in the peculiarities of the American polity within which twentieth-century expanders of the state's role in the social sphere have had to work. As developed in the nineteenth century, this polity had lodged power with judges, patronage organizations, and local authorities, dispersed opportunities for initiatives and vetoes among a variety of institutions and political actors, and carried on its ordering and modernizing functions without an autonomous bureaucratic core, programmatic parties, or collaborating peak associations. It was not a structure well suited to dealing with the market-produced social problems that were becoming national concerns as America entered the twentieth century. Yet it proved highly resistant to calls for restructuring and, as a result, made the creation of new administrative realms of the type being used abroad exceedingly difficult. At best, these had to be jerrybuilt by taking advantage of fortuitous openings and conjunctures and accepting constraints that minimized the threat that their creation posed to the existing pattern of authority. And much of the "national bureaucracy" that emerged from this process not only accommodated itself to continuing roles for patronage organizations and subnational units but became their ally in resisting the creation of national planning institutions and the attempted importation of national welfare models from abroad.[20]

The way that administrative capacity developed, moreover, helps to explain the comparatively heavy reliance in America on quasiprivatist machinery. A weak administrative sector sought to enhance its capacity by bringing private administrative resources into "public service." And probably of greater importance, there was an understandable reluctance on the part of America's reform elements to entrust the performance of new social tasks either to patronage organizations or to the kind of jerrybuilt bureaucracy that the American polity was producing. There were efforts to find an alternative in a set of "public service" organizations that combined the attributes of private associations with those of governmental bureaus. And while these organizations, too, have frequently come under attack as ineffective or improper performers of the tasks assigned them, they have continued to be formed and a residue of them has remained part of the solution to a persisting administrative problem rooted in a solidly established state framework.[21]

A focus on state frameworks, then, appears to be a highly promising line of inquiry, capable of adding much to our understanding of why America's twentieth-century liberal state developed as it did and why its efforts to alter the social output of the market have involved arrangements and instrumentalities differing from those found in other liberal democracies. A complementary line of inquiry with similar promise has been that focusing on the peculiarities of American political culture, particularly in regard to the sense of the state found among active participants in the political process, and how these have worked both to sustain America's peculiar state framework and to rule out arrangements and instrumentalities that have become characteristic of twentieth-century state action in other liberal democracies. This seems to have grown out of the general revival in recent years of "culture studies," the extension of them into new areas, and a new willingness to recognize cultural formations as independent determinants. And it seems especially encouraging in that it has gotten beyond explanations stressing the almost complete dominance of liberal values in America's political culture and begun to analyze the complex interplay of differing formations of these values and the effects of this on state development.

The first point of course is still worth making. Modern welfare states, it has been argued, embody and reflect complex amalgams of liberal, socialist, and Tory values;[22] and in the American case the liberal component seems to have been almost the whole mix. So far at least, efforts to identify American counterparts to the socialist and Tory influences operating in the European cases have not been very persuasive, and their absence helps to explain some of the "incompleteness" of the American state. But more can be understood if one recognizes that this liberal component has consisted of not one but several value structures that in practice have been invoked against and helped to check and balance each other, the result being a policy and administrative output that lacks internal coherence and reflects the persisting tensions in the political culture.

One analysis of this sort has stressed the interplay and tension between a free-market libertarianism and a market-modifying republicanism, both liberal and both capable of becoming popular as well as class or interest ideologies, but one inclined to idealize the market's workings and defend its social output as being in line with liberal goals, while the other idealized citizens' assemblies and participatory politics and held them capable of improving on the market's decisions.[23] This is perceptive and gets at part of what we need to understand. But I would add to it a third major value structure interacting and existing in tension with the two already noted, one that for want of a better name might be called "managerial developmentalism." In it the mechanisms idealized as capable of improving on the liberal quality of the market's social output have been the technical survey, the "harmonization" council of functional representatives, the science-based educational institution, and the social-minded "private government." And while this is not as deeply rooted in America's past as the other two structures, there being only weak foreshadowings of it prior to the 1890s, it has, I would argue, been very much a part of American political culture in the twentieth century. Like its rivals, moreover, it has at times showed the capacity to become a popular as well as a class or interest ideology.[24]

What seems particularly relevant here is the sense of the state that each of these ideological formations has brought to the interactive process. Each has for some purposes found a place for a "strong state," the first as a protector of property rights and enforcer of contracts, the second as a smiter of the people's enemies and restorer of personal and community "independence," and the third as a fosterer, protector, and servicer of managerial mechanisms. Yet in each there has also been a strong element of "antistatism," directed particularly against entrusting centralized statist bureaucracies with managerial or "social engineering" capacities. Each has tended to view the reach for such power not as an effective way to solve social problems but as a threat to the mechanisms really capable of solving them, and each has helped to block the emergence of a cultural formation in which a powerful bureaucratic core is regarded as a legitimate arm of the state and a suitable instrument for realizing liberal ideals under modern conditions. In this respect, the cultural milieu was as unpromising as the state framework when it came to creating the kind of administrative realms that existed abroad. And again the resulting bureaucratic formation had to be pushed through the cracks with appropriate concessions to cultural ideals, symbols, and fears, a process that also helps to explain the fragmented, competitive-minded, dependent, and often irrational character of what came out. The culture, it seems, was malleable enough to allow a bureaucracy geared to the performance of narrow, specific, and pragmatically justified tasks but not one that had much of a capacity for overall social management or for developing and implementing a coherent national welfare scheme.[25]

This kind of "antistatism," it can be further argued, has also worked to produce the peculiarly American notion that whatever planning and managerial capacities were required could be had without such a bureaucracy. One manifestation of this has been the use of emergency machinery viewed as unbureaucratic because of its reliance on private-sector "volunteers" or because of its avowedly temporary character. Another has been the "associative state" phenomenon of the Hoover period, the early New Deal, and the Eisenhower years, an approach that would avoid the "evils of bureaucracy" by building the needed capacities into the associative life of the private sector or by lodging them in prestigious state-private intersects. And a third has been the reliance on presidents and presidential agents serving as "crisis managers" or "popular tribunes" rather than "bureaucrats" and as such respecting the constraints intended to keep bureaucratic power in its place. Significantly, when presidential administrative reform has failed to respect these and moved toward creating a potential institutional base for a bureaucratic establishment with national managerial capacities, it has met with stiff and generally successful resistance.[26]

The peculiarities of the political culture, then, should be considered along with the peculiarities of the state framework. And together, they seem capable of explaining much about the peculiar arrangements and instrumentalities through which twentieth-century America has attempted to alter the market's social output. A better understanding of them seems to be moving us toward a more satisfactory explanation than can be had from socioeconomic analysis alone; and studies contributing to this ought therefore to be encouraged.

The other general question has to do with policy inputs and outputs, the patterns that have been discerned in these, and the explanations offered for these patterns. What, in other words, has America's peculiar variant of twentieth-century state intervention in the social sphere been used for or functioned as? By whom and for whom has it been used? And what have been the consequences, intended or unintended, of its use?

The first general interpretation to dominate historical writing about these matters was that associated with the so-called "progressive" explanation of the intervention's origins. It was a view in which the workings of the expanded liberal state became a twentieth-century counterpart of earlier struggles to secure equity, respect, and power for the "common man," an appropriately updated version, in other words, of such earlier phenomena as Jacksonian Democracy and Lincolnian Republicanism. And these workings, it was held, had succeeded in bringing about a "big change" in the lot of common people. They had given America not only a "people's government" with capacities to correct social injustices but also a "people's capitalism," in which the market's social output contributed to the realization of democratic ideals.[27]

As with the "progressive" view of origins, however, this view of inputs and outputs failed to stand up well under close scrutiny and since the 1950s has been in retreat or at least on the defensive. Its "democracy on the march" turned out to be of greater service to upper-middle-class elites than to common people. Its "people's government" was found to be serving a "people" from which the poor, the unorganized, and the socially oppressed had been largely excluded. At best, some studies concluded, it had merely enlarged the array of special interests having access to governmental resources, not subjected the "interests" to popular control or instituted a popularly based system of just rewards. And what had been characterized as a "people's capitalism" turned out, when closely scrutinized, to be producing an array of "social bads" that were often making the lot of common people worse instead of better. It was responsible, among other things, for reinforcing social oppression and injustice, impoverishing the people's public life, diverting national resources to antisocial uses, and lowering the quality of the environment in which the people lived and worked.[28]

This critique of the "democratization" view would eventually open the way to interpretations in which the expanded American state became an antidemocratic and antiprogressive force. But initially, as with the question of origins, its chief rival became a view of inputs and outputs that stressed interest-group interaction and roles for modernizing or threatened elites. And while this could in the hands of some make the twentieth-century American state an expanded and appropriately updated version of the nineteenth century's "pork barrel" or "great barbecue," the initial inclination among formulators of the view was to stress the positive nature of the inputs and outputs. The new state, it was argued, had given more of the people an opportunity to secure fair shares of the society's benefits, risks, and burdens; and its output had consisted not only of administrative "pork" but of a kind of interactive sharing that had enhanced social stability and solidarity, immunized American "democracy" from totalitarian temptations, and allowed scientific progress to be turned into social progress. If it had not functioned as the "democratization" model postulated, it had helped to save the "democracy" previously achieved by making that "democracy" workable in the twentieth century. And in some formulations, it had brought into being a better organized "political market," one that efficiently translated competing political demands for surplus goods into distributive outcomes reflecting the democratically developed strengths of the competitors.[29]

This view of the expanded state's workings still has much support in the interpretive literature; and some would argue that if it is not fully applicable to the state that had emerged from the reforms of the first half of the twentieth century, it does make good sense of what had emerged by 1975. Others, however, have strongly disagreed. They have pointed to inputs and outputs that seemed incompatible with such a patterning. And just as with explanations of origins, the 1960s brought a wave of interpretive works that tried to make sense of these observations by viewing the expanded state as an instrument of class power engaged in preserving social privileges, "regulating" the underprivileged, and creating the social conditions needed for continuing capitalist accumulation. It had functioned as a "stabilizer" not in the sense of correcting social injustices or providing democratic opportunities for doing so but rather in the sense of containing or deflating social forces that threatened the existing social order. And its claims to have avoided class bias through mechanisms of popular participation and disinterested professional expertise were without merit. The former had not been allowed to decide the questions that mattered, and the latter had in practice become mechanisms for making the existing system work rather than seeking social justice or social democracy.[30]

Again, though, the search for the machinery through which the socially privileged have differentiated important from unimportant matters, turned public officials into their agents, and seen to it that such agents served the interests of their principals has been a disappointing and generally unsuccessful one. Although one could find in social-policy outputs a good deal that had been undemocratic, unjust, or of service to the privileged, it was hard to find the conscious and systematic class action and the principal-agent relationships that were supposed to explain this. Nor was it easy to dismiss the remainder of the policy output as being something about which the privileged had not really cared. At best, it seemed, one could find little more than a biased configuration of social power that had disposed officials in need of upper-strata resources to be solicitous of those who could make them available.[31] And while an understanding of this could help to explain how advantage had perpetuated itself, it amounted essentially to a mechanism of constraint rather than one of control or direction.

Still, as with the question of origins, the unpersuasiveness of the class-power patterning has not meant a general return to the "democratic pluralism" or "people's democracy" views. Instead, we have had a growing insistence that "politicians and bureaucrats matter," that the state as an autonomous set of institutions and values must be brought "back in," and that by doing so sense can be made of apparent chaos and irrationality. The key, it is argued, lies in understanding the behavior of public officials whose use of the state apparatus takes place within a historically changing structure of legal, institutional, cultural, societal, intellectual, and ethical constraints but who are more than neutral agents of either public or special interests and who acquire and use varying degrees of discretionary power to serve a variety of individual needs and purposes. The constraints can explain some of the contours of the input-output pattern and some of the contradictions, tensions, and inconsistencies in it. But for an understanding of the rest, one must focus on the ways in which officials have acquired and sustained political power bases and what they have chosen to do with the discretionary power at their command. What the expanded state has functioned as and the interests it has served through its social interventions has depended in part on the needs, worldviews, judgments, ambitions, and whims of the officials in charge of its operations. And given the continued dispersion of power among many such officials and diverse types and subtypes of them, the policies emerging from their choices are unlikely to have had much internal coherence or to be easily capturable under such rubrics as democratization, stabilization, or rationalization. They are likely, in other words, to look much like the aggregation of observed policy experience that has been used to cast doubt on conceptions of the state as a provider or enhancer of a particular social quality.

Such a focus has given us a number of valuable studies illuminating the accumulation and use of discretionary power by public officials. It has also begun to generate theories about the kinds of officials likely to want and be rewarded with such power under given sets of circumstances, the uses to which given kinds of officials will put the power at their command, and the imprints that these uses of official power have left on the workings of social programs.[32] In both of these respects, it promises to get us closer to an intellectually satisfying conception of what the expanded state has functioned as and why it has functioned that way. And in the process, it may provide knowledge of use to those who would make the American version of the liberal state a more effective social problemsolver. It may, however, be doing something else as well, namely, providing a picture of incoherence, bumbling, and unintended consequences that can be used to justify pronouncements of governmental failure or incapacity in the social sphere and to support calls on the one side for returning social tasks to the market and on the other for entrusting them to a new kind of apolitical, depoliticized, or debureaucratized agency. In a variety of ways, the "officials matter" view has been linked to ideologies that regard the American state's social interventionism as being part of a worsening set of "social problems" rather than a prospective solver of them. At best, these regard it as having once helped to improve social conditions but, because of processes analogous to the overloading of electrical circuits or the hardening of human arteries, as having long since lost the qualities and capacities needed for such a task.[33]

Still, the approach seems promising, particularly if the story of incoherence and disappointment can be disentangled from the judgmental application of ideal models, set in a history that also illuminates the likely workings of the alternatives, and rescued from analyses so structured as to render negative verdicts about costs and benefits.[34] If these things can be done, it promises to provide us with more satisfying answers as to how state power has been used in the social sphere, why it has been used that way, and what such use has been effective and ineffective in doing.[35]

On that note, then, I end this exercise. My purpose has been not to provide a history of the liberal state in twentieth-century America but to review our efforts to understand its past development and workings, indicate where we seem to be in this regard, and suggest promising lines of future inquiry. The general movement has been from a scholarly rejection of personalities and happenings as offering adequate explanations to conceptions in which the state became the product or agent of social forces and then back to a recognition of its relative autonomy and efforts to understand this as an independent force. Few, I suspect, would deny that America's twentieth-century polity has had roots in the society and been responsive to social transformations and conflicts. Nor would many deny that a fuller understanding of the social constraints on state action can contribute to a better understanding of state development and functioning. But a truly adequate understanding of these matters would seem to require a merger of social with political history and a renewed effort to understand the independent political factors that have also been at work; and this, so the indications are anyway, is a direction in which current scholarship is moving.

NOTES

1. Stephen L. Elkin, "Pluralism in Its Place: State and Regime in Liberal Democracy," in Roger Benjamin and Stephen Elkin, eds., The Democratic State (Lawrence: University of Kansas Press, 1985), 179.

2. See Stephen Skowronek, *Building a New American State* (Cambridge: Cambridge University Press, 1982), 19–35, and Charles C. Bright, "The State in the United States during the Nineteenth Century," in Charles Bright and Susan Harding, eds., *Statemaking and Social Movements* (Ann Arbor: University of Michigan Press, 1984), 121–158.

3. See the discussion in John W. Chambers, *The Tyranny of Change: America in the Progressive Era* (New York: St. Martin's Press, 1980), 1–42. See also Harold U. Faulkner, *The Decline of Laissez Faire* (New York: Rinehart, 1951), and David P. Thelen, *The New Citizenship* (Columbia: University of Missouri Press, 1972), 55–129.

4. For a discussion of comparative state building in terms of burdens and capacities, see Reginald J. Harrison, *Pluralism and Corporatism: The Political Evolution of Modern Democracies* (London: Allen and Unwin, 1980), 1–14.

5. See the chapter entitled "A New Middle Class," in Robert H. Wiebe, *The Search for Order, 1877–1920* (New York: Hill and Wang, 1967), 111–132. See also Donald Stabile, *Prophets of Order* (Boston: South End Press, 1984).

6. The classical statement of the view was Arthur M. Schlesinger, Sr., "Tides of American Politics," *Yale Review* 29 (December 1939). See also his *Paths to the Present* (New York: Macmillan, 1949); Arthur M. Schlesinger, Jr., "Sources of the New Deal," *Columbia University Forum* 2 (Fall 1959); Basil Rauch, *The History of the New Deal* (New York: Creative Age, 1944); and Robert S. McElvaine, *The Great Depression: America, 1929–1941* (New York: Times Books, 1984), especially pp. 3–7. A representative of the conservative version is Edgar E. Robinson, *The Roosevelt Leadership, 1933–45* (Philadelphia: Lippincott, 1955).

7. See McElvaine, *Great Depression*, and Arthur M. Schlesinger, Jr., in *New York Review of Books*, August 16, 1984, 35–37.

8. See, for example, Peter G. Filene, "An Obituary for 'The Progressive Movement,' " *American Quarterly* 22 (Spring 1970), 20–34.

9. See, for example, Arthur S. Link, "What Happened to the Progressive Movement in the 1920s?" *American Historical Review* 64 (July 1959), 833–851.

10. See, for example, the chapter entitled "The Politics of Adjustment," in Samuel P. Hays, *The Response to Industrialism* (Chicago: University of Chicago Press, 1957), 140–162.

11. See Samuel Hays, "The New Organizational Society," in Jerry Israel, ed., *Building the Organizational Society* (New York: Free Press, 1972), 1–15; Robert H. Wiebe, *Businessmen and Reform* (Cambridge: Harvard University Press, 1962); John Braeman, "The New Deal and the 'Broker State,' " *Business History Review* 46 (Winter 1972).

12. See, for example, Louis Galambos, *America at Middle Age* (New York: McGraw-Hill, 1984); Arthur S. Link, *American Epoch* (New York: Knopf, 1955); and Milton Friedman, *Capitalism and Freedom* (Chicago: University of Chicago Press, 1962). This view of the state's origins was also accepted in such critical works as Grant McConnell, *Private Power and American Democracy* (New York: Knopf, 1966), and Theodore Lowi, *The End of Liberalism* (New York: W. W. Norton, 1969).

13. See Barton J. Bernstein, ed., *Towards a New Past* (New York: Random

House, 1967); Ronald Radosh, "The Myth of the New Deal," in Ronald Radosh and Murray Rothbard, eds., A New History of Leviathan (New York: Dutton, 1972), 146–187; G. William Domhoff, The Higher Circles (New York: Random House, 1971); James Weinstein, The Corporate Ideal in the Liberal State (Boston: Beacon Press, 1968); Theda Skocpol, "Political Response to Capitalist Crisis: Neo-Marxist Theories of the State and the Case of the New Deal," Politics and Society 10 (1980), 155–201.

14. See the discussion in Skocpol, "Political Response to Capitalist Crisis," 163–169, and Elkin, "Pluralism in Its Place," 184–186. See also my discussion in "The New Deal and Business," in John Braeman et al., eds., The New Deal: The National Level (Columbus: Ohio State University Press, 1975), 75–76.

15. Examples include Theda Skocpol and John Ikenberry, "The Political Formation of the American Welfare State in Historical and Comparative Perspective," Comparative Social Research 6 (1983), 87–148; Ann Shola Orloff and Theda Skocpol, "Why Not Equal Protection? Explaining the Politics of Public Social Spending in Britain, 1910–11, and the United States, 1880s–1920," American Sociological Review 49 (December 1984), 726–750; Benjamin and Elkin, eds., The Democratic State; Barry D. Karl, The Uneasy State: The United States from 1915 to 1945 (Chicago: University of Chicago Press, 1983); Albert U. Romasco, The Politics of Recovery: Roosevelt's New Deal (New York: Oxford University Press, 1983); Thomas E. Borcherding, ed., Budgets and Bureaucrats: The Sources of Government Growth (Durham: Duke University Press, 1977); Gary Walton, ed., Regulatory Change in an Atmosphere of Crisis: Current Implications of the Roosevelt Years (New York: Academic Press, 1979); and Christopher Leman, "Patterns of Policy Development: Social Security in the United States and Canada," Public Policy 25 (Spring 1977), 261–291.

16. See especially Elkin, "Pluralism in Its Place," 186–206. The argument is a refinement of the "post-pluralist" view set forth by Charles Lindblom in Politics and Markets (New York: Basic Books, 1977) and the theory of power set forth in Clarence Stone, "Systemic Power in Community Decision Making," American Political Science Review 74 (December 1980), 978–990.

17. To explain the American state's expansion, it has become clear, one must combine an understanding of legitimation and incremental growth processes with an understanding of the periodic political explosions during which the major additions to and deletions from it have been made. These have come, it appears, when general perceptions that something must be done have coincided with the presence of officials able and willing to do something and of a policy intelligentsia with saleable prescriptions as to what this should be. At the federal level, such conjunctures can be noted during the years 1913–16, 1919–22, 1933–36, 1945–47, 1964–67, and 1970–71. But whether these are the products of contingency or of some underlying political or social dynamic is less clear.

18. See Peter Flora and Arnold Heidenheimer, The Development of Welfare States in Europe and America (New Brunswick: Transaction Books, 1981); Norman Furniss and Timothy Tilton, The Case for the Welfare State (Bloomington: Indiana University Press, 1977); Skocpol and Ikenberry, "Political Formation of the American Welfare State in Historical and Compara-

tive Perspective"; Gerhard Lambruch and Philippe Schmitter, eds., *Patterns of Corporatist Policy-Making* (Beverly Hills: Sage, 1982), especially the essay by Robert Salisbury; and Harold Wilensky and Charles N. Lebeaux, *Industrial Society and Social Welfare* (New York: Free Press, 1965 ed.).

19. See Furniss and Tilton, *Case for the Welfare State,* 153–183; Wilensky and Lebeaux, *Industrial Society,* v–xvii; Skocpol and Ikenberry, "Political Formation of the American Welfare State in Historical and Comparative Perspective."

20. Works helping to make this clear include John Ikenberry and Theda Skocpol, "From Patronage Democracy to Social Security" (November 1984), forthcoming in Raymond Duvall, ed., *States and Economies;* Karl, *Uneasy State;* Otis L. Graham, Jr., *Toward a Planned Society* (New York: Oxford University Press, 1976); and Skowronek, *Building a New American State.*

21. See Furniss and Tilton, *Case for the Welfare State,* 155–158, 173–176; Barry Karl, "Presidential Planning and Social Science Research: Mr. Hoover's Experts," *Perspectives in American History,* vol. 3 (1969); Ellis Hawley, "Herbert Hoover, the Commerce Secretariat, and the Vision of an 'Associative State,' 1921–1928," *Journal of American History* 61 (June 1974); Kim McQuaid, "Businessman and Bureaucrat: The Evolution of the American Welfare System, 1900–1940," *Journal of Economic History* 38 (March 1978); Robert Griffith, "Dwight D. Eisenhower and the Corporate Commonwealth," *American Historical Review* 87 (February 1982); and Hal Draper, "Neo-Corporatists and Neo-Reformers," *New Politics* 1 (Fall 1961).

22. Hugh Heclo, in Flora and Heidenheimer, eds., *Development of Welfare States,* 392–393.

23. McElvaine, *Great Depression,* 196–223.

24. See my "The Discovery and Study of a 'Corporate Liberalism,' " *Business History Review* 52 (Autumn 1978), 309–320. See also the other essays in the same issue of *Business History Review;* David A. Horowitz, "Visions of Harmonious Abundance" (Ph.D. dissertation, University of Minnesota, 1971); Griffith, "Eisenhower and the Corporate Commonwealth"; Patrick D. Reagan, "The Architects of Modern American National Planning" (Ph.D. dissertation, Ohio State University, 1982); and Guy Alchon, *The Invisible Hand of Planning* (Princeton: Princeton University Press, 1985).

25. See Graham, *Toward a Planned Society,* 28–68, and Skocpol and Ikenberry, "Political Formation of the American Welfare State in Historical and Comparative Perspective." Elizabeth Sanders argues that even this kind of bureaucracy was mostly a legacy of the depression period, when a large white-collar class was in economic distress and sought meaningful positions in government. See Elizabeth Sanders, "Businesss, Bureaucracy, and the Bourgeoisie: The New Deal Legacy," in Alan Stone and Edward J. Harpham, eds., *The Political Economy of Public Policy* (Beverly Hills: Sage, 1982), 115–140.

26. See Karl, *Uneasy State;* Hawley, "Hoover and the 'Associative State' "; Griffith, "Eisenhower and the Corporate Commonwealth"; Robert Cuff, "American Mobilization for War: Political Culture vs. Bureaucratic Administration," in Royal Military College of Canada, *Military History Symposium* (1980), 73–86; Barry Karl, "In Search of National Planning," paper presented at Organization of American Historians convention, April 1983; and Peri Arnold, "Ambivalent Leviathan," in J. David Greenstone,

ed., *Publlic Values and Private Power in American Politics* (Chicago: University of Chicago Press, 1982), 109–136.

27. See, for example, John D. Hicks, "The Third American Revolution," *Nebraska History* 36 (1955), 227–245; Frederick Lewis Allen, *The Big Change: America Transforms Itself, 1900–1950* (New York: Harper and Row, 1952); and Dwight Dumond, *America in Our Time, 1896–1946* (New York: Holt, 1947).

28. See, for example, Rexford G. Tugwell and E. C. Banfield, "Grass Roots Democracy—Myth or Reality?" *Public Administration Review* 10 (Winter 1950), 47–55; Henry Kariel, *The Decline of American Pluralism* (Stanford: Stanford University Press, 1961); John K. Galbraith, *The Affluent Society* (Boston: Houghton Mifflin, 1958); Gabriel Kolko, *Wealth and Power in America* (New York: Praeger, 1962); Michael Harrington, *The Other America* (Baltimore: Penguin, 1963); Paul Conkin, *The New Deal* (New York: Crowell, 1967).

29. See, for example, Peter Viereck, "A Third View of the New Deal," *New Mexico Quarterly* 26 (1956), 44–52; Daniel Bell, *The End of Ideology* (New York: Free Press, 1960); Seymour Lipset, *Political Man* (Garden City: Doubleday, 1960); and Robert A. Dahl, *Pluralist Democracy in the United States* (Chicago: Rand McNally, 1967). See also the discussion in Richard H. Pells, *The Liberal Mind in a Conservative Age* (New York: Harper and Row, 1985), 130–147.

30. See, for example, Bernstein, ed., *Towards a New Past;* Weinstein, *Corporate Ideal;* Domhoff, *Higher Circles;* Francis Fox Piven and Richard Cloward, *Regulating the Poor* (New York: Pantheon Books, 1971); Gabriel Kolko, *The Triumph of Conservatism* (New York: Free Press, 1963); and Kolko, *Main Currents in Modern American History* (New York: Harper and Row, 1976).

31. See Stone, "Systemic Power."

32. See, for example, Robert MacKay and Joseph Reid, "On Understanding the Birth and Evolution of the Securities and Exchange Commission: Where Are We in the Theory of Regulation?" in Walton, ed., *Regulatory Change in an Atmosphere of Crisis,* 101–127; Borcherding, ed., *Budgets and Bureaucrats;* Benjamin and Elkin, eds., *The Democratic State;* Samuel P. Hays, "Political Choice in Regulation," in Thomas McCraw, ed., *Regulation in Perspective* (Cambridge: Harvard University Press, 1981), 124–154; Thomas McCraw, *Prophets of Regulation* (Cambridge: Harvard University Press, 1984); and Theda Skocpol, "Bringing the State Back In," *Items* 36 (June 1982).

33. See Raymond Seidelman, "Pluralist Heaven's Dissenting Angels: Corporatism in the American Political Economy," in Stone and Harpham, eds., *Political Economy of Public Policy,* 49–70; Richard A. Musgrove, "Leviathan Cometh—Or Does He?" in Helen Ladd and Nicolaus Tideman, *Tax and Expenditure Limitations* (Washington, D.C.: Urban Institute Press, 1981); Norman Furniss, "The Political Implications of the Public Choice-Property Rights School," *American Political Science Review* 72 (June 1978), 399–410; E. S. Savas, *Privatizing the Public Sector* (Chatham: Chatham House Publishers, 1982); and Charles Murray, *Losing Ground: American Social Policy, 1950–1980* (New York: Basic Books, 1984).

34. See Kenneth J. Meier, "Political Economy and Cost-Benefit Analysis," in Stone and Harpham, eds., *Political Economy of Public Policy*, 143–162.

35. As to just how the society has been changed by state intervention in the twentieth century, there is still much disagreement. The current wisdom, however, seems to be that it has not reduced income or wealth inequality by very much (but see Edgar Browning and William Johnson, "Taxes, Transfers, and Income Inequality," in Walton, ed., *Regulatory Change in an Atmosphere of Crisis*, 129–152), has not provided much protection for groups threatened by modernization processes, and has not had much success at moral engineering and value inculcation—but that it has reduced the risks and burdens of urban-industrial life (especially for the middle classes), redistributed some of the social costs of economic development, widened opportunities for education and state-of-the-art health care, facilitated new kinds of associational life, helped to reduce discriminatory social practices, and established entitlements moving the society away from the concept of "decent provision" toward that of a "citizen's wage." As to whether doing these things has made the market and associative sectors work better or worse, there is much less agreement. In addition, the whole assessment has been complicated by differing views as to what the market and associative sectors might have become in the absence of state intervention.

JACK L. WALKER

Interests, Political Parties, and Policy Formation in American Democracy

IN the aftermath of the political upheavals
of the 1960s and 70s, there is an unsettling
lack of agreement on national priorities in the United States. We are
experiencing a period of divided partisan control of the national
government, an era of painful transition from international economic hegemony to stiff competition with the Japanese and the
Western Europeans and an ever more threatening military confrontation with the Soviet Union. Just as in earlier troubled periods of
American history, questions are being raised about the staying
power of our political system. America faces today, however, a

This paper grows out of research on interest groups funded by grants from
the Earhart Foundation and National Science Foundation. Thanks are also
due to the Program in American Studies at the Woodrow Wilson International Center for Scholars, where I spent a stimulating year of research, and
to the Guggenheim Foundation for a fellowship that helped to pay for it all.
Special thanks go to Thomas L. Gais and Mark Peterson, doctoral students
who have assisted in my interest-group project and also taught me a great
deal about this subject. The Institute of Public Policy Studies, my home
base at the University of Michigan, paid certain costs of reproducing this
paper, and important editorial assistance was given by Mark Peterson and
Jackie Brendle. The paper was produced through the University of Michigan's word-processing system through the wizardry of John Hankins.

fundamentally different kind of governmental challenge than in the past, not only because of the grave social and economic problems emerging in both the international and domestic realms but also because our population is better mobilized and organized for political action in the 1980s than ever before.

While much alarm has been expressed about the decline in turnout at national elections, not much notice has been given to the extraordinary growth in recent years in the electorate's *active core*— the people who follow political news, contribute to political organizations, and make gifts to campaigns. The system's politically engaged, attentive public has been steadily growing, and there has also been an unprecedented expansion in the number of professional advocates who claim to represent this growing pool of citizen activists. Many groups and organizations have been created that can marshall the skills and the resources necessary to compete—sometimes quite effectively—with the President and other elected officials for the attention and loyalty of the public. Although there has never been an accurate census, it seems likely that the number of such political organizations operating in Washington may have *tripled* during the past thirty years.

American political parties have undergone great changes as a result of these developments, causing some to believe that they are collapsing, leaving the country with no stabilizing institutions to provide shape for our public life. Recent critics warn that the government may become overloaded with the demands from all of these conflicting interests, leading eventually to policy "gridlock" or "political bankruptcy" (Huntington, 1973; King, 1975; and Rose and Peters, 1980). They warn that our contentious system cannot produce coherent foreign or domestic policies, and speak of a "systemic condition of paralysis that must be corrected if we are ever to regain our national confidence and fulfill our national promise" (Sorensen, 1984, 28).

In order to arrest what they regard as a serious decline in governmental capacity, critics recently have proposed constitutional amendments that would increase the length of presidential or congressional terms, prevent leaders from succeeding themselves, and alter the traditional division of powers between the executive and legislative branches. Fundamental reforms are needed, in the eyes of these observers, in order to reverse a dangerous trend toward the fragmentation of American political institutions. These critics believe that as the leading nation among Western democracies in the 1980s, the United States cannot afford to indulge itself with a political system which was designed in the eighteenth century to govern a small agricultural society; a system that now frustrates all attempts at leadership and produces aimlessness, drift, and inconstancy in crucial public policies—not in this age of people's wars, international terrorism, and nuclear confrontation.

Are these complaints about our political system justified? Does the great increase in the number of interest groups and the growth of the attentive public in recent years warrant major changes in the country's policies toward political participation? Are American political parties collapsing, setting the political system adrift? Do we really need a stronger, centralized, national authority with the power to harness our national resources and enforce a clear set of national priorities?

Policymakers in Washington are fond of saying: "If it ain't broke, don't fix it." I do not believe that the American system is overloaded, or that there is need for fundamental constitutional changes in order to provide greater authority for the Washington political establishment. This essay presents reasons for my skepticism about the complaints of critics who lament the effect of recent trends in the political mobilization of the American public. I believe that they have misunderstood the modern history of American political parties and do not understand why the system of interest groups at the national level has expanded so rapidly in recent years. Once these developments are placed in proper perspective, it will become clear that the American political system actually is stronger as a result of these changes. The American policy-making system has several serious structural weaknesses—it is far from perfect—nevertheless, American political leaders have succeeded, through their efforts to accommodate the demands of many new emerging political forces, in creating a system that is much better adapted than the older one to the needs of a modern democracy in an age of mass communication.

POLITICAL PARTIES VERSUS INTEREST GROUPS AS AGENTS OF MOBILIZATION

Critics of the contemporary American political system express great misgivings about the prevalence of interest groups in the national policymaking system. In their minds, there is little doubt as to whether political parties or interest groups are preferable as mechanisms for political mobilization in a democracy. The parties are better, without doubt. Interest groups have been an important object of research for more than a century, but from the beginning most scholars have been noticeably uncomfortable about the phenomena they were studying (Garson, 1978). Most believe that the hundreds of lobbyists who pack the hearing rooms of the Capitol represent narrow, selfish interests and have little concern for the public interest. Some have argued that conflict among these advocates produces restraint, and that a balanced portrait of popular desires will emerge from the interaction of all these voices; but most political scientists agree with E. E. Schattschneider, who charged that the interest-group system is seriously unbalanced because it includes mainly those who are affluent and educated enough to become involved in voluntary associations. "The flaw in the pluralist heaven," he argued, "is that the heavenly chorus sings with a strong upper class accent" (Schattschneider, 1960, 35).

Only the parties, with their goal of winning elections, could be expected to reach out to the poor or the many other unorganized segments of the population. They are also the only institutions capable of aggregating demands from conflicting interests, coordinating the constitutionally divided branches of the government, concentrating authority, and allowing for the exercise of leadership in American democracy.

The advocates of party government, however, are not united. Some argue that parties in such a complex society can never be more than pragmatic coalitions of regional, ethnic, commercial, and professional interests, whose major purpose should be to preserve national unity and provide for a consistent ruling majority. Because of their diversity, such parties naturally will contain ideologically incompatible elements that will prevent their advancing a consistent set of programs or policies. Other writers, however, do not believe that ensuring stability within the ruling elite is so valuable as long as members of this inner circle are in fundamental disagreement over the party's values and purposes. These writers have called for parties built around ideologically consistent programs of social policy that will provide clear-cut signals to the public about who is responsible for the government's successes and failures.[1]

Party advocates also disagree about the value of citizen participation in important party decisions. Some favor greater participation on principle, simply because democracy demands it, while others believe participation is the best way to encourage consent and build support for the party's candidates. In recent years these advocates of participation have been countered by those who fear that the parties have been seriously weakened and believe that party leaders must be granted the power they need to direct all the organization's resources toward the pursuit of electoral victories. An active debate continues over these procedural issues, but all factions agree on one proposition: strong political parties are desirable, and they are the best way to counter threats to democracy posed by an unrestrained system of interest groups.[2]

A highly questionable assumption underlies these debates over the organization and functions of political parties and the proper role of interest groups in the American system. Many seem to believe that if the parties could only be strengthened, they would somehow temper or reduce the fragmenting influence of interest groups. The two systems are thought to be fundamentally at odds. When groups flourish, parties go into decline; if only parties could be strengthened, the group system would begin to wither. Much of the scholarship on this subject, especially by persuasive writers like Schattschneider, has contrasted descriptions of the grubby details of interest-group lobbying with an idealized vision of responsible parties, striving to mobilize the disadvantaged and dedicated to the pursuit of the public interest. The group system, however, taken as a whole, is not as selfish and narrow as it is portrayed in these accounts, and the party system is not so consistently dedicated to mobilizing the public or coordinating the government as its advocates assert. The two systems also are not fundamentally antithetical. Many politically active people take part in party politics and belong to several interest groups at the same time. In recent years, as parties began to offer more consistent programs to the public and exercise more discipline over their members in the Congress, thus threatening the vital interests of many established constituencies, the group system, far from fading away, has expanded and become more active.

A CAPSULE HISTORY
OF THE PARTY SYSTEM IN TRANSITION

Warnings about the weakening of American political parties have become more persistent during the past ten years, but the historical evidence suggests that the parties are not collapsing. Rather, their relationship with the major interest groups and their role and function in the political system is being transformed.[3]

Assuming their modern form in the 1830s and 1840s, the parties entered a golden age as the chief organizing devices of American politics soon after the Civil War. For more than three decades, until the Republican party achieved hegemony after the political realignments of 1896, the outcomes of most national elections were in doubt; precinct level organizers were hard at work for both sides; large numbers of recent immigrants were mobilized into the political system; turnout at elections soared; and the policy agendas in Washington and many state capitals emerged almost entirely from the clash of the two major parties.

These powerful nineteenth-century parties were decentralized organizations composed of largely autonomous state and local units. They were built upon ethnic, religious, and regional loyalties, but the key to their success was the vast supply of material resources at the disposal of party leaders in the form of patronage jobs, government contracts, exclusive franchises for local services and utilities, and privileged access to judges and other public officials. Party leaders were able to reward those who cooperated and to punish their opponents. They used this power to maintain their organizations, control party nominations, and shape the policy agenda, but their methods were not always within the law. The "boss," the "machine," the "gerrymander," the "graveyard vote," and many other unsavory metaphors became part of common parlance in America during this golden age of party government, and politicians acquired a sinister reputation that lingers on today.

As the twentieth century began, a cultural transformation was underway in almost all realms of American life. Large, centrally managed, bureaucratic hierarchies were emerging in the business world with names like International Harvester or United States Steel; and national professional communities were being formed in fields like education, finance, engineering, and the law, based largely upon technical or scientific values (Hays, 1957; 1969). Pressures soon arose for the creation of government agencies in which these new professional specialties could be pursued without the corrupting interference of partisan politicians. The slogan of the advocates of reform in urban government was: "There is no Democratic or Republican method of paving a street!" Educational leaders wanted to get the public schools "out of politics," just as military planners, public health officers, policemen, forest rangers, and other managers of the new public services wanted to free themselves from kickbacks, graft, partiality, and all the other tainted aspects of partisanship (Skowronek, 1982).

As these debates over the delivery of public services intensified in the first decades of the twentieth century, political parties were usually depicted as the chief enemies of good government. Party leaders were under attack for corruption, but the conflict actually ran much deeper. Reformers did not believe that such parochial, decentralized, geographically limited organizations could serve as the centerpieces of representative democracy in an industrial society. Local and state political machines often opposed the expansion of government into new services like public health or city planning, especially if it meant the incorporation of more professionals into the public service who would refuse to submit to party discipline (McDonald and Ward, 1984). In the eyes of those who wished to meet the social problems of an industrial society or exploit the nation's potential as a world power, the political parties developed in the nineteenth century were among the chief obstacles to the modernization of business, government, and the professions in America.

The clash between party leaders and reformers that began in the late nineteenth century did not end in one climactic battle. It dragged on in isolated struggles in cities and states all over the country during the next fifty years. As sources of patronage were eliminated and social services were expanded and professionalized at the state and local levels, the material resources required by party leaders to maintain their organizations began to disappear. Political machines collapsed one by one, party organizations fell into disrepair, and their capacity to mobilize potential voters or control their own nominating procedures steadily declined.

By the 1950s, the party system that had emerged from the New Deal realignment of the 1930s had not only suffered many organizational setbacks but also was unable to control the agenda of American politics. During the Truman administration and throughout the 1950s and early 1960s, stubborn resistance from an alliance of southern Democrats and northern Republicans successfully prevented most efforts at domestic reform, creating what James MacGregor Burns called in 1963 a "deadlock of democracy" that frustrated liberals and, above all, prevented resolution within the legislative arena of one of the country's most serious and potentially explosive domestic problems—racial segregation in the southern states (Burns, 1963). Factions within the Democratic party urgently wanted to address this problem, and majorities in favor of national civil-rights legislation clearly existed after World War II, but the ruling party was unable to produce legislation on this subject out of fear that its supporting coalition would be blown to pieces by the conflict created by such a debate. Far from being a force for further mobilization of the unorganized and disadvantaged, the party system became a major obstacle to change. Proponents of civil rights were forced to look to the Presidency, the courts, and eventually the streets as the only forums where the dilemma of racial segregation might be resolved.

At the state and local level, party organizations were also unable to adjust to the rapid shifts in population and the growth of suburbia after World War II. Representatives of the burgeoning suburban middle class were demanding expensive new government programs in education, health care, transportation, recreation, natural-resource conservation, pollution control, and land-use planning. Once again, sufficient public support existed to enact these new programs, but established party leaders resisted and delayed, refusing to begin the tremendous expansion of state and local government that such new programs would require. Pressures mounted to reapportion state legislatures according to population so that suburbanites and city dwellers would have a greater voice. In many states during the 1950s large popular-vote majorities failed to produce a majority of legislative seats. Party leaders who profited from these arrangements defended declining rural interests against the rising urban and suburban middle class. When the Supreme Court decided in *Baker v. Carr* (1962), *Reynolds v. Sims* (1964), and subsequent rulings, that state and local legislative bodies must be apportioned according to equal population size, it also opened the policy agenda in these jurisdictions to new issues that leaders of the majority parties had either ignored or bitterly resisted.

The immediate impact of reapportionment was rapid turnover in all representative bodies. Prior to reapportionment in the 1959 General Election in New Jersey, 20% of those elected to the state Senate were new members, while in 1967, soon after reapportionment, 75% of those elected were serving for the first time. Many southern states were engaged in elongated disputes that required many court orders and several reapportionments. No sooner was the issue settled than the 1970 census figures became available, requiring yet another round of district drawing. The Tennessee state legislature, for example, was redistricted six times in the nine years from 1962 to 1973. This constant shifting of district lines fractured local political organizations, sent many politicians into early retirement, and led to the unsettling of state party systems for more than a decade (O'Rourke, 1980). These decisions had their greatest impact on southern states, such as Georgia and Mississippi, that had long been controlled by a single dominant Democratic party, or northern states such as New Jersey and Michigan, where carefully constructed coalitions based in heavily Republican rural areas and small towns had blocked proportional representation for predominantly Democratic urban areas. The decade-long turmoil emerging from the process of reapportionment fractured local political organizations in all these states, leaving their party systems in shambles.

The wrenching experience with legislative reapportionment was but another of a long series of organizational body blows sustained by the party system in the twentieth century. With the disappearance of the kind of material inducements organizers had always used, some other bases were needed upon which party workers might be recruited. It soon became apparent that "Amateur Democrats" who wanted to achieve programmatic policy goals through political action would also expect to have a voice in party affairs and could not be counted upon for loyal support of all decisions by party leaders (Wilson, 1962). During the 1970s a search began in both parties to find a new formula for organizational viability. Through a series of reforms and re-reforms of their nominating procedures, Democrats opened their party to an unprecedented amount of participation by volunteer workers and citizens who took part in caucuses, conventions, and direct primaries. Republicans began highly successful experiments with direct-mail solicitation for funds, the use of telephone banks, polling, special publications, and other techniques of mass persuasion.[4] Party organizers soon learned that blanket calls for volunteers or financial support could seldom be based upon blatant appeals to religious, ethnic, regional, or racial loyalties but rather must deal in some way with the substance of public policy. A new model of party organization began to evolve in the 1970s, aimed at the growing middle class, built around the latest techniques of mass communication, and based much more than ever before upon broadly ideological appeals.

A CAPSULE HISTORY
OF THE MODERN SYSTEM OF INTEREST GROUPS

Interest groups have been a part of American life from the country's origins, but the modern system began to take shape only in the late nineteenth century, during the golden age of party government. The rapidly developing industrial economy, besides luring the millions of immigrants to whom the parties were making their appeals, was also spawning a great many new commercial and scientific specialties that served as the foundations for a number of trade and professional societies. These new associations were meant to exercise control over unruly competition; provide forums for the exchange of information and the development of professional reputations; create knowledge about the latest methods or techniques in the field; and represent the occupational interests of their members before legislative committees or government bureaus (Johnson, 1972; Mosher, 1968). There is evidence that the membership of these groups waxed and waned with the economy and that there were spurts of development, especially around the national mobilization during World War I, when dozens of these groups were formed each year (Berry, 1977; Schmitter and Brand, 1982). A new set of linkages between government and the citizenry was emerging, based squarely upon the rapidly growing occupational structure of the industrial society.

Mobilization of Occupational Interests: The Profit versus the Not-for-Profit Realms: The new occupationally based interest-group system grew in response to several different forces. From the beginning, occupations carried on mainly in the public sector or in not-for-profit institutions organized separately from those in the profit-making sector. Interest groups usually contained members who were mostly from one sector or the other, and often conflict between the two sectors stimulated the growth of even more interest groups (Walker, 1983).

Beginning in the 1940s, for example, a coalition of occupationally based organizations in the not-for-profit sector, led by the American Cancer Society and the American Heart Association, began a concerted campaign to reduce cigarette smoking because of its links to cancer and heart disease. This campaign gained wide publicity and was joined by officials in the U.S. Public Health Service, including the Surgeon General. The six large firms that dominated the tobacco industry—together accounting for 98% of domestic cigarette sales—immediately realized that there was a grave threat of government intervention in their affairs. To combat this threat they joined forces in a defensive coalition and jointly funded both the Tobacco Research Council, a corporation designed to conduct research under industry auspices, and the Tobacco Institute, a trade association that would coordinate their lobbying efforts in Washington. A struggle began between these two coalitions—public-sector professionals, not-for-profit institutions, and government agencies on one side, and large corporate and commercial interests on the other—that has continued for more than thirty years, causing many additional organizations to spring up and causing elaborate coalitions to be built on both sides (Fritschler, 3d ed., 1983; Miles, 1982).

This controversy over the use of tobacco bears little relation to the cleavages around which the political parties are organized because it unites all regional interests, Republican and Democratic, where the tobacco industry is dominant. It also invites log-rolling tactics in the Congress with other bipartisan, regional-industrial blocs, such as the oil or dairy industries, that wish to protect generous subsidies or obtain favorable government regulations.

Most studies of the formation of business interest groups or trade associations have concluded that they tend to form not so much in response to conflict with organized labor but rather as responses to threats of unwanted government intervention, as in the case of the tobacco industry, or when factions of an industry seek government aid or protection from their competitors. Antitrust laws prevent some openly collusive joint political efforts, but trade associations tend to form within relatively homogeneous industrial domains where firms perceive the threats emanating from their political environment in much the same way. Associations are also more likely to be established within industries where a few large firms predominate, presumably due to their willingness to bear a disproportionate share of the costs of organizing because they expect to gain a disproportionate share of any benefits that result (Gable, 1953; Pfeffer and Salancik, 1978; and Schmitter and Brand, 1982).

The expanding scope and size of government not only stimulated the organization of business interests; it encouraged even more directly the rapid increase of new organizations in the not-for-profit or public sectors. The growth during the twentieth century of the public schools, parks and forest preserves, agricultural research stations, public hospitals, and social-welfare agencies of all kinds stimulated the creation of numerous professional associations made up of the providers of these new public services. These groups often were created at the suggestion of public officials who realized the political value of organized constituents working to promote their programs from outside of government.

Government Sponsorship of Political Mobilization: The mobilization of the elderly provides a good example of this process at work. The creation of the first pensions for federal civil servants during the 1920s soon led to the establishment of the National Association of Retired Federal Employees, which could lobby for increases in the program. A system of neighborhood centers for the elderly begun in New York State during the 1930s led to the organization of the social workers who managed these centers. This new professional society not only encouraged the exchange of information about professional techniques but also pressed for greater financial support from all levels of government. A piecemeal process of mobilization of interests representing the elderly began, with the service providers taking the lead in the effort.

Mobilization of the elderly was spurred on by ambitious civil servants in the Federal Security Agency, and eventually through a series of White House Conferences in 1951, 1961, and 1971. Organizations were created with the federal government's assistance to plan and conduct these national meetings. In each case, these organizations continued in existence afterward as independent interest groups, remaining heavily dependent upon grants and contracts from government agencies or private foundations for their continued maintenance. Almost three decades after the process of mobilization had begun, groups designed to enlist the elderly clients themselves came into being. One of these groups was formed with the aid of trade unions and the presidential campaign for John F. Kennedy, while the largest one—the American Association of Retired Persons, currently the largest single voluntary association in the country— began as a marketing device for a private insurance company.

By the 1980s a large, potent array of interest groups representing both the providers and recipients of government services to the elderly had grown up in Washington. The system is heavily subsidized by private foundations, churches, business firms, trade unions, and the federal government itself through the Department of Labor and the Agency on Aging. Most of these interest groups were founded *after* the great legislative breakthroughs of Social Security, Medicare, and the Older Americans Act of 1965. In this case, there was no steady buildup of a gathering force of lobbyists and citizens associations that finally achieved their goals after decades of pressure upon the government. Much of the initiative for legislation in this field came from *within* the government itself. The associations representing the elderly—especially those that represent the clients of these programs rather than the professionals who deliver the services— were more the consequence of legislation than the cause of its passage (Pratt, 1976).

The prominent role of government officials, activist legislators, and presidents in creating the interest groups associated with the public sector matches the role of large national and multinational corporations in stimulating the organization of trade associations in the business and commercial sector. But government leadership in the mobilization of interests has not been confined to creating groups that advocate an expansion of the welfare state. While business firms have mainly been successful in organizing themselves around narrowly defined market sectors where homogeneous interests exist, leadership from the government has been necessary for creating almost all broadly based associations meant to represent the collective interests of all businesses in the management of the economy.

Secretaries of Commerce not only complained throughout the twentieth century about the weak and indifferent participation of business leaders in discussions at the highest governmental levels, but many took action to strengthen the voice of business—and presumably increase their own influence within their administrations. These entrepreneurial cabinet members provided the energy required to establish the U.S. Chamber of Commerce during the Taft administration, a number of trade associations during the Coolidge-Harding administrations, the Business Council and the Committee for Economic Development during the Roosevelt administration, the Labor-Management Group under the Kennedy administration, the National Alliance of Businessmen during the Johnson administration, and at the strong urging of Secretary of Treasury John Connally and Federal Reserve Chairman Arthur Burns, the Business Roundtable during the Nixon-Ford administrations (Arnold, 1982; McConnell, 1966; McQuaid, 1982; and Silk and Silk, 1980).

Government leadership has also been crucial in the creation of many other broadly based organizations meant to represent the collective interests of distinctive sectors of American life. The American Farm Bureau Federation began as a network of official advisory committees to county agents from the Department of Agriculture; the National Rifle Association was launched in close consultation with the Department of the Army to encourage familiarity with firearms among citizens who might be called upon to fight in future wars; and the American Legion was begun during World War I with government support to encourage patriotism and popular support for the war effort. One of the most important results of the New Deal was the relatively peaceful organization of large industrial unions under the supervision of the newly created National Labor Relations Board, following years of bitterly violent resistance from employers.

Even feminist organizations, representatives of a powerful social movement with access to many committed volunteers, received millions of dollars of support in their early years from a series of White House Conferences during the Kennedy administration; from federal legislation sponsored by President Kennedy assisting in the creation of Commissions on the Status of Women in every state; from large grants to the International Women's Year; from both statewide and national conferences on women's issues paid for with public funds during the 1970s and 1980s; and from grants and contracts between federal agencies and feminist organizations for research, data gathering, and the conduct of demonstration projects. The National Organization for Women was created during one of the annual national conventions of State Commissioners on the Status of Women by a group of commissioners frustrated by the limits on political action placed upon them by their official status. The women's movement would undoubtedly have made an important mark upon American life without this early leadership and financial support from the government, but the organizations representing it almost certainly would have been more narrowly focused, smaller, and more parochial. In addition, they would have found it much more difficult to attract the attention of the communications media or the political leadership (Carden, 1974; Freeman, 1973; and Gelb and Palley, 1982).

The Rise of Citizen Movements: Most of the groups seeking to represent women in Washington have emerged from social movements and are open to all citizens regardless of their occupations or status. Other groups of this kind, such as the Anti-Saloon League, Marcus Garvey's Negro Improvement Association, the Townsend Movement, the Committee of One Million, the Society Against Nuclear Energy, or the Students for a Democratic Society, made a dramatic impact upon the political life of their times. These groups often motivated thousands of people to put forth great efforts in intense political activities, but soon they collapsed and disappeared, often with few discernible results. Not all "cause" or citizen groups experienced such rapid cycles of hyperactivity and collapse, but those that did manage to persist often were relatively small, or were the exclusive preserve of a circle of dedicated activists sponsored by a few wealthy individuals or institutional patrons.

Citizen groups—organizations built around a compelling moral cause or a "single issue"—have always been outnumbered in the modern interest-group system by associations founded upon occupational communities. While they still are, citizen groups now constitute a larger proportion of national lobbying organizations than ever before. Evidence for such a shift in the composition of the group system is difficult to find because there has never been a comprehensive census of interest groups operating in the American political system. One important piece of circumstantial evidence showing an increase in the proportion of citizen groups in the system comes from a survey I conducted in 1980 of interest groups operating in Washington, D.C., in which each group in the sample was asked for its founding date. In Figure 1 these dates are cumulated over time to compare the rate of growth of groups based upon occupational communities with those organized around a cause. Figure 1 shows that occupationally based groups have been steadily increasing in number since the turn of the century, with about half of them founded before World War II and half within the past forty years. Over half of the citizen groups, however, have been formed within the past twenty to twenty-five years in a dramatic surge that began in the late 1960s. These data are flawed because they do not include groups that were created in earlier years but disappeared before 1980, when the sample was taken. Since citizen groups have always been unstable, it might be expected that any reconstruction of history from a single point in time would display a pattern of this kind, although such a sharp increase in the number of citizen groups probably could not be caused entirely by a statistical quirk.

It is clear that groups like Common Cause, the Sierra Club, NOW, the Moral Majority, and the NAACP are important participants in the national debate over public policy and also appear to have achieved a degree of administrative stability that is unprecedented. With the growth of a large, well-educated middle class since World War II, and with the development of many new techniques of carefully targeted mass communication, such as computerized mailing systems, closed-circuit video conferences, and WATS long-distance telephone lines, it has become possible to organize large, highly dispersed formations of citizens united only by their dedication to a cause or common beliefs about the appropriate direction of public policy. It appears that more than 100,000 households now make routine contributions to groups advancing the causes of consumer protection, environmental conservation, and civil rights, and there is evidence of a similar, perhaps even larger body of supporters willing to make contributions to groups advancing conservative social issues. Common Cause has managed to stay in existence for a decade relying almost solely upon direct-mail solicitation. There have been ups and downs, but the group had almost 270,000 members in 1984 (McFarland, 1984). The Committee for a Sane Nuclear Policy (SANE), originally founded in the 1950s, was still in operation in 1984, with an expanding list of over 80,000 members (*New York*

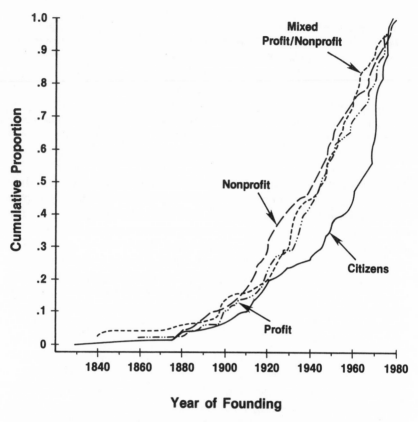

Figure 1   A cumulative count by founding date of all national interest groups divided by sector types from the typology of occupational roles

Times, April 16, 1984, 16). The leaders of both political parties and interest groups are discovering that ideological commitment, under some circumstances, can serve as a sound basis for long-term organizational membership.

The Catalytic Effect of the Civil-Rights Movement: The demands of civil-rights organizations for the immediate implementation of the American democratic creed inspired many other groups in the population who also believed they were victims of discrimination to make similar appeals, thus bringing many formerly quiescent elements of the population into closer contact with the nation's political leaders. The National Organization for Women has been described as the "NAACP of the women's movement" (Carden, 1974), and the Mexican-American Legal Defense and Education Fund (MALDEF), one of the most active of the new Hispanic groups, was incorporated by a former staff member of the NAACP (Broder, 1980). Hundreds of other groups were formed representing Hispanics, women, the handicapped, homosexuals, and other disadvantaged elements of the society in attempts to make the same kind of gains for their constituents that they believed blacks were achieving through the civil-rights movement. They used class-action lawsuits, acts of civil disobedience, initiatives and referenda, as well as conventional electoral politics, the same mixture of tactics pioneered by civil-rights organizations.

Once this process of political mobilization of the disadvantaged was well underway, other kinds of social movements began to arise. At the beginning these came mainly from the educated middle class, and they were dedicated to promoting the rights of consumers against the power of large business firms, placing restraints on the ability of businesses and individuals to exploit the environment, or granting the government extensive powers to ensure higher standards of industrial health and safety. Many of the groups in fields such as civil rights or environmental protection had been in existence for decades, and there had been a steady buildup throughout this century in broad public support for the values underlying these movements. The political atmosphere of the 1960s, however, provided the catalyst needed to create organizations dedicated to advancing these values.

The Political Consequences of Increased Mobilization: The elaborate networks of associations and advocacy groups that grew up during the 1960s provided hundreds of new channels through which public preferences and opinions could be both molded and transmitted to the political leadership. The degree to which they transformed the political system was graphically illustrated by the striking differences in the reactions of the American public to the wars in Korea and Vietnam. When public-opinion polls measuring support for the war in Korea in the 1950s are compared with the results of similar polls measuring support for the war in Vietnam more than a decade later, the patterns are remarkably similar. As casualties mounted and frustration grew over the limited goals of American forces in both conflicts, the numbers of citizens expressing disapproval of the war effort began to rise at about the same rate (Mueller, 1973). Public approval of Presidents Truman and Johnson, as measured by the Gallup Poll, dropped rapidly as each war dragged on (*The Gallup*

Opinion Index, Report No. 182, October-November 1980). Voters in both the national elections of 1952 and 1968 shifted toward those candidates who promised to end the fighting, but in the 1960s the more highly mobilized public, accustomed to unconventional forms of political expression, erupted in an angry series of demonstrations. Members of Congress immediately began to receive questioning letters from their constituents, heard outspokenly negative testimony in congressional hearings, and were visited by delegations of concerned citizens. Political leaders found that they were no longer as well insulated from the shifting tides of public opinion as they had been only a little more than ten years before.

The Conservative Counter-Mobilization: Most of the groups formed in the 1950s and 1960s were dedicated to liberal causes, but they were matched almost immediately by conservative countermovements, which grew even stronger in the 1970s. Planned Parenthood was soon confronted by the National Right to Life Committee; The Fellowship of Reconciliation encountered The Committee on the Present Danger; the National Council of Churches was matched by the Moral Majority. These new conservative groups, often employing organizing techniques introduced by the liberals, such as computer-assisted direct-mail solicitation for funds, began campaigns of opposition to most of the central policies of the Kennedy-Johnson years. The New Christian Right, a complex of voluntary associations and not-for-profit corporations centered around the Moral Majority, was similar in some ways to the civil-rights movement. It grew up around an established network of fundamentalist churches, TV evangelists, and bible colleges, each with its own sources of income and strong community ties. These established institutions provided the administrative and financial foundations upon which a national movement could be built (Liebman and Wuthnow, 1983).

Several new policy initiatives were launched by this rapidly growing network, and some, such as the tax limitation movement, began to have a major impact on the course of political debate in the country. These conservative movements, like the liberal ones .nat preceded them, drew many elements of the population—housewives concerned over abortion, formerly apolitical business executives and Protestant evangelicals—into active participation in political life for the first time. With the help of sympathetic business firms and foundations, an imposing network was created consisting of think tanks, public-interest law firms, and political magazines dedicated to conservative causes. This conservative movement, rising in opposition to the liberal movements that preceded it, was an extension of the process of political mobilization begun with the Montgomery bus boycott in 1955. The civil-rights movement had a profound impact on the American political system that has reverberated throughout the society for decades afterward, steadily expanding the boundaries of the active political community.

INSTITUTIONAL PATRONAGE AND POLITICAL MOBILIZATION

The history of political mobilization in America clearly demonstrates that mobilizing efforts often come from the top down, rather than the bottom up (Cameron, 1974). Many groups are begun at the instigation of the leaders of large corporations or government agencies, who often even recruit the entrepreneurs and sponsor their efforts in order to achieve policy goals that are meant to enhance their institutions' well-being. Political participation should not be conceived only as the spontaneous result of the psychological and social characteristics of individuals but also as the result of the incentives, constraints, and opportunities created by the society's legal system and the intervention in political life of its largest economic, social, and governmental institutions.

One of the most important reasons for the rapid increase in the total number of groups and the increasing prominence of citizen groups during the 1960s and 1970s was the emergence of many new patrons of political action willing to support efforts at social reform. Numerous private foundations were just being founded, for example, when the civil-rights movement began, and their staffs saw in this and subsequent movements a significant opportunity for their institutions to play an important role in public affairs (Marris and Rein, 1973). These new patrons, along with wealthy individuals, churches, trade unions, government agencies, and business firms, made an effort to direct into useful channels the frustration being expressed by participants in the political insurgencies of the time. They began to support experiments in social activism and political mobilization that would have been impossible to finance even a few years earlier. Once this process of mobilization began, it had a contagious effect upon political activists representing other disadvantaged groups, leading to the creation of more organizations making appeals to additional patrons, whose support added further to the process of mobilization.

The patrons who helped to create these new interest groups did not confine their advocacy to the support of voluntary associations. The same institutions that patronized interest groups also greatly increased their purchases of the services of lawyer-lobbyists, public-relations specialists, and other political guns-for-hire that are available in both the national and state capitals. Several large corporations and trade unions launched major advertising campaigns designed to combat what they believed to be prejudices against them among those in the mass media who write and interpret the news. Many new political magazines and newsletters, study centers, and think tanks were created, representing both liberal and conservative views, all financed mainly by wealthy individuals, private foundations, and business firms. The same institutions, in other words, that subsidize the formation and maintenance of membership associations have contributed as well to the recent flowering of many other types of nonmembership political organizations. These groups must also be included in any comprehensive inventory of the devices through which interests are formulated and communicated to the government.

Institutional patrons try to advance their interests through many different channels, and in recent years some institutions have supplemented these efforts by entering directly into the political arena to represent themselves. Large cities not only join associations like the National League of Cities or the U.S. Conference of Mayors, but they also send members of their own staffs to Washington to lobby for their interests. Agencies in the federal government not only play important roles in coordinating lobbying campaigns but also use their own personnel to contact legislators or their staffs. Most of the larger corporations mount large lobbying operations with extensive staffs operating out of their own offices of public affairs, and sometimes they even conduct grass-roots lobbying campaigns—something unheard of even a few years ago—in which their employees, suppliers, and customers are encouraged to contact legislators to urge the passage of important legislation. Record amounts of mail have been received in recent lobbying campaigns run by the banking industry, AT&T, and Chrysler, rivaling any grass-roots campaign ever mounted by organized labor or any citizen interest group. With the new authority granted private corporations by the courts to spend treasury funds to advance public-policy positions deemed to be in the interest of the firms, and to operate political action committees, business firms themselves are becoming important devices, in some ways like parties and interest groups, that serve as direct links between individual citizens and their government.[5]

Even social movements—the most spontaneous form of collective political activity—cannot be fully understood unless one accounts for the role of private and public institutions in stimulating their emergence, affecting their choice of tactics, and determining their success. Most explanations offered by political scientists depict social movements mainly as upwellings from below and ignore the significance of the broader political environment in determining their behavior. Samuel Huntington's elaborate cyclical theory of what he refers to as outbursts of "creedal passion" in American politics, for example, conceives of these movements as a kind of fever that breaks out within the population from time to time, often instigated by marginal figures who are venting their frustrations through anomic, disruptive acts of political deviance (Huntington, 1981). Such theories leave the distinct impression that during periods when no organized protest movements exist, and there are no signs of outright repression by governmental authorities, one may conclude that the country is united, support exists for the social and economic order, and the public is satisfied with its leadership.

The rise and fall of political insurgencies and their ultimate success in obtaining their goals, however, depends not so much on the character, attitudes, or motives of those who lead or participate in them; rather, it is a function of the amount of assistance they obtain from sympathetic third parties and the reaction of authorities to their challenges. Jenkins and Perrow, in their study of efforts to organize farm workers, found that movements during World War II and those in the 1960s led by César Chavez were remarkably similar in every detail, yet the earlier movement made little progress and attracted few followers, while Chavez was ultimately successful. The differences in result did not stem from greater determination among the protest leaders, more distress among workers, more money, better organization, or different tactics. The crucial differences seem to have been, first, the mounting of an effective boycott of nonunion lettuce and grapes by a huge, national, liberal constituency mobilized during the 1960s through the efforts of many groups working on many diverse issues; and second, divisiveness in the 1960s among the authorities who dealt with the challenge from the farm workers about how to respond (Jenkins and Perrow, 1977).

We must conclude that political insurgencies are not exclusively the result of social changes that create distress, eventually leading individuals to engage in protest. Farm workers had been distressed for years and, if anything, were better off in the 1960s than they had been in the 1940s. The same could be said of the southern blacks or the Appalachian whites who also mounted protests in the 1960s. Distress and anger over perceived injustice is a persistent fact of life among disadvantaged elements of any society and is only one of a number of factors that must exist before a social movement begins. A comprehensive explanation of unconventional political movements must reach beyond the motives and inclinations of individuals who lead or join the movement to include a description of changes in the larger political environment and the intervention of sympathetic patrons who provide fresh resources and crucial assistance for entrepreneurial leaders at critical times. Movements that receive aid from outside sources and are able to achieve a few initial breakthroughs begin to attract followers because the presence of potent allies provides enough hope for success to prompt their sympathizers to risk engaging in potentially dangerous political actions (Gamson, 1975; Gaventa, 1980; McAdam, 1982; McCarthy and Zald, 1979; and Oberschall, 1973).

The vast increase in the level of political mobilization in the American system during the past thirty years resulted from fundamental social changes, such as the growth of a large new educated middle class, the emergence of many new institutions prepared to subsidize political organizations, and, above all, from the steady expansion of the power and responsibility of the federal government. Elaborate networks of policy professionals have grown up around policy areas like agriculture, housing, or national security, or around constituencies like the handicapped, or Hispanic-Americans. These policy networks or communities bring together public officials and policy specialists from the Congress, bureaucracy, the Presidency, university research centers, private consulting firms, think tanks, interest groups, law firms, and state and local governments (Heclo, 1978; Walker, 1981). Some groups within these communities specialize in collecting data, while others conduct mid-career training for professionals in the field; others engage in campaigns of public education, or serve as consultants for public bureaucracies, leaving a few groups to take the lead in the more conventional tasks of legislative lobbying. As the representational system in each policy area matures, policy entrepreneurs and their patrons are able to devise many different formulas for organizational maintenance, creating highly specialized membership and nonmembership groups that are only viable because they fill a niche in a larger policy community (Hannan and Freeman, 1978; Knoke and Laumann, 1982; and Ross, 1970).

Increases in the number of specialized membership and nonmembership organizations involved in policy formulation and advocacy have led to a dramatic increase in the range of interests being represented and the number of issues being debated in Washington. In the past, most citizen groups that emerged from social movements simply faded away once the intense enthusiasm of their followers began to cool, or when a string of policy defeats caused marginal supporters to lose interest. In the 1980s, however, many of the citizen groups born during the 1960s and 1970s are still in business, with help from their patrons, even though public interest in their causes has declined. These groups promote concern for their issues and stand ready to exercise leadership whenever there is a new burst of public enthusiasm. As a result of the expansion of the interest-group system, the processes of passing legislation and evaluating public policies have become much more complicated, and policy formulation has become much more conflictual than ever before (Gais, Peterson, and Walker, 1984).

POLITICAL PARTIES IN AMERICAN DEMOCRACY

Political parties have not been collapsing under the impact of this great upsurge of political mobilization—rather, they have been transforming themselves. Realizing that it is unlikely that parties will ever receive large public subsidies, or that restrictive legislation will be passed that would restore the virtual monopoly on representation enjoyed by political parties in the late nineteenth century, both the Republicans and Democrats launched efforts during the past decade to rebuild their organizations by employing many of the same techniques being used by many successful interest groups.

Rather than trying to re-create the precinct organizations of a century ago, parties have tried to recruit millions of people willing to make small contributions. This money is being used to develop large sophisticated staffs that are seeking to coordinate national election campaigns, provide consultation for local and state parties, and provide advice for PACs and other sympathetic contributors who want to back promising new candidates. This new approach to organizational viability must be founded on ideological appeals, or at least upon more consistent approaches to public policy than American parties have used in the past. The continued loyalty of small contributors, who are receiving mainly moral or ideological reinforcement in exchange for their support, can be assured in no other way. Parties, by adopting this approach, are beginning to compete with the ideologically based citizen interest groups for the loyalty of the affluent new middle class, the electorate's active core.

No matter how successful the parties are in adapting to the demands of campaigning in the age of mass communications and programmatic politics, however, it is hard to imagine a set of issues or ideological appeals that could divide the highly mobilized, contemporary electorate neatly into only two political camps. The social issues of abortion and public support for religious institutions cut across the constituency that supports national health insurance, and environmental issues divide this group in yet another way. None of these issues is likely to go away and all are promoted by well-financed policy communities made up of dozens of interest groups and other political organizations. These policy communities make the American system more adaptive and responsive by allowing citizens loyal to different political parties an opportunity to voice passionately felt concerns. They supplement, rather than weaken, the political parties by ensuring that debate about issues not consistent with society's basic partisan divisions takes place in democratic legislative forums, rather than in the streets.

Furthermore, if party politics does center more around fundamental public-policy questions, and if national elections increasingly appear to pose significant choices between different ideological paths, there is good reason to expect an *increase* in interest-group activity, not a reduction, in response to the reinvigoration of political parties. Political parties might find a new role as coordinators of large coalitions of interest groups, PACs, and other political organizations, but if institutional patrons are left free to sponsor political action, and the futures of many government programs enacted during the recent expansion of the welfare state are put in jeopardy at each election, those that support these programs will respond vigorously, using all the resources at their command.

COPING WITH THE DEMOCRATIC DILEMMA

Walter Lippmann in *Drift and Mastery*, written in 1914, complained about the inability of the sprawling American political system to establish coherent goals or carry out comprehensive plans.

Complaints about political fragmentation are not new, but it is important to see that this is only one side of a fundamental governmental problem that no democracy can entirely escape. Coordination is especially difficult in the American system because government in a democracy amounts to much more than simply making optimal decisions about the allocation of scarce resources. Besides deciding who gets what, when, and how, democratic leaders must also strive to maintain the public's commitment to the very procedures through which decisions are made. If sacrifices are called for, and it is pain rather than pleasure that is being allocated, democratic leaders must somehow persuade those who will be damaged by their decisions that these new policies are in harmony with the broad public interest.

It obviously would be simpler to impose sacrifices on those who have no effective representatives in the councils of government than upon those who are mobilized for political action and can retaliate at the polls against legislators who fail to support them. Policymaking has become more hazardous for elected officials in recent years as advocates have appeared in ever-increasing numbers speaking for the interests of blacks, the handicapped, consumers, environmentalists, and many other interests seldom heard from in the past. Those who have encouraged this process of mobilization argue that the American political system will suffer a permanent loss of legitimacy unless it responds positively to many newly mobilized elements of the population whose needs have been ignored in the past. They believe that these rising political forces should receive a greater share of society's benefits and privileges, but they are also trying to bring these groups out of the streets and into the system's established democratic forums, where policy decisions are made peacefully through discussion and compromise. Throughout the country's history America has been experiencing a steady trend toward increasing democratization, and the reformers believe that attempts to thwart this trend would place popular institutions of government in jeopardy. They stress the importance of fairness and equality of political rights, and they see themselves as the ultimate guardians of the legitimacy of the democratic process.

Critics of the mobilization process believe that it has increased the dangerous tendency of the American system to drift aimlessly from one policy to another, often producing decisions that flatly contradict each other. They warn that all efforts to formulate coherent goals or exercise national leadership may be frustrated by the political deadlock that will result from our chaotic system, and ultimately the government will be prevented from dealing successfully with the many serious social and economic problems that face the country. Should the government be consistently unsuccessful in meeting domestic and international challenges, public confidence and trust in democratic institutions eventually will collapse. Democratic governments, no matter how responsive they strive to be, cannot maintain the trust and allegiance of their citizens unless they can deliver the goods. Both sides in this debate fear an ultimate breakdown in public confidence, but each sees the danger arising from different sources—one side is concerned about inequitable access to policy-making forums, unjustified privileges, and arbitrary discrimination against vulnerable groups, while the other warns of the excessive fragmentation of authority leading to paralyzing governmental incompetence.

This fundamental difference in the evaluation of recent developments in the American political system illustrates a fundamental dilemma that faces all democratic systems of government. The principal force that diffuses authority and fragments power in a democracy—active citizen participation—is also the fundamental justification for authority and leadership. Popular sovereignty provides the system its reason for being, but at the same time it can prevent any collective goals from being reached. Participation can lead to a renewed sense of community involvement, or it may deteriorate into a selfish, aimless scramble for private gain. Throughout the country's history, critics of American political institutions have shifted back and forth in their concern about the system, reflecting their estimate of which of these closely linked problems of democratic involvement and governability is more prevalent at the time.

It is tempting to believe that authority and leadership can be restored in the American system simply by re-creating a simpler political era that prevailed before the political upheavals of the 1960s, before so many narrow special-interest groups emerged, cluttering the scene with their selfish demands. Their numbers might be checked by creating legal obstacles that would make it difficult to bring them into being, or by restricting their access to the funds needed to finance their activities. Subtle forms of political suppression of this kind might succeed in reducing the competition felt by the President or other national leaders for the attention and loyalty of the public, but they could have dangerous consequences because they restrict opportunities for participation and breed alienation, thus ignoring the other side of the democratic dilemma.

We take for granted the fact that in America during the 1980s there are few organized, violent clashes between racial or sectarian groups of the kind that are prevalent in many other countries with culturally diverse populations. Given the extreme disparities of wealth and status in the United States, it is remarkable that the level of revolutionary terrorism is as low as it is. Detroit, Philadelphia, or Boston has much of the explosive potential of Belfast or Beirut, and although there are extremely high levels of interpersonal violence in American cities, and millions of private citizens own firearms, it is a remarkable political achievement that there are only rare instances of persistent internal war. There are many reasons for America's political stability, most of which have little or nothing to do with its system of government, but surely part of the explanation must be found in its permeable political institutions, made all the more accommodating by many organizational developments of the past two decades.

The country has passed through a serious crisis of participation during the last thirty years that pressed our democratic traditions to their limits. A form of access to government has been provided for many social groups that in the past had either been ignored, or, as with blacks, forcibly excluded from politics. There seems little prospect that groups emerging from the growing specialization of our occupational structure will soon disappear—especially those that have emerged as a direct result of the growth of government. The many newly founded citizen groups also have shown remarkable resiliency. Political parties must accommodate to this new, highly engaged, conflictual political environment and accept the elaborate bargaining and the intrusive role of the mass media that it involves. America continues its risky experiment with democracy in the modern world. We have moved to a higher plateau of political participation from which there is no turning back.

NOTES

1. For a review of the debate over parties, see Epstein (1983).

2. The best recent statements are Pomper (1980); Kirkpatrick (1978); and Ladd (1977).

3. The following section is based upon my interpretation of Chambers and Burnham (1972) and several of the essays in Kleppner (1981).

4. For recent developments, see Crotty and Jacobson (1980); Harmel and Janda (1982); and Gibson et al. (1983).

5. The most significant recent expansion of the discretion of the manag-

ers to involve their firms directly in politics is in the Supreme Court decision: *First National Bank of Boston* v. *Bellotti*, 435 US 765 (1978).

REFERENCES

APSA (1950). "Toward a More Responsible Two Party System: A Report of the Committee on Political Parties," *American Political Science Review* 44 (September), Supplement.

Arnold, Peri E. (1982). "Herbert Hoover and the Positive State," in J. David Greenstone, ed., *Public Values and Private Power in American Politics* (Chicago: University of Chicago Press), 109–138.

Berry, Jeffrey M. (1977). *Lobbying for the People* (Princeton: Princeton University Press).

Broder, David S. (1980). *Changing of the Guard: Power and Leadership in America* (New York: Simon and Schuster).

Burns, James McGregor (1963). *The Deadlock of Democracy* (Englewood Cliffs: Prentice-Hall).

Cameron, David (1974). "Towards a Theory of Political Mobilization," *Journal of Politics* 36, 138–171.

Carden, Maren Lockwood (1974). *The New Feminist Movement* (New York: Russell Sage).

Chambers, William Nisbet, and Walter Dean Burnham, eds. (1972). *The American Party Systems: Stages of Development* (New York: Praeger).

Crotty, William J., and Gary C. Jacobson (1980). *American Parties in Decline* (Boston: Little, Brown).

Epstein, Leon D. (1983). "The Scholarly Commitment to Parties," in Ada Finifter, ed., *Political Science: The State of the Discipline* (Washington, D.C.: The American Political Science Association), 127–154.

Freeman, Jo (1973). "Origins of the Women's Liberation Movement," in John Huber, ed., *Changing Women in a Changing Society* (Chicago: University of Chicago Press).

Fritschler, A. L. (1983). *Smoking and Politics* (Englewood Cliffs: Prentice-Hall), 3d edition.

Gable, R. W. (1953). "N.A.M.: Influential Lobby or Kiss of Death?" *Journal of Politics* 15, 254–273.

Gais, Thomas L., Mark A. Peterson, and Jack L. Walker (1984). "Interest Groups, Iron Triangles, and Representative Institutions in American National Government," *British Journal of Political Science* 14 (April), 161–185.

Gamson, William (1975). *The Strategy of Social Protest* (Homewood, IL: Dorsey).

Garson, G. David (1978). *Group Theories of Politics* (Beverly Hills: Sage).

Gaventa, John (1980). *Power and Powerlessness: Quiescence and Rebellion in an Appalachian Valley* (Urbana: University of Illinois Press).

Gelb, Joyce, and Marian Lief Palley (1982). "Feminist Mobilization," in

Women and Public Policies (Princeton: Princeton University Press), 14–36.

Gibson, James L., Cornelius P. Cotter, John F. Bibby, and Robert J. Huckshorn (1983). "Assessing Party Organizational Strength," *American Journal of Political Science* 27 (May), 193–222.

Hannan, Michael T., and John Freeman (1978). "The Population Ecology of Organizations," in *American Journal of Sociology* 82, 924–964.

Harmel, Robert, and Kenneth Janda (1982). *Parties and Their Environments: Limits to Reform?* (New York: Longman).

Hays, Samuel (1957). *The Response to Industrialism: 1885–1914* (Chicago: University of Chicago Press).

Hays, Samuel (1969). *Conservation and the Gospel of Efficiency: The Progressive Conservation Movement: 1890–1920* (New York: Atheneum).

Hays, Samuel (1981). "Politics and Society: Beyond the Political Party," in Paul Klepner, ed., *The Evolution of American Electoral Systems* (Boston: Greenwood Press), 243–267.

Heclo, Hugh (1978). "Issue Networks and the Executive Establishment," in Anthony King, ed., *The New American Political System* (Washington, D.C.: The American Enterprise Institute), 87–124.

Huntingdon, Samuel (1973). "The Democratic Distemper," *Public Interest* 14 (Fall), 9–38.

Huntingdon, Samuel (1981). *American Politics: The Promise of Disharmony* (Cambridge: Belknap, Harvard University Press).

Jenkins, J. C., and Charles Perrow (1977). "Insurgency of the Powerless: Farm Workers Movements: 1946–1972," *American Sociological Review* 42, 248–268.

Johnson, Terrence J. (1972). *Professions and Power* (London: Macmillan).

King, Anthony (1975). "Overload: Problems of Governing in the 1970s," in *Political Studies* 23 (June–September), 162–174.

Kirkpatrick, Jeane J. (1978). *Dismantling the Parties: Reflections on Party Reform and Party Decomposition* (Washington, D.C.: American Enterprise Institute).

Kleppner, Paul, ed. (1981). *The Evolution of American Electoral Systems* (Boston: Greenwood Press).

Knoke, David, and Edward Laumann (1982). "The Social Organization of National Policy Domains," in Peter V. Marsden and Nan Lin, eds., *Social Structure and Network Analysis* (Beverly Hills: Sage), 255–270.

Ladd, C. Everett, Jr. (1977). " 'Reform' is Wrecking the U.S. Party System," *Fortune* (November), 177–188.

Lippmann, Walter (1914). *Drift and Mastery* (New York: Mitchell Kennerley).

Marris, Peter, and Martin Rein (1973), *Dilemmas of Social Reform* (Chicago: Aldine), 2d edition.

McAdam, Doug (1982). *Political Process and the Development of Black Insurgency: 1930–1970* (Chicago: University of Chicago Press).

McConnell, Grant (1966). *Private Power and American Democracy* (New York: Alfred A. Knopf).

McDonald, Terrance J., and Sally K. Ward, eds. (1984). *The Politics of Urban Fiscal Policy* (Beverly Hills: Sage).

McQuaid, Kim (1982). *Big Business and Presidential Power* (New York: William Morrow).

Miles, Robert H. (1982). *Coffin Nails and Corporate Strategies* (Englewood Cliffs: Prentice-Hall).

Mosher, Frederick C. (1968). *Democracy and the Public Service* (New York: Oxford University Press).

Mueller, John E. (1973). *War, Presidents and Public Opinion* (New York: John Wiley).

Oberschall, A. (1973). *Social Conflict and Social Movements* (Englewood Cliffs: Prentice-Hall).

O'Rourke, Timothy G. (1980). *The Impact of Reapportionment* (New Brunswick, NJ: Transaction Books).

Pfeffer, J., and G. R. Salancik (1978). *The External Control of Organizations* (New York: Harper and Row).

Pomper, Gerald M., ed. (1980). *Party Renewal in America* (New York: Praeger).

Pratt, Henry J. (1976). *The Gray Lobby* (Chicago: University of Chicago Press).

Rose, Richard, and Guy Peters (1978). *Can Government Go Bankrupt?* (New York: Basic Books).

Ross, Robert L. (1970). "Relations Among National Interest Groups," *The Journal of Politics* 32, 96–114.

Schattschneider, E. E. (1960). *The Semi-Sovereign People* (New York: Holt, Rinehart and Winston).

Schmitter, Philippe C., and Donald Brand (1982). "Organizing Capitalists in the United States: The Advantages and Disadvantages of Exceptionalism" (University of Chicago: mimeo.).

Silk, Leonard, and Mark Silk (1980). *The American Establishment* (New York: Basic Books), 226–267.

Skowronek, Stephen (1982). *Building a New American State* (Cambridge: Cambridge University Press).

Sorensen, Theodore C. (1984). *A Different Kind of Presidency* (New York: Harper and Row).

Walker, Jack L. (1981). "The Diffusion of Knowledge, Policy Communities and Agenda Setting: The Relationship of Knowledge and Power," in John Tropman, Milan Dluhy, and Roger Lind, eds., *New Strategic Perspectives on Social Policy* (New York: Pergamon Press).

Walker, Jack L. (1983). "The Origins and Maintenance of Interest Groups in America," *The American Political Science Review* 77 (June), 390–406.

Wilson, James Q. (1962). *The Amateur Democrat* (Chicago: University of Chicago Press).

Zald, Mayer N., and J. D. McCarthy, eds. (1979). *The Dynamics of Social Movements* (Cambridge, MA: Winthrop).

EDWARD D. BERKOWITZ

Social Welfare and the American State

TO write the social history of the twentieth century, historians will need to
bring the federal government into the picture. Consideration of an
important social-welfare program, such as Social Security, clinches
the point. "Social security has become a central feature of American
life," writes historian W. Andrew Achenbaum, who notes that Social Security payments are the single most important source of income for people over 65, accounting for $42 of every $100 they
receive. Achenbaum refers specifically to old-age and survivors' insurance, which is run entirely by the federal government, without
the help of state or local intermediaries. A huge bureaucratic entity
that reaches more than 36 million people, it also conditions the
individual daily lives of nearly all Americans, affecting how long
they plan to work and how much financial responsibility they feel
toward their parents. Without considering Social Security, recent
American social history would be incomplete.[1]

In terms of the federal government's importance, the story of the
twentieth century differs significantly from the story of earlier centuries. Writing about the eighteenth century, for example, Robert
Wiebe has stated flatly that the center of society was "the family in a
community." Each of these communities "set family units to manage
the particulars of every day life in a manner that constrained each unit

by the values all of them held in common." In the nineteenth century, these hermetically sealed localities developed into "island communities" that formed parts of America's "segmented society." As for Washington, D.C., it served as a "clearing house for a quite limited range of problems."[2] Wiebe's famous images of America in the pre-Progressive Era do not contradict those of political scientist Stephen Skowronek, who writes of a late nineteenth-century state in which courts and parties loosely held America together, or of historian Michael Katz, who describes a nineteenth-century governmental social-welfare system in which no state (never mind the federal government) "even gathered together in one source financial information and other data about its activities, let alone tried to coordinate or control its policies toward dependence."[3]

Even in the twentieth century, a large federal presence in social-welfare activities came late. A crisis developed in American society toward the end of the nineteenth century. At the heart of this crisis lay the imposition of a national economy on a "polity," to use Morton Keller's phrase, that lacked what Skowronek calls the "administrative capacity" to handle national problems. Among the manifestations of change that initiated a "search for order" in late nineteenth-century America were a disruption in labor-management relations, the growth of cities, and a depression during the 1890s that affected nearly every part of the country and produced an unprecedented misery. This crisis did not usher in an American welfare state with the federal government at its center. Private professional organizations, rather than the state itself, pointed a way toward the resolution of the predicament. Even into the 1920s, private groups, rather than federal agencies or programs, supplied the engine for what Ellis Hawley has called the "associative state."[4]

Nor did the depression jolt an American welfare state into existence, as the gap between the onset of the depression in 1930 and the passage of the Social Security Act in 1935 demonstrated. Even if President Roosevelt had wanted to do so, he lacked the administrative means to command the economy in a Keynesian manner and use federal funds for direct service programs. The New Deal, like Herbert Hoover's old deal, bargained with private groups and produced a version of the associative state. The results were such early New Deal programs as the National Industrial Recovery Act and the Agricultural Adjustment Act: government acquiescence in private self-regulation.[5]

When the New Dealers got past the old barriers of Congress and the courts and passed federal programs that would have a lasting impact on American life, federal social-welfare programs such as Social Security remained relatively small. In 1940, for example, total government spending for social welfare amounted to 9.2% of the country's gross national product. Yet in that year the nation spent more than six times as much on state workers' compensation payments as on federal Social Security. Veterans programs, products of a tradition in which only a select few received benefits, cost fifteen times as much as Social Security in 1940 and remained more costly until the mid-1950s.[6]

American federal social-welfare programs arrived late, stayed small for a long time, and then grew large quickly. A sketch of twentieth-century federal social-welfare policy illuminates America's path from island communities to a nation in which federally administered Social Security became an important feature of daily life.

This essay neglects traditional topics. It does not emphasize intellectual attitudes toward unemployment, poverty, or voluntarism or the fates of the elderly, women, or the handicapped under various policy regimes.[7] If an intellectual bias underlies these choices, it is that federal programs form important categories in and of themselves. What towns have been to the social history of the colonial period, federal programs might be to twentieth-century history: not exclusive fields of vision but important organizing constructs nonetheless.

Institutional details can overwhelm more general themes, but consideration of the administrative demands that programs make on the federal government broadens the analysis. To place a program within a reform category, such as national health insurance or civil-service reform, tells only part of the story. One might also wish to place the program within the confines of American federalism. Where do the responsibilities for administering the program lie, on the federal, state or local levels, and which level of government pays most of the bill? How does the government raise the money to fund the program? Another relevant dimension concerns the extent to which the public sector performs an activity itself. Do government officials supply social-welfare services or do they "franchise" this activity to private insurance companies or voluntary organizations such as hospitals?[8] Still another dimension centers on the branch of the federal government that takes the lead in initiating and maintaining a program.

All programs pass through three stages: passage, implementation, and modification. As programs pass through these stages, they alter their characteristics. Congress, for example, may play a large role in the passage of the program; external factors unforeseen by Congress may affect the way in which a program gets implemented; and the bureaucracy often figures prominently in a program's modification. All programs pass through these stages and possess distinctive dimensions, and all programs are subject to administrative and fiscal constraints. Historians have the unique ability to move beyond universal categories and add the clarifying dimension of time to discussions of individual programs.

THE DISTINCTIVE NATURE
OF THE PROGRESSIVE ERA

Although the programs of the Progressive Era took many different forms, one important strain of progressive reform consisted of a call on the part of newly created professional groups for the reassignment of functions previously performed by "generalists" in the old polity to "specialists" who would initiate a new polity. Progressive reform, conducted on the state and local levels, also had a national dimension. Assisted by private groups and even by the federal government, states imitated one another and passed similar laws.[9]

In this manner, the National Association of Manufacturers, a newly created occupational organization, and the American Association of Labor Legislation, a newly minted professional organization, participated in the fight for workers' compensation. Passed in many states around 1912, this new type of law represented a reassignment of the function of compensating victims of industrial actions from the courts to specialized industrial commissions. Injured workers received quicker, more certain compensation in return for accepting lower average payments. The programs did not strain the existing capacity of the state because private employers and private insurers performed most of the necessary administrative and financial work. This law, in common with many Progressive Era social-welfare laws, set minimum standards of conduct which private employers were expected to follow. It conditioned private behavior without increasing public responsibilities.[10]

The change from earlier laws becomes evident in a comparison with Civil War veterans' pensions. In 1862 Congress passed a law, traditional in form and content, that provided pensions to soldiers who were wounded or killed in battle. In the last quarter of the nineteenth century, Congress, bidding for votes, made the pensions more liberal, raising the benefit level and making the benefits easier to get. Congress also passed an inordinate number of laws granting pensions to people whose requests had been denied by the Pension Bureau. In this way, Congress became personally involved in the administration of the program and extended its boundaries. Veterans' pensions resembled expenditures for rivers and harbors: programs of direct benefit to local constituents for which individual congressmen could take personal credit and in which the wide distribution of benefits took precedence over their careful administration. With the passage of time, expenditures for veterans' pensions mounted. In 1890 veterans' pensions consumed 34% of the federal budget, and veterans' pensions became the largest single item (with the exception of debt service) in the federal budget every year between 1885 and 1897. Over time, as well, Congress loosened the relationship between a disability pension and wartime injury until, by 1906, any Civil War veteran over 62 automatically qualified for a pension. Veterans' pensions had become a large and loosely managed program.[11]

Workers' compensation, by way of contrast, represented a conscious effort to reduce political influence over disability pensions. By World War I, most states had removed the administration of the laws from the control of the courts and instead allowed nonpartisan industrial commissions to settle disputed cases. This action lessened the chance that a state legislature would consider an injured worker's plea for relief and made it more likely that benefits would be awarded for actual injuries rather than for political loyalties. In reducing political discretion, workers' compensation also made eligibility for benefits more universal. Civil War pensions applied only to the families of northerners who served in the Civil War. This category tended to exclude southerners and Eastern European immigrants. Workers' compensation contained less ethnic or regional bias. For all of these reasons, the proponents of workers' compensation viewed their laws as improvements over earlier social-welfare programs.[12]

The aspirations of progressive reformers did not exempt their laws from political realities. Since the laws were made at the state level with little or no federal government involvement, the contents of the laws differed widely from state to state, not only in the benefit levels but in the relationship between particular disabilities and the receipt of benefits. Some states based benefits on a worker's loss of earning power; other states related benefits directly to the presence of an impairment, such as the loss of an arm.[13]

Regulatory government, it became clear, did not represent a complete break with the politics of the past. The quality of administration depended on the competence of the industrial commissioners. By the mid-1930s social reformers had written critiques of workers' compensation administration that resembled Progressive Era exposés of the court system. An investigator for the Commonwealth Fund found that four of the Illinois officials who heard disputed compensation cases had little knowledge of the compensation law, close contacts with the local political machine, and a questionable command of written English.[14]

The problem of political power arose in other ways as well. As technology enabled epidemiologists to discover links between illness and occupational conditions, employers and insurance companies used their political clout to limit the benefits for industrial illnesses under the state workers' compensation laws. As workers with such conditions as asbestosis grew frustrated with the workers' compensation laws, they turned increasingly to the courts to remedy their problems. Yet, for all that the courts and the federal government eroded the jurisdiction of workers' compensation laws, they remained costly items for private employers, so much so that the governor of Maryland recently made reduction of workers' compensation costs a priority.[15]

Although workers' compensation laws represented the cutting edge of change in 1912, they soon became difficult to modify in a significant way and gradually became a force against change. When federal bureaucrats proposed the creation of a national disability law that would remedy the patchwork quality of the state compensation laws, workers' compensation administrators refused to surrender their turf and insisted on the preservation of state laws. In other words, even laws launched with great expectations soon came to exhibit defensive bureaucratic behavior. Once in place, workers' compensation laws became permanent memorials to the Progressive Era.[16]

THE NEW ERA
OF FEDERAL SOCIAL-WELFARE PROGRAMS

Workers' compensation laws had only a limited effect on the federal government. With the significant exceptions of the District of Columbia and federal workers themselves, federal responsibility for workers' compensation laws remained advisory. The Department of Labor assisted in the formation of a national organization of state workers' compensation officials, but neither the Department nor the Congress could change the contents of the state laws. A similarly indirect relationship between the federal government and the states applied to other Progressive Era laws, such as minimum wages for women, maximum labor laws, and child-labor laws.[17]

Beginning in the 1920s, the federal government became more directly involved in the provision of social-welfare services with the passage of federal laws in the areas of health, education, and welfare. In the field of health, Congress passed the Sheppard-Towner Act in 1921, hoping through the provision of prenatal and child health centers to reduce infant and maternal mortality rates. In the field of education, Congress began federal support for vocational education with the passage of the Smith-Hughes Act in 1917, and in welfare Congress created a federal vocational rehabilitation program in 1920. This last program resembled vocational education. It allowed handicapped individuals to receive counseling and training that enabled them to enter the labor force and hold a job.[18]

Certain characteristics united these programs. All of them represented additions to the nation's social-welfare system that expanded upon but did not conflict with the basic responsibilities of the state and local governments. The patchwork structure of local public and private programs that provided aid to the poor remained intact; no one suggested that the federal government interfere with local school systems. To these established systems, special programs for national purposes, such as reducing the infant mortality rate and increasing the supply of trained manpower, were now added. Each of the programs operated through a grant-in-aid structure that enabled the state and federal governments to share the costs of the program and allowed the states to operate the programs. The federal supervisory offices remained small; nearly all of the program employees worked for state or local governments. In 1924, for example, the entire Washington, D.C., office of the infant and maternal health program consisted of four physicians, a nurse, an accountant, a secretary, and a stenographer.[19]

For all of the limitations, the new programs represented significant breaks from previous federal programs. In the nineteenth century, the federal government dispensed pensions to its wards, such as veterans or Indians, and made individual grants to local institutions. Grants of land, the major asset the federal government had at its disposal, played a large role in nineteenth-century social-welfare activities. In 1819, for example, the Connecticut Asylum for the Deaf and Dumb received a federal grant of 23,000 acres of land and promptly sold it for some $300,000.[20] Beginning in 1889, the Red Lake Band of the Chippewa Indians of Minnesota received annuities, education, and health services from a fund created by the sale of lands that had previously been reserved for this tribe.[21] In the new twentieth-century programs, the government did not pay annuities to its wards or deal in the provision of lands. Instead, the government dispersed cash to the states. Further, federal legislators were responding to a new constituency, professional social-welfare providers. All of the laws owed their origins to the organized activities of groups that had come into existence in the Progressive Era. Social-welfare workers, such as Florence Kelley and Lillian Wald, helped to create the federal Children's Bureau in 1905, which in turn lobbied for passage of the Sheppard-Towner Act.[22] In a similar manner, workers' compensation administrators were important proponents of the vocational rehabilitation law.[23] Finally, the laws, unlike the earlier laws, did not represent grants to specific localities so much as federal aid to professional administrators across the nation.

Although the laws enabled the federal government to cross important thresholds, they remained products of their times, with all the implied restrictions on federal activity. The federal government paid cash to the states, but the clients of the various programs received services in kind, usually in the form of advice or training. Funding for the programs was limited. In the case of vocational rehabilitation, the states could not spend all of the federal money available to them in the 1920s because of an inability to appropriate matching funds. Congress neglected to appropriate any federal funds for vocational rehabilitation in the first half of 1925, and in 1929 Congress refused to renew the Infant and Maternal Health Program. None of the programs could be described as an entitlement. Instead, each of the programs exercised great selectivity in the clients who received its services, with the result that none of the three programs served a high percentage of the people eligible for its services.[24]

The programs developed distinctive rationales for their continued existence based not on humanitarian so much as on efficiency grounds. This process went furthest in the vocational rehabilitation program, which came to be viewed as an antidote to welfare programs rather than as a welfare program itself. According to the official ideology that developed to justify its existence, it kept handicapped people off welfare and therefore served as a good investment of government funds. "Curing the disability is far and away the more economic procedure," federal vocational rehabilitation officials wrote in the 1920s (using revealing medical rhetoric), "and in this case sound economics is clearly sound public policy."[25] Such claims encouraged the officials to undertake formal cost-benefit demonstrations. In 1926 federal officials noted that it was only natural to "raise the question whether the investment of federal and state funds in the civilian rehabilitation program brings adequate return."[26] A year later the federal bureaucrats produced a study that demonstrated "scientifically and beyond question that the vocational rehabilitation program in the States is permanently economically sound."[27] More than twenty-seven years later, the federal officials made the same claims, arguing that "vocational rehabilitation is an investment in human welfare that is wholly self-liquidating."[28] By that time, accountants had produced a calculation based on the federal income tax. Vocational rehabilitation, described as "pyramiding profits in . . . an investment in human welfare," brought returns of ten dollars in federal income taxes alone for each federal dollar expended.[29] Here was a federal welfare program that owed its success to the fact that it reduced welfare expenditures, an important precedent for future efforts at welfare reform.

Indeed, vocational rehabilitation illustrated how a program could change from its enactment, to its implementation, to its modification. Passed with grand rhetorical flourishes about rehabilitating injured workers, the program and its state counselors soon learned that they had neither the funds nor the technological means to transform a significant percentage of the handicapped into labor-force participants. The program remained small and selective through the 1920s, managing only to place 5,852 people in jobs in its best year. By the estimates of program officials, more than 70,000 cases arose each year that might benefit from rehabilitation. At the operational level, the uses to which federal funds could be put were circumscribed, limited for the most part to counseling, training, and the purchase of artificial limbs. Faced with many constraints and eager to win funds and expand the program, federal officials, whose role was far from clear in a program where all actions occurred at the state level, seized on the notion of cost-benefit analysis. Performing the data gathering and statistical operations for cost-benefit analyses gave the federal officials definite responsibilities and provided a demonstration of the program's worth that differentiated it from other programs and increased its attractiveness to congressional sponsors.[30]

While federal officials spent their time gathering data, state rehabilitation officials used the principles of scientific casework to advise their handicapped clients on how best to adjust to their disabilities. Implemented in the 1920s, the program naturally turned to methods of operation, such as scientific casework and industrial psychology, that were accepted professional practices of the time. Through the 1950s and 1960s, the program continued to benefit from its professional image. One early commentator argued, for example, that vocational rehabilitation counselors could not "work in a dirty noisy office where the men stand at a desk with a line of applicants trailing off behind them." The counselors needed an "attractive office very much like the office of the better type of physician." "Effective placement," noted federal officials, "is not an amateur job." To make sure that professionalism held sway in the program, the federal government eventually funded rehabilitation training programs for state rehabilitation counselors. By 1965 forty universities were offering graduate degrees in rehabilitation counseling; between 1958 and 1968, 1,413 articles on the function of the rehabilitation counselors appeared in newly established rehabilitation journals.[31]

As these figures demonstrated, practices invented in the program's implementation brought success and shielded the program from significant modification. When more federal money became available in the late 1940s through the 1960s, the program grew, but it did not change. The clientele expanded to include the socially disadvantaged, and counselors were authorized to provide more services at federal expense, yet the reliance on scientific casework remained unaltered from the 1920s. Between 1960 and 1973, the program's federal expenditures rose from 80 million to 730 million in current dollars. By the 1970s, the program was serving one million people a year.[32]

The growth of vocational rehabilitation exemplified a process that political scientists call incremental expansion, a process that in this particular case proceeded without the President's involvement. Even President Eisenhower, who chose to highlight vocational rehabilitation, depended heavily on analyses prepared by bureaucrats in the executive agencies, and, by the time Kennedy arrived, the White House simply processed requests for White House ceremonies and submitted bills prepared by federal vocational rehabilitation administrators to Congress. At most, the presidents gave the program tacit approval. Martha Derthick has persuasively argued that vocational rehabilitation owed this tacit approval to an ambiguity that program administrators exploited. To liberals, vocational rehabilitation represented an important social service that was not incompatible with their efforts to expand social-welfare services; to conservatives, vocational rehabilitation deserved support because it was designed to lessen the nation's dependence on other social-welfare services. Supporters and detractors of the welfare state collaborated to expand vocational rehabilitation.[33]

The very success of vocational rehabilitation blocked other approaches toward social welfare. Locked into a 1920s mode of operation, the program implicitly rejected societal solutions to the problems of disability, such as modifying the physical environment so as to permit accessibility on the part of the physically handicapped. Psychological adjustment, in the manner of scientific casework, clashed with the idea of civil rights. As modern commentators have expressed this idea, activists in the handicapped community and program administrators disagreed on where the problem lay. Was it in the handicapped individual or society itself? In the 1970s, handicapped activists, who strongly believed that civil rights and not psychological counseling represented the best approach, attempted to force modifications in the vocational rehabilitation program. They hoped to make the program depend less on discretionary acts by professional counselors and become more a source of entitlements which all handicapped citizens could receive (a college education, a van, a motorized wheelchair might qualify). Congress somewhat reluctantly placed such features as a civil-rights statute for the handicapped and a special program of legal aid for program clients into the basic legislation. Few people, including the handicapped activists themselves, understood the significance of the first action, and the second was accomplished over the objections of professional groups representing vocational rehabilitation counselors. Despite these congressional mandates, the program clung to its traditions. The effects of the program's implementation in the 1920s continued to linger.[34]

SOCIAL SECURITY: DELAYED IMPLEMENTATION AND SUBSTANTIAL MODIFICATION

Vocational rehabilitation, like the other products of the 1920s, was largely irrelevant to the social-welfare efforts of the 1930s. New Deal officials conducted an agonized search for a social-welfare policy, struggling first with industrial self-regulation, only to find it impractical and, because it delegated so much power to the executive branch, unconstitutional as well. The New Dealers, in other words, found old barriers to the expansion of the federal government. In addition to the courts, these barriers included the primacy of state and local governments in social-welfare policy and the limited administrative capacity of the federal government itself.[35]

The Social Security Act of 1935 reflected those constraints. The Act expanded the power of the federal government, but only in a limited sense. It introduced federal funds into state programs and provided permanent legislative authorization for the programs of the 1920s, such as vocational rehabilitation. In the process, however, the Act encouraged the states to start programs, such as unemployment compensation, that existed in only a few states, and allowed states to make their welfare benefits more liberal, particularly for the elderly. In other words, the authors of the Social Security Act borrowed ideas from existing policy networks, such as state workers' compensation administrators and social workers associated with the Children's Bureau, in order to expand and to strengthen local social-welfare programs. This did not imply an expansion of the federal government's administrative capacity.[36]

Its importance can be minimized, its contents linked to the limited state of the times, yet the Social Security Act represented a major point of discontinuity in American social welfare. The federal programs of the 1920s affected basic welfare programs only at their margins; the programs authorized by the Social Security Act involved the federal government in the most basic aspects of local social-welfare programs, such as the provision of aid to dependent children. The federal involvement was indirect, limited to channeling money to local authorities, but it still gave the federal government some influence over local public welfare. Activities subsidized by the Social Security Act enjoyed significant advantages over activities that the states paid for themselves, as the subsequent histories of state mental-health hospitals and federal-state welfare programs demonstrated. Implicit choices of 1935 made a difference to the long-run development of the American welfare state.

The Social Security Act also provided for old-age insurance, which turned out to be the most important program of all. Unlike the other programs, this one left everything to the federal government, with no local intermediaries except for the employers whose payrolls would be taxed to pay for the new program. The idea was to gather money from a payroll tax of 2%, with the burden divided equally between employee and employer, on the first $3,000 of each employee's wages. By collecting money in this way for five years, the federal government hoped to overcome its limited fiscal capacity and have enough money on hand to pay pensions to retirees over 65. Collection would start in 1937, and the first pensions were to be paid in 1942. In the meantime, program officials hoped to develop the administrative expertise necessary to sustain such a program. The fact that experts such as Walton

Hamilton from the Brookings Institution, I. S. Falk from the Committee on the Costs of Medical Care and the Milbank Memorial Fund, and Arthur Altmeyer from the Wisconsin Industrial Commission joined political figures such as John Winant, the former governor of New Hampshire, and Vincent M. Miles from the Democratic National Committee provided some encouragement.[37]

The old-age insurance program of 1935 proved impossible to implement, and it never was. Because of the problems, the 1935 Act was substantially revised, even before the 1942 starting date for the payment of pensions. The problems centered on the means of funding. As I have explained at length elsewhere, the 1935 Act was designed to be "fully funded," in the sense of not ever having to rely on general revenues. Avoiding general revenues was easy in the beginning of the program. In 1937, for example, Congress appropriated $511 million into the Social Security account, of which only $6 million was needed for current expenses, such as lump-sum payments to people who died before they could receive their pension. In 1980, however, things would not be so simple. A much larger percentage of the retired industrial and commercial workers would be entitled to receive Social Security pensions. In fact, actuaries projected the amount coming in that year would fall $1.5 billion short of the money needed to pay the benefits. The solution envisioned in the 1935 Act consisted of gradually raising tax rates and the establishment of a large reserve. The interest on this large reserve would fund the short-fall in Social Security's "current account," when it appeared in 1967. The problem with this plan was that the amount of money in the reserve account would eventually reach $47 billion, a figure beyond the public's imagination. It amounted to eight times the amount of money then in circulation. No one knew if the federal government could maintain the fiscal discipline to invest such a sum prudently or whether it would not simply collect Social Security taxes and then spend them, leaving future generations with only a previous generation's empty promises to pay. In 1939, liberals and conservatives joined to modify the program and eliminate the large reserves, in part by beginning the payments sooner and in part by raising benefit levels and changing their nature.[38]

The change was crucial to Social Security's future. It meant that, instead of being fully funded, the system would move much closer to a pay-as-you-go plan in which today's workers supported today's retirees. It also allowed the system to achieve welfare objectives previously beyond its reach. In the original plan, people who paid less money to the program received a greater return on their investments, but workers with similar records of labor-force participation were treated in the same way. If two workers earning similar wages went to work, retired, and died at exactly the same times, they received exactly the same benefits under the 1935 Act, regardless if one was a bachelor and the other a married father with fourteen children. Under the 1939 rules, the worker with the family would, in all likelihood, receive substantially more than the bachelor, even though the two workers paid exactly the same amount in the plan. Because of this feature and the other aspects of its "family protection," Social Security mimicked welfare and departed from the actuarial features of private insurance.

In the 1940s, old-age insurance was a money-making machine for the federal government, yet it still encountered serious problems that led to substantial modifications. As the labor force expanded, more people paid into the program. As wage levels rose, more and more workers paid the maximum amount of money into the system. The result was an increase in the amount of money coming into the system, even though Congress refused to raise the level of Social Security taxes and the taxable wage base (the $3,000 limit on a worker's wages subject to the Social Security tax). The amount in the Social Security trust grew steadily during the 1940s, increasing from $2 billion to well over $13 billion.[39]

The people who worked for the Social Security program viewed their progress during the decade in far less sanguine terms. They failed to get what they wanted from Congress in three different senses. Congress refused to make retirement benefits more liberal, to extend coverage to new groups, and to expand the range of benefits beyond old age and into health and disability. By the end of the 1940s, Social Security administrators spoke in terms of a crisis. In a careful memoir published in 1966, Arthur Altmeyer, who directed the Social Security program from 1937 until 1953, wrote that the events of 1949 would be "decisive as to whether the old age and survivors' insurance system would survive as a contributory, wage-related system."[40]

Altmeyer's fears concerned the place of Social Security within the American social-welfare service. As he noted, more than twice as many people were on the state welfare rolls, receiving old-age assistance, than were receiving retirement benefits from the federal government under Social Security. The reasons had to do with the passage and implementation of the two programs. Old-age assistance covered any needy elderly person; Social Security limited coverage to industrial and commercial workers who had contributed into the system. Congress refused to raise Social Security benefits significantly; many of the state legislatures did not hesitate to respond to their elderly constituents by raising the level of old-age assistance. By the end of the 1940s, just over a fifth of the elderly received old-age assistance payments, and in a few states it was over half. The surprising result was that the average monthly welfare payment was $42 in 1949, compared to an average Social Security benefit of $25.[41]

America had not yet come to accept Social Security as its primary means of providing aid for the elderly, and a strong possibility existed that a different form of pension, one based more directly on need, would replace the social insurance principles of Social Security. As one of Truman's advisers noted in 1949, the "race between insurance and pensions" was "nip and tuck."[42] Congressmen echoed these sentiments. "We are at the crossroads," said Representative Thomas Kean of New Jersey. "The old-age assistance program has grown by leaps and bounds." Representative Doughton of North Carolina said that Congress faced a decision "whether the insurance program of the social security system can be strengthened and reinforced against the assaults of old age pensions."[43]

Responding to this crisis, Congress substantially modified the Social Security program in 1950, choosing to raise the level of benefits and extend coverage. Altmeyer noted with some relief that eight million workers, most of whom were self-employed, were brought into the system and that average benefits were increased by about 80%. The Social Security system picked up almost immediately. The old-age-assistance rolls declined as soon as the new Social Security law went into effect, and, for the first time, the number of Social Security beneficiaries exceeded the number receiving old-age assistance in February 1951.[44]

The battle between public assistance and old-age insurance illustrated how social-welfare politics had changed between 1935 and 1950. None of the alternatives in 1950 involved exclusive reliance on the private sector. In 1935, by way of contrast, Congress gave serious consideration to exempting those already covered by a private pension plan from Social Security. Fifteen years later, both liberal and conservative critics of Social Security wanted to move to a pay-as-you-go system with universal coverage. Although they disagreed on how generous the benefits should be, all the participants agreed on a continuing federal role. Increasingly, social-welfare debates involved the question of which level of government should take the lead on the provision of social-welfare services, not the question of whether the federal government should be involved.

Indeed, Social Security now benefited from the same sort of ambiguity that supported the extension of federal programs from the 1920s. Liberals regarded its notion of an implied contract between the government and the elderly as a sure means of expanding social-welfare expenditures; conservatives saw its contributory insurance features as a means of controlling the growth of future expenditures. Both sides made an implicit comparison with veterans' compensation and state welfare programs: Social Security expenditures could not be bid up, the conservative fear, or bid down, the liberal worry, as easily as expenditures in the older programs.

The Social Security Amendments of 1950 changed the following for federally run programs. Before the postwar era, federal programs embodied the Progressive Era notion that social-welfare programs responded to industrialism. Either they corrected a problem of industrial development, as in workers' compensation, or redressed the imbalance between urban and rural areas of the country, a lack of health care in rural areas, for example. By limiting coverage to industrial and commercial workers, Social Security continued this tradition. In 1985, Senator Daniel Patrick Moynihan, himself an astute student of social-welfare programs, acknowledged Social Security's heritage when he described the program as a response to the problems of urban America.[45] Before 1950, universal coverage had never existed for any federal social-welfare program. After 1950, Social Security held the potential to break the Progressive Era mold and become a universal program.

Extending Social Security coverage to the self-employed represented the key 1950 breakthrough. Program officials had long realized that incomplete coverage exacerbated the dilemmas of funding the Social Security program. It would be difficult to ask a farmer to pay taxes to support the pension of a retired steelworker when the steelworker did not have to do the same for a retired farmer. That meant that the program would never be able to utilize general revenues. One Social Security bureaucrat noted in 1937 that "if we are going to tax [the self-employed] to pay the subsidy necessary but not include this group in the benefits, I think we are going to find that we will have a very difficult problem on our hands. I think that the problem of providing a subsidy from the general revenue is likely to have a lot of dynamite in it."[46] The solution was to broaden coverage under Social Security to cover farmers as well as steelworkers, the self-employed as well as industrial and commercial workers. But how? Few precedents existed for collecting a payroll tax from the self-employed who, by definition, had no payroll. The income-tax system was one remedy, but not a good one. A 1938 Social Security advisory council could not determine a satisfactory way of collecting contributions from farmers, self-employed shopkeepers, and others. The United States was not far removed from the world in which, according to the Lynds, only 12% to 15% of the residents in Muncie, Indiana, reported incomes large enough to make filing income-tax returns necessary. World War II marked a watershed in the federal government's ability to collect taxes. In 1948, when another advisory council studied Social Security, it reported, "The fact that almost all full-time and a large proportion of part-time self-employed persons have for the last few years been required to file income-tax returns has radically altered the outlook for extending coverage to this group. It has been demonstrated that income reports can be obtained from the great majority of the self-employed."[47] The technology of tax collection facilitated the expansion of Social Security to cover the self-employed; a major bottleneck of the American social-welfare system was broken in the process.

THE GOLDEN AGE OF SOCIAL SECURITY AND THE HALO EFFECT

After 1950, Social Security entered its golden age.[48] It was the one welfare program in which every member of Congress had a stake. That made political coalition-building easier to achieve. It enabled the program to take advantage of rising wage rates, low unemployment, and an expanding labor force and become the nation's largest social-welfare program. Benefit increases in 1952, 1954, and 1958 testified to the program's success.

Although program administrators collaborated with Congress on benefit increases and other incremental changes, their success was limited in convincing Congress to pass health and disability insurance. Even as Congress proved willing to expand retirement benefits for the elderly, it refused to allow younger people to receive disability pensions. Congress routinely blocked efforts to create a national health insurance program that would cover people of all ages. In each case, the problems centered on the politics of enactment. A shifting coalition of private professional groups, notably insurance companies and medical doctors, and of state administrators, opposed the enactment of both measures.[49]

Consideration of disability insurance, for example, began almost immediately after the passage of the Social Security Act in 1935.

Certain factors mitigated against its immediate passage, however. With the federal government's limited administrative capacity, few people believed it had the ability to separate the disabled, those worthy of special aid from the state, from the nondisabled, those expected to participate in the labor force, even in periods of unemployment. Such administrative considerations delayed passage of disability insurance, as did the active opposition of the insurance industry, which wished to protect its prerogative to supply disability protection privately, and the American Medical Association, which worried about federal regulation of its professional services.

Social Security bureaucrats bargained with these various interests and, when the popularity of Social Security increased in the 1950s, arrived at a compromise in which states, acting through the established and trusting vocational rehabilitation program, would certify people as disabled. The doctors who would be needed to participate in this process could work with a state bureaucracy, with which they felt relatively comfortable, rather than directly with the Social Security Administration. The new disability program could be comfortably wrapped in the rhetoric of cost-cutting and efficiency that surrounded the vocational rehabilitation program. Furthermore, the program would initially cover only those above 50 years of age, a group largely abandoned by the private insurance industry as too risky to cover. Not only did this age compromise lessen the opposition of the insurance industry, which at one time had supported a disability program for younger workers, it also heightened the resemblance between disability insurance and old-age insurance. Disability, it was argued, represented only a small change from old-age insurance. The program which once covered the elderly now covered the "pre-old," who because of disability now needed to drop out of the labor force just short of the retirement age. The robust shape of the Social Security trust funds, although not a major factor in the passage of disability insurance, made it possible for the Social Security Administration to argue that disability insurance was financially feasible, even as the various compromises allowed congressmen to maintain that the program was administratively feasible.

After many rounds of bargaining, Congress acquiesced in the passage of disability insurance in 1956, and the President reluctantly went along. It may be that Eisenhower felt about this matter as he did about subsequent expansions of Social Security in his administration: "If we just say no," he told his cabinet, "we'll get rolled."[50]

Even though disability insurance emerged only after much political compromise, it still followed the general pattern of American social-welfare policy. Because Social Security was so successful, many areas of social policy were cast in its image, and disability was no exception. To be associated with Social Security was to gain respectability; it was the halo effect in social welfare.

Social Security's halo brought gains and losses to America's social policy. Disability policy became an adjunct of Social Security policy and hence of the nation's retirement policy. Passed with attention to the possibilities of rehabilitating the disabled, disability insurance never developed into an effective rehabilitation program. Here again the program, as implemented, differed from the program promised during the political process of passage. Once part of the Social Security program, however, disability insurance benefited from the same politics of incremental expansion that characterized the entire Social Security program. Within a decade, it became a full-fledged retirement program for disabled workers of all ages, with benefits as liberal—often more liberal—than old-age benefits. As a result of what happened to disability insurance during its passage, implementation, and modification, the American policy toward physical disability consisted largely of paying premature retirement benefits to people judged to be disabled. Other alternatives, such as encouraging the participation of the handicapped in American society, never were funded as lavishly or as enthusiastically as retirement pensions for disability.[51]

Health insurance was an even looser fit with Social Security, yet it too was forced into the Social Security mold. By 1950, Social Security administrators realized that passage of health insurance would be impossible without substantial compromise. They chose to make what in retrospect looks like an obvious compromise, and that was to limit health-insurance benefits to the elderly. Even with this compromise, it took many years of negotiations with the American Medical Association to produce even a modest health-insurance program. This program, like the Social Security Act itself, came in a year in which the President enjoyed one of the largest congressional majorities in American history.

In the Medicare program, the federal government used Social Security funds to reimburse hospitals for medical care. The elderly also had the option of contributing to a second insurance program, popularly known as Part B, that paid for doctors' bills. Both of these programs intruded very little on the existing systems of providing and paying for medical care, except to pump more money into the systems and bid up costs. Where before doctors prided themselves on treating some of the elderly for free, now Medicare stood ready to pay the bills at "customary" rates over which the federal government had little influence.[52]

More than other parts of the Social Security program, health insurance followed strict insurance principles. Medicare took a very traditional and hence conservative approach to the problems of health insurance. Mechanisms designed to discourage frivolous use of health care in which the consumer shared some of the costs of paying for medical care were built into the program, just as they were in most private health-insurance coverages. Medicare consisted of reimbursement for up to ninety days of hospitalization for each "spell" of illness, and it featured both co-payments and deductibles. The initial deductible was $40, and the act required the patient to pay $10 per day after the sixtieth day of hospitalization. If the illness led directly to a stay in an extended-care facility, then Medicare reimbursed the patient for up to twenty days. Like the hospital-insurance part of the act, Part B contained both deductibles and co-payments, in this case a deductible of $50 a year and a co-payment of 20% of the cost.[53]

Unlike disability insurance, Medicare remained limited to the elderly; no easy means existed to extend it further. To qualify for Medicare, one had to be a Social Security beneficiary, and the only way to be a Social Security beneficiary was to be old, disabled, or the dependent of someone who was old or disabled. Others qualified only for a state-run welfare program known as Medicaid, which helped to finance hospital and doctor's care for the recipients of welfare (families with dependent children, the permanently and totally disabled, the blind, and the elderly) and others whom states deemed medically indigent. Like Medicare, Medicaid was linked to an existing program. Despite many years of trying, Social Security officials and other policymakers never managed to extend the federal reimbursement system much beyond the one implemented in the late 1960s.

EXPANDING THE SOCIAL WELFARE SYSTEM IN GOOD TIMES AND BAD

With the passage of Medicare in 1965, the modern American social-welfare system was largely completed, but it would be a mistake to think of this system in static terms. Change came through many channels, such as the initiation of federal wars against old problems for which solutions now appeared to be in sight. President Kennedy wanted to "solve" the problems associated with mental retardation, President Johnson hoped to eradicate poverty, and President Nixon led a search for a cancer cure.

Noting that it was now possible "to attack the causes of mental retardation and improve its treatment," Kennedy managed to push mental retardation to the top of the policy agenda. In so doing, he forced the bureaucracy and congressional committees to readjust their routines to take mental retardation into consideration. By 1963, Congress had passed comprehensive mental-retardation legislation, although the solution took traditional administrative forms. Amendments to the Social Security Act allowed states to receive mental-retardation planning grants. Amendments to the child and maternal-health and crippled children's programs provided money for prenatal care and basic research into the causes and cures for mental retardation. Congress also passed a bill initiating grants for the construction of mental-retardation research centers, university clinics, and treatment and training centers, not to mention three types of education grants, such as money to train teachers of the handicapped. Each of the grants was firmly linked to established professional groups or local providers.[54] In this manner, the President's war on mental retardation blended imperceptibly into the standard incremental politics of existing programs.

As with mental retardation, so with the other social-welfare wars. In all cases, the President worked through HEW's operating machinery and through the congressional proprietors of existing programs. Departures from this practice produced the most fragile programs of the 1960s and 1970s, such as the Community Action Program.

The politics of incrementalism, whether of the War on Poverty variety or of the type that sustained programs such as vocational rehabilitation or Social Security, depended on expanding federal expenditures. In the period between 1946 and 1974, the growth of social-welfare expenditure easily outdistanced the growth of the gross national product. Between 1950 and 1975, for example, social-welfare expenditures at all levels of government rose from 8.9% to 20.0% of GNP. A high-watermark year was 1974, when assets in the Social Security trust fund reached an all-time high of $37.8 billion.[55]

Then came the period of stagflation and reduced economic expectations, both of which induced changes in the social-welfare system. In Social Security, for example, stagflation led to the near bankruptcy of the system. After 1972, benefits were indexed to the rate of inflation. In the next years, wages, which represented money coming into the system, failed to rise as rapidly as the prices which determined the amount of money going out of the system. Coupled with a spectacular rise in the number of people seeking early retirement through disability benefits, the result was a drain in the Social Security trust funds. Economic crisis and talk of bankruptcy undermined the confidence of young people in the system, particularly those members of the Baby Boom generation, for whom retirement was a long way off and for whom the notion of forced savings in a time of high inflation made little sense. Talk of generational inequity disturbed the consensus on which Social Security had been built. As a result, it took heroic political sacrifices to preserve the incremental politics of Social Security in 1983.[56]

Few people bothered to go to great lengths to preserve the welfare system, yet it too survived. The Aid to Families with Dependent Children program (AFDC) became a popular target for those who wanted to reduce the budget in times of relative austerity. In the late 1960s and 1970s, interest centered on the creation of work incentives. No longer was the notion of keeping mothers at home with their children a worthy goal of social policy. Indeed, the Baby Boom experience forced many couples into a two-career marriage, which meant that even in affluent families mothers worked. The notion that poor mothers should be allowed to stay home grated against the sensibilities of people who had been welfare's staunchest defenders. The drive toward work incentives began in earnest in 1962, when policymakers hoped to provide the poor with social services and improve their performance in the labor market. By the end of the decade, economists had designed programs, many of which were never passed by Congress, in which work incentives were to come from lowering the "marginal tax rates" for working welfare recipients. Finally, in the eras of Presidents Carter and Reagan, those expected to work (primarily the able-bodied) were to be separated from those not expected to work. Working would become a condition for the receipt of welfare benefits.[57]

Particularly in the austere fiscal times from the fall of Richard Nixon to the departure of Jimmy Carter, changes in the social-welfare system depended on congressional initiative. The absence of popular cries for broad social-welfare measures in the depression mode (Social Security) or the prosperity mode (the War on Poverty) tended also to coincide with the absence of strong presidential leadership, which in turn heightened the importance of Congress. Getting a program through Congress required fashioning a compromise that appealed to a wide spectrum of political beliefs.

A good example of how change came about in such a setting involved medical care. Passed with strong executive and bureaucratic leadership, Medicare was nonetheless geared to the traditional health-care system. Medicare consequently depended on retrospective payment: payment after the fact on permissive terms. With the government pumping money into the health-care system and with inflation in the cost of hospital services, the costs of health care soon began to rise. The rise in costs produced a search for a method of delivering health care equitably yet efficiently. No one should be denied access, but everyone should receive only necessary medical care. Just as in welfare, reformers in the Nixon administration hoped to use the market as an instrument of reform.[58]

The search ended with the rediscovery of prepaid group health, an idea that had been widely discussed in health-reform circles since the late 1920s. Prospective payment, payment in advance, provided an incentive to keep costs within the limits that had been set; group practice made for efficient utilization of specialists.[59] A permissive system of hospital care would be replaced with a controlled system. Further, nothing about prepaid group practice restricted access to health care, particularly if the government decided to pay the premiums for its special clients: the elderly and the indigent. Prepaid group practice, with far fewer special payments than traditional health care and with rates that did not overtly discriminate against heavy health-care users, was particularly attractive to "high risk" groups. These arguments persuaded health experts to put a new label on prepaid group practice and call it the Health Maintenance Organization (HMO).

The Health Maintenance Organization Act of 1973 mandated that employers of twenty-five persons or more who were subject to the federal minimum wage offer a prepaid group-practice plan to their employees as one of their health-insurance choices, provided that such a plan was operating in a particular area. To assist in the creation of such plans, the government provided loans and grants to HMOs that met federal requirements. The rationale behind this part of the legislation hinged on creating competition in the health-care market; the large private health-insurance carriers, including Blue Cross and Blue Shield, would no longer enjoy a near monopoly in the health-insurance field. At the same time, however, the law acted as a force for social uplift by setting standards for plans certified as HMOs.

Community rating was one such requirement. The idea here was to apply the same rates to high-risk, underserved groups as to other groups and, in a sense, to use the HMO as a way of subsidizing medicine for the less advantaged. As authority Lawrence Brown has explained, the HMO Act required that HMOs offer prepaid services at premiums "fixed under a community rating system." The law defined community rating as a system of payments under which "rates of payments may be determined on a per-person or per-family basis and may vary with the number of persons in a family, but . . . must be equivalent for all individuals and for all families of similar composition."[60]

The HMO, in other words, was both liberal and conservative, in much the same way that the welfare programs of the 1920s swung both ways, depending on the predilections of a particular proponent. On the one hand, HMOs served as forces for social uplift and means of bringing medical care to the poor and the elderly. On the other hand, they were forces contributing to the efficiency of the health-care system and a means of reducing health-care costs. As such, they served as a means of limited compromise in a troubled area of social welfare at a time of congressional leadership. The dynamics of workfare were similar. Liberals saw workfare as a means of providing training, conservatives as a way of deterring people from entering the welfare rolls. Although a person's point of view could shift at any point in the process and cause a retreat from support for workfare or HMOs, both sorts of programs provided structures on which to rest political compromises.

In both cases, furthermore, the federal government sought a means of controlling the costs of its own programs. Passage of legislation and the implementation of programs marked responses to crises created at least in part by previous legislation. In this sense, an era of federal activism that might be described as liberal led to a new era of federal activism that might be described as conservative. New programs arose both in times of prosperity and times of austerity, in times of presidential and in times of congressional leadership.

CONCLUSION: THE HISTORIAN AND SOCIAL-WELFARE POLICY

The result was considerable confusion as policymakers added layer upon layer to these programs, each with its complicated network of political support, each with its complex relationships to other programs. No wonder that James Patterson concluded his overview of social-welfare policy by noting that programs had developed "helter skelter and overlapped in ways that few people had foreseen and fewer yet could untangle."[61]

When historians focus on the development of government programs, they have advantages over other policy analysts in untangling social-welfare programs. They understand in ways that other policy analysts do not that we live with the remnants of social-welfare programs from many different eras. Even as the cutting edge of political debate centers on workfare and controlling health-care costs, programs such as workers' compensation, direct inheritances from the Progressive Era at the turn of the century, continue to function. Because of the politics of incrementalism, old programs continue to operate at modern levels of expenditure.

It therefore falls to historians to remember the political circumstances of a program's passage and the rhetoric that this passage called forth. And it is the historian's responsibility to separate the reality of a program's implementation from the rhetoric of a program's passage and to observe the persistence and modification of the program over time. When historians concentrate on a program's performance in what Hugh Heclo has called the "operational reality" of the bureaucracy, they may come to understand that, in Martha Derthick's words, policymaking and program extensions have acquired a "continuity, momentum and political logic of their own."[62] Historians, some would contend, have the necessary skills to uncover the logic and explain the continuity and momentum.

At the very least, good historical scholarship demands a critical understanding of the development of American social-welfare policy from the rudimentary programs of the nineteenth-century state to the profusion of costly and consequential modern programs run by the federal government in the twentieth century. We might not be able to foresee all of the consequences of the federal government's growth, as James Patterson suggests, but we are in position to outline the broad contours of that growth. At least that hope has animated this volume's final effort at social policy history: a note of scholarly optimism on which to conclude.

NOTES

1. W. Andrew Achenbaum, *Social Security: Visions and Revisions* (New York: Cambridge University Press, 1986), 4.

2. Robert Wiebe, *The Segmented Society* (New York: Oxford University

196   EDWARD D. BERKOWITZ

Press, 1975), 15, 36; James Sterling Young, *The Washington Community, 1800–1828* (New York: Harcourt Brace Jovanovich, 1966).

3. Stephen Skowronek, *Building a New American State: The Expansion of National Administrative Capacities* (New York: Cambridge University Press, 1982); Michael B. Katz, *In the Shadow of the Poorhouse: A Social History of Welfare in America* (New York: Basic Books, 1986), 86.

4. Morton Keller, *Affairs of State: Public Life in Nineteenth-Century America* (Cambridge, MA: Harvard University Press, 1977); Robert Wiebe, *The Search for Order* (New York: Hill and Wang, 1967); Ellis W. Hawley, *The New Deal and the Problem of Monopoly: A Study in Economic Ambivalence* (Princeton: Princeton University Press, 1966); Ellis W. Hawley, "Herbert Hoover, the Commerce Secretariat, and the Vision of an 'Associative State,' 1921–1928," *Journal of American History* 61 (June 1974), 116.

5. In addition to the Hawley sources already cited, see Bernard Bellush, *The Failure of the NRA* (New York: W. W. Norton, 1975).

6. *Social Security Bulletin: Annual Statistical Supplement, 1981* (Washington, D.C.: Department of Health and Human Services, 1981), 53, 54.

7. Such topics have a long tradition in the literature as the succession of Robert Bremner's *From the Depths* (New York: NYU Press, 1956) and James T. Patterson's *America's Struggle Against Poverty, 1900–1980* (Cambridge, MA: Harvard University Press, 1981) make clear. Although Patterson's book continues Bremner's focus on attitudes toward the poor, it also contains valuable insights on social-welfare programs themselves. A similar combination of intellectual and policy history can be found in two classic works on social-welfare history: Roy Lubove, *The Struggle for Social Security* (Cambridge, MA: 1968), which has been recently reissued in paperback by the University of Pittsburgh Press, and Daniel Nelson, *Unemployment Insurance: The American Experience* (Madison: University of Wisconsin Press, 1969).

8. I have taken this concept from Katz, *In the Shadow*, p. x, and he has taken it from Alan Wolfe.

9. Wiebe, *The Search for Order*; Keller, *Affairs of State*; William Graebner, "Federalism and the Progressive Era: A Structural Interpretation of Reform," *Journal of American History* 64 (1977), 331–357.

10. Edward Berkowitz, *Disabled Policy: America's Programs for the Handicapped* (New York: Cambridge University Press, 1987), chapter 2; Edward Berkowitz and Monroe Berkowitz, "The Survival of Workers' Compensation," *Social Service Review* 58 (June 1984), 259–280; Edward Berkowitz and Kim McQuaid, *Creating the Welfare State: The Political Economy of Twentieth-Century Reform* (New York: Praeger, 1980), 33–36. The leading scholar of workers' compensation is Robert Asher. See Robert Asher, "Business and Workers' Welfare in the Progressive Era: Workmen's Compensation Reform in Massachusetts, 1880–1911," *Business History Review* 43 (1969), 452–475.

11. More than any other scholar, Theda Skocpol is responsible for the rediscovery of this nineteenth-century version of a welfare state. See Theda Skocpol and John Ikenberry, "The Political Formation of the American Welfare State in Historical and Comparative Perspective," in *Comparative Social Research: An Annual Publication, The Welfare State, 1883–1893,*

Volume Six, 1983 (Greenwich, CT: JAI Press, 1983), Richard Tomasson, ed., 94–97.

12. Edward Berkowitz and Monroe Berkowitz, "Challenges to the Survival of Workers' Compensation: A Historical Analysis," in *Workers' Compensation Benefits: Adequacy, Equity, and Efficiency* (Ithaca, NY: ILR Press, 1985), John D. Worrall and David Appell, eds., 158–180.

13. Edward Berkowitz, *Disabled Policy*, chapter 2.

14. Walter Dodd, *Administration of Workmen's Compensation* (New York: The Commonwealth Fund, 1936), 222–286.

15. One authority estimated national workers' compensation expenditures for 1982 at $7.3 billion. See Monroe Berkowitz and M. Anne Hill, "Disability and the Labor Market: An Overview," in *Disability and the Labor Market: Economic Problems, Policies, and Programs* (Ithaca, NY: ILR Press, 1986), Monroe Berkowitz and Hill, eds., 13.

16. Edward Berkowitz, "Disability Insurance and the Social Security Tradition," in *Social Security: The First Half Century* (Albuquerque: University of New Mexico Press, forthcoming, 1987), Richard Tomasson et al., eds.

17. See Edward Berkowitz and McQuaid, *Creating the Welfare State*, 39–41.

18. Edward Berkowitz and McQuaid, *Creating the Welfare State*, 63–75; Katz, *In the Shadow of the Poorhouse*, 142–143. In the infant and maternal-health programs, women trained in the scientific care of children would teach expectant mothers rules of hygiene and child care. See Sheila Rothman, *Woman's Proper Place: A History of Changing Ideals and Practices, 1870 to the Present* (New York: Basic Books, 1978), 136–153.

19. Edward Berkowitz and McQuaid, *Creating the Welfare State*, 65.

20. Walter I. Trattner, "The Federal Government and Social Welfare in Early Nineteenth-Century America," *Social Service Review* 50 (June 1976), 243–255; Trattner, *From Poor Law to Welfare State: A History of Social Welfare in America* (New York: The Free Press, 1984), 3d edition, 47–76.

21. "The Nelson Act," 25 Stat., 642; "Past and Present Indian Policy," address delivered at the Annual Meeting of the American Missionary Association, Hartford, CT, 1892, Dawes Papers, Box 50, Library of Congress, Washington, D.C.

22. Trattner, *From Poor Law to Welfare State*, 203–208.

23. Edward Berkowitz and Kim McQuaid, "Bureaucrats as Social Engineers: Federal Welfare Programs in Herbert Hoover's America," *American Journal of Economics and Sociology* (October 1980), 321–335.

24. Ibid.

25. U.S. Federal Board for Vocational Education, *Report of the Federal Board for Vocational Education* (Washington, D.C.: Government Printing Office, 1921), 27.

26. Federal Board for Vocational Education, *Annual Report 1926* (Washington, D.C.: Government Printing Office, 1926), 123.

27. Federal Board for Vocational Education, *Bulletin 132, Civilian Rehabilitation Series 16, A Study of Rehabilitated Persons: A Statistical Analysis of the Rehabilitation of 6,391 Disabled Persons* (Washington, D.C.: Government Printing Office, 1928).

28. Department of Health, Education, and Welfare, *Report of the Depart-*

ment of Health, Education, and Welfare 1953 (Washington, D.C.: Government Printing Office, 1954), 229.

29. Federal Security Agency, *Annual Report of the Federal Security Agency, Office of Vocational Rehabilitation, 1948* (Washington, D.C.: Government Printing Office, 1948), 586.

30. Lawrence I. Mars, *An Exploratory Cost-Benefit Analysis of Vocational Rehabilitation* (Washington, D.C.: Rehabilitation Administration, Division of Statistics and Studies, mimeo., 1968); Edward Berkowitz and Monroe Berkowitz, *Benefit Cost Analysis: Rehabilitation Research Review* (Washington, D.C.: National Institute of Handicapped Research, 1983).

31. For the quotations and statistics, see Edward Berkowitz, *Disabled Policy*, chapter 6. See also Edward Berkowitz, "Rehabilitation's Past: History as a Factor in the Future," in *If . . . the future of VR*, Proceedings of the Twelfth Institute on Rehabilitation Issues, October 29–30, 1985, Louisville, L. Robert McConnell and Elizabeth B. Minton, eds., distributed through the West Virginia University Research and Training Center, Dunbar, 9–18.

32. Edward Berkowitz, "Rehabilitation's Past."

33. "The services approach was appealing because it united conservatives and liberals, the former believing that services would reduce dependency, the latter believing that they would succor the poor. . . . Ambiguity was the great advantage of social services as public policy," writes Martha Derthick in *Uncontrollable Spending for Social Service Grants* (Washington, D.C.: The Brookings Institution, 1975), 13.

34. Edward Berkowitz, *Disabled Policy*, chapters 6, 7, 8; Joseph Stubbins, "The Clinical Model in Rehabilitation," in *The Clinical Model in Rehabilitation and Alternatives* (New York: World Rehabilitation Fund, 1983); Harlan Hahn, "Paternalism and Public Policy," *Society* (April 1983), 36–46; Gerben Dejong, "Independent Living as Analytic Paradigm," *Australian Rehabilitation Review* 6 (1982), 45–50. For an excellent examination of the unintended effects of the civil-rights statute for the handicapped (Section 504 of the Rehabilitation Act of 1973), see Richard Scotch, *From Goodwill to Civil Rights* (Philadelphia: Temple University Press, 1984). Scotch's monograph is exemplary in every way and one of the best efforts to examine the realities of the policy process that I have found.

35. Katz, *In the Shadow of the Poorhouse*, 218, 238; Patterson, *America's Struggle*, 75–77.

36. Achenbaum, *Social Security*, 13–26.

37. In my account of old-age insurance, I rely on Achenbaum, *Social Security*; Edward Berkowitz and McQuaid, *Creating the Welfare State*; Carolyn L. Weaver, *The Crisis in Social Security* (Durham, NC: Duke University Press, 1982); Arthur J. Altmeyer, *The Formative Years of Social Security* (Madison: University of Wisconsin Press, 1966); Edwin E. Witte, *The Development of the Social Security Act* (Madison: University of Wisconsin Press, 1963); William Graebner, *A History of Retirement* (New Haven: Yale University Press, 1980).

38. See Edward Berkowitz, "The First Advisory Council and the 1939 Amendments," in *Social Security After Fifty: Successes and Failures* (Westport, CT: Greenwood Press, 1987), Edward Berkowitz, ed., 55–78. This chapter updates an earlier version, "The First Social Security Crisis," *Prologue* 15 (Fall 1983), 133–149.

39. *Social Security Bulletin, 1981,* 79.

40. Altmeyer, *Formative Years,* 169. See also Christopher Leman, "Patterns of Policy Development: Social Security in the United States and Canada," *Public Policy* 25 (Spring 1977), 261–290.

41. Altmeyer, *Formative Years,* 169–170; Mark H. Leff, "Historical Perspectives on Old-Age Insurance: The State of the Art on the Art of the State," in Edward Berkowitz, ed., *Social Security After Fifty,* 42.

42. Staff Comments, "Expansion and Extension of the Social Security System," February 14, 1949, Charles Murphy Papers, Harry S. Truman Library, quoted in Leff, "Historical Perspectives on Old-Age Insurance," 41.

43. Both of these October 4, 1949, speeches from the *Congressional Record* are quoted in Edward Berkowitz, "Introduction: Social Security Celebrates An Anniversary," in Berkowitz, ed., *Social Security After Fifty,* 20.

44. Altmeyer, *Formative Years,* 185; Achenbaum, *Social Security,* 45.

45. Senator Daniel P. Moynihan, *Congressional Record,* June 19, 1985, p. S 8347. When I speak of Social Security here and elsewhere, I mean old-age and survivors' insurance and not the programs authorized by the Social Security Act of 1935: social insurance, not welfare. Welfare, it can be argued, did cover nonindustrial workers before 1950, but it was highly selective in its coverage and applied to people outside of the labor force, such as children, the elderly, and the blind.

46. Wilbur Cohen to Arthur Altmeyer, February 10, 1937, Record Group 47, Records of the Social Security Administration, Box 98, Chairman's Files, File 705, National Archives, Washington, D.C.

47. *Old Age and Survivors Insurance,* Summary, Report to the Senate Committee on Finance from the Advisory Council on Social Security, 80th Congress, 2d Session, 1948, in *Readings in Social Security* (New York: Prentice-Hall, 1948), William Haber and Wilbur Cohen, eds., 250, 266–267; Robert S. Lynd and Helen Merrill Lynd, *Middletown: A Study in Modern American Culture* (New York: Harcourt, Brace and World, 1929), 84.

48. Here the undisputed best source is Martha Derthick, *Policymaking for Social Security* (Washington, D.C.: The Brookings Institution, 1979), one of the true masterpieces of social policy history.

49. In what follows, I rely heavily on Edward Berkowitz and Wendy Wolff, "Disability Insurance and the Limits of American History," *The Public Historian* 8 (Spring 1986), 65–82, and on chapter 3 of Edward Berkowitz, *Disabled Policy.*

50. Folder "L-49 (3) June 10, 1958," 45, White House Office, Legislative Meeting Series, Box 5, Dwight D. Eisenhower Library, Abilene, Kansas, quoted in Leff, "Historical Perspectives on Old-Age Insurance," 15.

51. For the implementation of disability insurance, see Edward Berkowitz, "Disability Insurance and the Social Security Tradition" and *Disabled Policy,* chapter 4.

52. Achenbaum, *Social Security,* 161–178; Theodore R. Marmor, *Politics of Medicare* (Chicago: Aldine, 1973). The source that dominates the field of health care is Paul Starr, *The Social Transfiguration of American Medicine* (New York: Basic Books, 1982).

53. In addition to Starr, *Transformation,* and Marmor, *The Politics of Medicare,* see Richard Harris, *A Sacred Trust* (New York: New American Library, 1966), 55, 69–72.

54. Edward Berkowitz, "Mental Retardation Politics and the Kennedy Administration," *Social Science Quarterly* 61 (June 1980), 128–143, inquires into this legislation at length.

55. *Social Security Bulletin, Annual Statistical Supplement, 1981,* 79, 53–54.

56. Eric Kingson et al., *The Common Stake: The Interdependence of Generations (A Policy Framework)* (Washington, D.C.: The Gerontological Society, 1986); Paul Light, *Artful Work* (New York: Random House, 1985).

57. See, for example, President's Commission for a National Agenda for the Eighties, *Government and the Advancement of Social Justice, Health, Welfare, Education and Civil Rights in the Eighties* (Englewood Cliffs: Prentice-Hall, 1981); Edward Berkowitz, "Changing the Meaning of Welfare Reform," in *Maintaining the Safety Net: Income Redistribution Programs in the Reagan Administration* (Washington, D.C.: American Enterprise Institute, 1984), John Weicher, ed., 23–42; Gilbert Steiner, *Social Insecurity: The Politics of Welfare* (New York: Rand McNally, 1966), 34–37; Daniel P. Moynihan, *The Politics of a Guaranteed Annual Income: The Nixon Administration and the Family Assistance Plan* (New York: Random House, 1973).

58. Here I depend heavily on my research into the history of the group health association and on Lawrence D. Brown, *Politics and Health Care Organization: HMOs as Federal Policy* (Washington, D.C.: The Brookings Institution, 1983).

59. See Daniel M. Fox, *Health Policies, Health Politics: The British and American Experience, 1911–1965* (Princeton: Princeton University Press, 1986), 21–36.

60. Brown, *Politics and Health Care Organizations,* 296–297.

61. Patterson, *America's Struggle,* 168.

62. "Aggrandizement," she goes on to say, "is inherent in the modern state," in *Policymaking for Social Security,* 12.

Contributors

W. ANDREW ACHENBAUM, Department of History, University of Michigan, Ann Arbor, is director of the Aging Society Policy Studies Center at the Institute of Gerontology. Author of several books and articles on the history of old age in the United States, he recently published a Twentieth-Century Fund Study, *Social Security: Visions and Revisions* (Cambridge University Press). Achenbaum serves on the editorial board of the *Journal of Policy History.*

BRIAN BALOGH, Department of History, Harvard University, did his graduate work in history at the Johns Hopkins University. Prior to that he administered income-maintenance programs for the New York City Department of Social Services.

EDWARD D. BERKOWITZ, Director of the Program in History and Public Policy at George Washington University, writes on social-welfare history and policy. He is editor of *Social Security After Fifty* (1987) and the author of *Disabled Policy: America's Programs for the Handicapped* (1987), as well as the co-author of the forthcoming *Cooperative Competitor: Group Health Associations and American Health Care.* In 1987–88 he served as a Robert Wood Johnson Foundation Faculty Fellow in Health Care Finance at Johns Hopkins University.

DONALD T. CRITCHLOW, Department of History, University of Notre Dame, currently serves as editor for the *Journal of Policy History*. He is the author of *The Brookings Institution, 1916–1952: Expertise and the Public Interest in a Democratic Society* (1985) and editor of *Socialism in the Heartland: The Midwestern Experience, 1890–1920* (1986).

ELLIS W. HAWLEY, Department of History, University of Iowa, is the author of *The New Deal and the Problem of Monopoly* (1966) and *The Great War and the Search for a Modern Order* (1979). He is currently working on a study of Herbert Hoover as Secretary of Commerce and President and on a social history of the American people in the 1920s.

MORTON KELLER, Department of History, Brandeis University, is the author of numerous articles and books, including *Affairs of State: Public Life in Nineteenth-Century America* (1977), *The Art and Politics of Thomas Nast* (1968), and *In Defense of Yesterday: James M. Beck and the Politics of Conservatism, 1861–1937* (1958).

ROBERT KELLEY is co-founder and Chairman of the Graduate Program in Public Historical Studies at the University of California, Santa Barbara. A frequent contributor to many journals, including the *American Historical Review*, he has authored *Gold vs. Grain* (1959), *The Transatlantic Persuasion: The Liberal Democratic Mind in the Age of Gladstone* (1969), and *The Cultural Pattern in American Politics* (1979).

JUDITH SEALANDER, Department of History, Wright State University, is the author of *As Minority Becomes Majority: Federal Reaction to the Phenomenon of Women in the Work Force, 1920–1963* (1983), and she recently completed a book manuscript examining business and progressivism at the turn of the century.

JACK WALKER serves as Chairman of the Department of Political Science, University of Michigan, Ann Arbor. His work focuses on interest groups and political mobilization in the American political system.

Index